Labour and the left in the 1980s

Labour and the left in the 1980s

Edited by Jonathan Davis and Rohan McWilliam
Foreword by Peter Tatchell

Manchester University Press

Copyright © Manchester University Press 2018

While copyright in the volume as a whole is vested in Manchester University Press, copyright in individual chapters belongs to their respective authors, and no chapter may be reproduced wholly or in part without the express permission in writing of both author and publisher.

Published by Manchester University Press
Altrincham Street, Manchester M1 7JA
www.manchesteruniversitypress.co.uk

British Library Cataloguing-in-Publication Data is available

ISBN 978 1 5261 0643 8 hardback
ISBN 978 1 5261 5144 5 paperback

First published by Manchester University Press in hardback 2018

This edition first published 2020

The publisher has no responsibility for the persistence or accuracy of URLs for any external or third-party internet websites referred to in this book, and does not guarantee that any content on such websites is, or will remain, accurate or appropriate.

Typeset by Toppan Best-set Premedia Limited

Contents

Notes on contributors	*page* vii
Foreword by Peter Tatchell	x
Preface	xiii
Introduction: new histories of Labour and the left in the 1980s *Jonathan Davis and Rohan McWilliam*	1

Part I: The crisis of the Labour Party

1	Retrieving or re-imagining the past? The case of 'Old Labour', 1979–94 *Eric Shaw*	25
2	Leading the Labour Party in the 1980s *Martin Farr*	44
3	Labour's liberalism: gay rights and video nasties *Paul Bloomfield*	69
4	Responsible capitalism: Labour's industrial policy and the idea of a National Investment Bank during the long 1980s *Richard Carr*	90

Part II: The British left in a global context

5	Neil Kinnock's *perestroika*: Labour and the Soviet influence *Jonathan Davis*	113

6 The international context: end of an era   132
   John Callaghan

Part III: Currents of the wider left

7 Militant's laboratory: Liverpool City Council's struggle with the
   Thatcher Government   151
   Neil Pye

8 'Fill a bag and feed a family': the miners' strike and its supporters   172
   Maroula Joannou

9 'Race Today cannot fail': black radicalism in the long 1980s   192
   Robin Bunce

   Index   210

Notes on contributors

Paul Bloomfield works at Anglia Ruskin University for the Faculty of Arts, Law and Social Sciences and is part of the Labour History Research Unit. Paul is currently completing a PhD thesis entitled 'The Breakaway of the Social Democratic Party between 1979 and 1982 in the Context of Post-war Labour Party History'.

Robin Bunce is a historian based at Homerton College, University of Cambridge, where he supervises work on the history of ideas. His monograph *Thomas Hobbes* was published by Continuum in 2009. Subsequently he has worked on black power as an ideology and a movement in Britain. His most recent book, written with Paul Field, *Renegade: The Life and Times of Darcus Howe*, is published by Bloomsbury in 2017.

John Callaghan is Professor of Politics and Contemporary History at the University of Salford. He is the author of *Socialism in Britain Since 1884* (1990), *The Retreat of Social Democracy* (2000) and *Labour and Foreign Policy: A History* (2007).

Richard Carr is a Senior Lecturer in History and Politics at Anglia Ruskin University. He has recently published a political biography of Charlie Chaplin with Routledge, and has written widely on interwar British conservatism, including a monograph *Veteran MPs and Conservative Politics in the Aftermath of the Great War: The Memory of All That* (2013). He co-authored *Alice in Westminster: The Political Life of Alice Bacon* with Rachel Reeves MP – which was named as one of the *Guardian*'s Political Books of 2016.

Jonathan Davis is Senior Lecturer in Russian History and co-Director of the Labour History Research Unit at Anglia Ruskin University. He is the author of *The Global 1980s: People, Power and Profit* (2019) and *Stalin: From Grey Blur to Great Terror* (2008), and co-editor with Paul Corthorn of *The Labour Party and the Wider World* (2008), and with John Shepherd and Chris Wrigley of *Britain's Second Labour Government, 1929–1931: A Reappraisal* (2011). He has published articles on delegates' visits to the Soviet Union in the 1920s in *Revolutionary Russia*, on the influence of the Russian Revolutions on Labour's ideology in *Scottish Labour History*, and on Labour's contemporary political thought in *Renewal*.

Martin Farr is Senior Lecturer in Contemporary British History at Newcastle University. He has published on political biography, government and Parliament before, during and after the First World War, the politics of strategic bombing in the Second World War, seaside resorts and declinism, and package holidays in the 1970s. He is currently writing a book entitled *Margaret Thatcher's World*, and articles on imperial tropes in 1960s Britain, the film version of *Oh! What a Lovely War*, the deaths of Hugh Gaitskell and John Smith, and the relationship of Barack Obama and David Cameron.

Maroula (Mary) Joannou is Emerita Professor of Literary History and Women's Writing at Anglia Ruskin University. She is the author of *Women's Writing, Englishness, and National and Cultural Identity: The Mobile Woman and the Migrant Voice, 1938–1962* (2012), *Contemporary Women's Fiction: From The Golden Notebook to The Color Purple* (2000), and *'Ladies Please Don't Smash These Windows': Women's Writing, Feminist Consciousness and Social Change 1918–1938* (1995). She is the editor of volume 8 of *The Palgrave History of British Women's Writing* (2012) and *Women Writers of the 1930s, Gender, Politics and History* (1998) and has published some forty book chapters and essays in peer-reviewed journals. In 1984 she was a member of both the St Albans Miners' Support Group and the Cambridge Miners' Support Group.

Rohan McWilliam is Professor of Modern British History at Anglia Ruskin University, Cambridge and co-Director of the Labour History Research Unit. He is a former President of the British Association for Victorian Studies. His publications include *Popular Politics in Nineteenth Century England* (1998), *The Tichborne Claimant: A Victorian Sensation* (2007) and articles on Victorian melodrama, Elsa Lanchester, Jonathan Miller and G. W. M. Reynolds. He is currently at work on a history of the West End of London since 1800.

Neil Pye completed a PhD in History at the University of Huddersfield which was published as *The Home Office and the Chartists, 1838–48: Protest and Repression in the West Riding of Yorkshire* (2013). Currently, he is conducting research about Metro Mayors and Combined Authorities, plus independent research about Michael Heseltine's role as the minister for Liverpool during the 1980s. Outside of academia, Neil previously served as a borough councillor in West

Lancashire during 2011–15 and chaired the West Lancashire Labour Group which in 2015 took control of the council.

Eric Shaw is Honorary Research Fellow in the Division of History and Politics at Stirling University. He is author of *Discipline and Discord in the Labour Party* (1988), *The Labour Party since 1979* (1994), *The Labour Party since 1945* (1996), *Losing Labour's Soul: New Labour and the Blair Government 1997–2007* (2008) and, with Gerry Hassan, *The Strange Death of Labour Scotland* (2012).

Peter Tatchell is a human rights campaigner and Director of the Peter Tatchell Foundation: www.PeterTatchellFoundation.org.

Foreword

Peter Tatchell

The 1980s were the heyday of the Thatcher counter-revolution, with mass deindustrialisation destroying Britain's manufacturing base. The consequent lay-offs, and Tory economic policies designed to bolster business interests and maximise profits, cast 3.2 million people onto the dole queues by 1983.

The post-war consensus was torn to shreds, with the privatisation of public utilities, curtailment of local democracy and trade union rights, Section 28, cuts to local councils and public services, the poll tax and restrictions on civil liberties and the right to protest.

But this inequality and repression also provoked resistance, rebellion and rage: huge mass protests against government cuts and nuclear weapons, the People's March for Jobs and widespread rioting by working-class youth in Brixton, Toxeth, St Paul's, Moss Side and Tottenham.

It was a period of significant setbacks for left politics, most notably the crushing of the miners' strike, Tony Benn's defeat in the Labour deputy leadership contest, abolition of the left-controlled Greater London Council, the surcharging and disqualification of councillors who resisted central government rate-capping, Labour's loss of the 1983 and 1987 general elections and my own defeat in the notorious 1983 Bermondsey by-election.

As Maroula Joannou's chapter 8 elucidates, the miners' strike, and the semi-police-state methods used to destroy it, was a pivotal moment – and in many unexpected ways, not least because it spawned new forms of working-class solidarity and self-help and forged new connections between different and often separate struggles, most notably in the sphere of sexual politics. Lesbians and Gays Support the Miners challenged macho old-labourist attitudes on the coalfields, as did Women Against Pit Closures, which drew strongly on suffragette traditions and on the history of women campaigners during the General Strike of 1926.

These were not the only glimmers of hope amid the debacles and gloom of Thatcherism rampant. Something big stirred within Labour itself during the 1980s. The Left revived and grew. Atrophied and nepotistic local Labour parties were democratised, right-wing Tammy Hall local Labour leaders and MPs were ousted and a whole new generation of social and community activists joined the party. Many became councillors in left-dominated Labour local authorities and proceeded to enact a ground-breaking, visionary late twentieth-century version of municipal socialism in major cities across the UK.

The Conservatives had power at Westminster but the left captured large chunks of the local state and, despite Thatcherism and the more cautious Labour national leadership, transformed it in ways that advanced popular participation, community empowerment, social justice and equality.

Ken Livingstone's Labour administration of the Greater London Council (GLC, 1981–86) epitomised this new left politics and its exhilarating experiment in local democracy, local equality and local socialism. The previously stuffy, remote and exclusive GLC offices and committees were opened up to public consultations and community groups.

For the first time in Britain, politicians in power sought to engage seriously with women's issues and the concerns of marginalised minorities. They sought to tackle the too-often ignored inequalities of race, gender, disability, sexuality and gender identity. The GLC pioneered equal opportunities policies that have since become standard. It set up women's and ethnic minorities' committees, with membership including outside experts and grass-roots community activists. It also created a Gay Working Party which later produced a report, Changing the World, recommending far-sighted and unprecedented policies to tackle anti-LGBT prejudice, discrimination and hate crime.

The GLC developed pioneering policies on housing, environmental protection and, especially, public transport. Its 'fares fair' policy cut travel costs by one-third, with the aim of aiding the mobility of low-income Londoners and incentivising people to not drive in central London, in order to cut congestion and pollution. It was hugely popular but was scuppered by a legal action brought by the Tories. A revised version was eventually implemented in 1983.

Livingstone's administration pioneered municipal economic planning; founding the Greater London Enterprise Board to create employment by investing in the industrial regeneration of London, mostly with money provided by the council and its staff pension fund. It proposed workers' co-operatives and the creation of London Community Builders to construct new council housing and regenerate existing housing stock.

Similar initiatives were spearheaded by left-wing Labour councils in Manchester, Sheffield and Liverpool (the latter, but not the GLC, is discussed at length in this book). Although their radical ambitions were often stymied by the Thatcher government's caps on local authority spending, they did nevertheless enact many tangible, positive reforms.

The 1980s was, in my mind, the most creative, exciting era for the left in many decades. It has had an impact on British politics and culture ever since. Many of its once trail-blazing radical ideas are the now mainstream consensus; especially around issues of equality, inclusion and diversity.

This book explores and illuminates some of these ideas and events – and many others – that collectively reshaped Labour in the 1980s and which, in some respects, still influence Labour today. The authors offer insights on the past that are issues for debate today regarding the future of progressive politics in the UK.

What happened in the 1980s has been made all the more relevant by the left-wing resurgence that led to the election of Jeremy Corbyn as Labour leader in 2015. In contrast to the 1980s, this new, twenty-first-century left renaissance has focused on winning national, not local, power. The explosion in party membership far exceeds that in the 1980s and Corbyn is putting an even greater premium on democratising the party and its processes, to make them more participatory, collaborative, transparent and accountable.

Jeremy Corbyn is arguably the most socialist leader of Labour since George Lansbury in the 1930s and his agenda for radical social reform echoes that of Attlee – minus the nationalisation of major industries. However, winning power in the Labour Party is one thing; winning power in the country and Parliament is a much tougher task.

The future of Labour depends, in part, on learning lessons – positive and negative – from the past. The authors of this volume offer a mix of different political and historical perspectives on the 1980s. While I don't share all their analysis, they make points that deserve to be heard and discussed. Go read.

December 2017

Preface

Labour and the left in the 1980s is the product of the Labour History Research Unit at Anglia Ruskin University. We are very proud of Anglia Ruskin and its role in hosting discussions and events that explore the great issues of our time. The aim of the Unit is to develop new ways of thinking about the British Labour Party and progressive politics by employing the insights of historians as well as scholars in other disciplines. The present volume is one of the first to reassess the experience of the political left in the crucial decade of Thatcherism. It is based on a conference held at Anglia Ruskin in November 2014 in association with the Society for the Study of Labour History. It was a great day of exploration which really opened up a new subject. There were a number of excellent papers delivered that we were unable to use but we remain very grateful to the speakers. Some of the issues in this book have been explored in dialogue with members of the Cambridge Labour Party, whom we also thank.

Apart from the contributors, there have been many others who have assisted in making this book through direct input, support or just inspiration. The following list is far from exhaustive but we would like to thank Peter Ackers (who wondered aloud at our conference whether his generation in the 1980s was 'too full of politics'), Alison Ainley, Tim Bale, Lucy Bland, Kelly Boyd, Marlene Buick, Anne Campbell, Luke Cooper, Paul Corthorn, Jon Cruddas MP, Nina Davis, Sharon Davis, Susan Flavin, Sean Lang, Keith Laybourn, Julia Long, the team at Manchester University Press, Daisy Payling, Emily Robinson, Sasha Roseneil, Robert Saunders, John Shepherd, Florence Sutcliffe-Braithwaite, Tony Taylor, Ian Thatcher, Nathalie Thompson and Michael Ward. Special thanks must also go to Anglia Ruskin University for granting Jonathan Davis a sabbatical which allowed him to work on this book, and the archivists at Churchill Archives Centre, Churchill College, Cambridge, where Neil Kinnock's papers are held. We are particularly grateful to Peter Tatchell for writing the passionate Foreword to our book.

As this book goes to press, the future of the Labour Party looks uncertain (just as it has done at many points in its history). Clearly, this is the right time to re-examine a comparable moment in Labour's past when it was in the wilderness. We do not claim that simple lessons can be learned, as the historical record is too complex, but we hope to prompt reflection on a decisive moment in the party's development. What we do believe is that histories of different forms of Labour and left-wing politics have a role to play in the ongoing search for social justice. This book is not exhaustive. We are very aware that we have not had space to consider many key issues. Tony Benn, the peace movement, environmentalism, grass-roots activism, the GLC, feminism and the issue of unemployment (to name just a few topics) need extensive treatment. The book lacks enough voices of working people themselves. We hope, however, that this book will kick-start a much-needed reconsideration of a formative moment in the history of the left.

Jonathan Davis
Rohan McWilliam
February 2017

Introduction: new histories of Labour and the left in the 1980s

Jonathan Davis and Rohan McWilliam

The forward march of Labour halted

In 1980, notwithstanding the defeat of the Labour government the year before, the political left in its various forms remained a major presence in British life. Local government, the media, trade unions, pressure groups, the arts and academia: all were often dominated by left-of-centre voices that created networks of opposition to the recently elected Conservative government of Margaret Thatcher. Since the reforming Labour government of 1945, the liberal left had some reason to believe that it had shaped the orthodoxies of modern Britain with the welfare state, Keynesian economic policy and the liberal reforms that abolished censorship and challenged gender and racial discrimination. It was still possible, in 1980, for some to believe that a socialist future beckoned.

By the end of the decade, a wrecking ball had shattered these assumptions completely. Not only did the Conservatives win landslide majorities against Labour in the elections of 1983 and 1987 but the organised labour movement was defeated time and again, its rights heavily reduced and its bargaining power diminished by mass unemployment. Labour's left-leaning manifesto in 1983 was dubbed by Gerald Kaufman MP, 'the longest suicide note ever penned', and the party received just 28 per cent of the popular vote, barely ahead of the centrist alliance of the Liberals and the new Social Democratic Party (SDP). Right-wing newspapers ran articles about a so-called 'loony left' obsessed with political correctness but out of touch with ordinary people and popular culture. Attempts at creating a left-wing mass newspaper, the *News on Sunday*, failed miserably, while Rupert Murdoch's newspaper, the *Sun*, would go on to claim that it won the 1992 election for John Major. At a global level, the socialist world was collapsing, a transformation marked by the fall of the Berlin Wall in 1989 and the Gorbachev reforms in the country that soon ceased to be the Soviet Union. The Communist Party of Great Britain actually wound itself up in 1991. Tony Benn argued that the challenge for the left was to win the argument for socialism. By any reckoning, the 1980s was the decade when the argument for socialism was lost.[1]

Yet the 1980s was in many ways a creative decade for the left. Victories may have been few but there was no lack of energy. The party managed to get the first black MPs elected to Parliament.[2] In 1984 Chris Smith, Labour MP for Islington, became the first openly gay MP. Opposition to nuclear weapons resurfaced as a major agitation while the possible hazards of nuclear power were highlighted.[3] The plight of the unemployed was placed at the top of the political agenda. Miners' support groups created networks of solidarity.[4] The Greater London Council (GLC) became a popular cause when faced with abolition and promoted new kinds of politics which helped to shape the wider social agenda.[5] Feminists and anti-racism campaigners fashioned a new common sense about personal identities. There was an assault on the idea that it was acceptable to pay women less than men, while issues around sexual harassment became more prominent later in the decade. AIDS and the introduction of Clause 28 changed the gay community and gave it a renewed political focus. Tony Benn, Michael Foot, Ken Livingstone, Derek Hatton, Beatrix Campbell and Arthur Scargill were key figures of the age. Labour (while diminished by the defection of members to the SDP) ended the decade as the main opposition party, a position that had seemed in doubt after the 1983 election. The early years of Channel 4 television provided a platform for alternative forms of politics and social identity to be expressed. Films like *The Ploughman's Lunch* and plays like David Hare's *Pravda* challenged the Thatcherisation of society. Red Wedge, alternative comedians, Band Aid, television series like *Spitting Image*, *Edge of Darkness*, *The Boys from the Blackstuff* and *A Very British Coup*: these were all part of a thriving left-of-centre popular culture.

Where Thatcherism prided itself on family values, Britain became a society in which divorce and cohabitation without marriage became more common. Where Thatcherism suggested private enterprise was the answer, the British remained doggedly attached to the National Health Service. Polls at the end of the decade suggested that, despite substantial victories (on a diminishing share of the popular vote), Thatcherism had still not transformed popular opinion, which continued to value public services and many aspects of the so-called 'nanny state'. The idea of a counter-culture is one that we associate with the 1960s, but it is fruitful to insist on the significance of alternative ways of living in the 1980s, evident in environmental activism (in 1989 the Green Party managed to get 14.5 per cent of the vote in the UK election for the European Parliament, although it gained no MEPs). After 1990, it was common to argue that the right had won the economic argument but the left had won the social and cultural argument.

The 1980s was therefore a contested and conflicted decade. Any account of the 1980s which simply looks at the triumph of Thatcherism is inadequate. Labour and the left may have failed electorally but they still mattered and shaped the political landscape. We need to think about the way in which Labour and the Conservatives defined themselves in relation to each other.[6] Both the right and the left abandoned the post-war consensus at about the same time. The SDP spoke for a renewed progressivism of the radical centre that was in danger of being eclipsed by the drift of the main parties towards the left and the right. This kind of politics was as much part of the period as Thatcherism.

Historians need to make sense of the cultures of the left and explore where they failed, and also where they had an impact. *Labour and the left in the 1980s* is an attempt to excavate this territory. The deeper academic study of the 1980s is now commencing, driven in part by the release of cabinet papers for the Thatcher years and also through the need to come to a reckoning with the most decisive decade in recent British history.[7] This book represents an attempt to make sense of this record and to establish the 1980s political left as a historical problem that requires rigorous research and analysis.

We adopt a wide understanding of the term 'left'. The volume takes the left to be the kaleidoscope of political institutions, ideologies and mentalities that challenged laissez-faire capitalism and promoted what it considered to be social justice in different ways on both a domestic and a global level. The left, for example, was formed by the international situation: the Cold War and the arms race, the decline of the Soviet Union, but also left-wing regimes in Latin America and the struggle against apartheid in South Africa.[8] The chapters by Callaghan (chapter 6) and Davis (chapter 5) in this volume document the ways in which the left mentally lived abroad, taking up issues of oppression around the world. In this sense, the radicals of the 1980s generation were heirs to a strand of internationalism that had been a feature of left-wing politics since the Chartists and which had shaped the Labour Party throughout its history.[9] It is difficult to understand the approach of Jeremy Corbyn as Labour leader after 2015 without understanding the way that he was formed by the left-wing internationalism of the 1970s and 1980s.

The decade was the moment when the left had to fully confront changes in class structure, when issues around race, gender, sexuality and environmentalism began to challenge class as the dominant left-wing paradigm. Neil Kinnock's Labour Party (particularly after the 1987–88 policy review) and intellectuals around the periodical *Marxism Today* offered a fundamental revision of the standard left-wing project.[10] Even before the decade began, Eric Hobsbawm's article, 'The Forward March of Labour Halted?' in 1978, had triggered a wave of debate on the left about whether class could provide the basis for mass mobilisation as it had previously done.[11] Political imagery based on the cloth cap was out of date in an age when workers bought their council houses, holidayed abroad and (briefly) purchased shares. This book recovers struggles that were sometimes unsuccessful but which were nevertheless an important part of the period. Despite the opprobrium directed at the so-called 'loony left', Labour remained true to the values of social liberalism, as Paul Bloomfield examines in chapter 3. Although liberal figures like Roy Jenkins defected to the SDP, it was Labour and the broader culture of the left which challenged sexism, racism and homophobia and stood for equal opportunities. This volume attempts an unsentimental analysis of the way that the forward march of labour was dramatically halted in the 1980s.

This Introduction (like this volume) does not claim to be exhaustive but sketches out some key ways of interpreting the trajectory of both Labour and the left in the age of Thatcherism. It begins with an examination of Labour's progress in the 1980s and the problems it ran into. We then seek to interpret the challenges of the decade by viewing them in terms of the longer history of Labour politics in Britain. Following that, we adopt an international lens, discussing Labour in the context of the global left in the era that saw the collapse of communism. The Introduction ends with an interrogation of the culture and ideology of the British left. We emphasise the kinds of identity that the left provided and suggest some leads that scholars of the future may wish to pursue.

Labour in the Foot and Kinnock era

> There are worrying signs that the labour movement is simply not willing to grasp, or is incapable of grasping, the seriousness of the position into which it has fallen. (Stuart Hall)[12]

Objects, places and moments that defined the left in the 1980s. Michael Foot's shabby 'donkey jacket' at the Cenotaph on Remembrance Day in 1981. The cardboard city of homeless people on London's South Bank. A policeman's truncheon. Tony Benn's claim that eight million people voted for socialism in the 1983 election. Gay's the Word bookshop. The use of the term 'The Cuts'. Riots at Toxteth in Liverpool. The branch meeting with uncomfortable seats in a cold community centre. The miners' walk-out at Cortonwood Colliery, South Yorkshire in 1984. The SDP accepting payments by credit card. The women's peace camp at Greenham Common. Neil Kinnock taking on Militant at the 1985 Labour Party conference. The Campaign for Nuclear Disarmament (CND) insignia. A car on fire during the Poll Tax riots in Trafalgar Square in 1990. The Labour Party's red rose emblem. Billy Bragg's melancholic but defiant rendition of 'Between the Wars'.

These are snapshots of the diverse left-wing culture in Britain. The Labour Party has never enjoyed a monopoly of the left. Many left-wing groups have been suspicious of it and even opposed to it. The SDP considered itself to be left of centre but felt compelled to abandon Labour as it seemed incapable of change. The left has often been fractured and subject to charges of betrayal.

For many in the public, the evident divisions within the Labour Party (brandished across the media) rendered it unelectable.

After the defeat of Jim Callaghan's government in 1979, his party shifted leftwards.[13] The 1974–79 Labour governments were believed by many to have failed. Labour was divided over Europe. In the 1975 referendum on the Common Market (as it was then called), Michael Foot and much of the left opposed Britain's continuing membership, while many on the right of the party (who would later join the SDP) supported remaining in Europe. But the divisions ran deeper still. Following the International Monetary Fund (IMF) crisis of 1976, Callaghan had been forced to make cuts in the welfare state which hit the very people Labour was meant to represent. The government had been elected in 1974 on the basis that it could deal with the unions, but this was fatally damaged by the chaos of the 'winter of discontent' in 1979, when rubbish piled up in the streets and flying pickets brought the country to a standstill.[14] Stagflation further undermined Labour's economic credibility although Chancellor of the Exchequer Denis Healey managed to reduce both inflation and unemployment (and to pay off the IMF loan) by 1979. After that year's general election, there was bitterness about the government's record, which the Conservatives attacked but few on the left were willing to defend.

This volume focuses on the long 1980s (from the general election of 1979 to that of 1992). There were two broad phases of left-wing activity. Faced with the coming of Thatcherism, there was a dramatic mobilisation of the left. Tony Benn emerged as the left's champion, damning the compromises of the Callaghan government of which he had been a part and insisting that policy should be driven by the views of the party itself (unions and ordinary members rather than the Parliamentary Labour Party). Michael Foot, the left's tribune since the 1950s, became Labour leader in 1980 (triggering a civil war within the party which led to the formation of the SDP).[15] The decision of the Conservative government to accept American cruise missiles led to the revival of the CND and Labour's decision to support unilateral nuclear disarmament (a cause Foot was associated with). Tony Benn, the new standard bearer of the left, challenged Denis Healey for the deputy leadership and was only narrowly defeated in 1981. The Militant Tendency emerged as a key left-wing movement in some cities, proving a challenge for the Labour leadership.[16] In 1979, Labour moved left as the centre of political gravity in the nation moved right. It had entered a wilderness in which it would stay for eighteen years (until 1997).

In retrospect, this leftward swing came to an end not with Labour's massive defeat in the 1983 general election or the selection of Neil Kinnock as Labour leader that followed, but with the miners' strike of 1984–85. There had been hopes by Labour activists that the miners could repeat what they had accomplished in 1974, when they in effect brought down the Conservative government of Edward Heath. The strike, however, was not mandated by a strike ballot, the miners ended up divided and the government had stockpiled sufficient coal to keep the country going. The miners were defeated just as they had been in the General Strike of 1926. The defeat of the print unions, who challenged Rupert Murdoch's move of his newspapers from Fleet Street to Wapping shortly after (in 1986), was no less momentous as it became a struggle over the introduction of new technology in which trade unions were perceived as the custodians of vested interests and restrictive practices. It was clear that the notion of extra-parliamentary opposition to the Thatcher governments was not going to work.

The labour movement and the left also had difficulty coming to terms with the larger economic forces unleashed by new technology and the global movements of capital epitomised by the Big Bang in the City of London. The left seemed backward looking, and Keynesian social democracy, which had once been considered so robust, now appeared fragile and a fleeting moment in Britain's post-war development. Opposition seemed increasingly futile because the left could not offer convincing alternatives to a world shaped by neo-liberalism. Yet this was a complex moment. The failure of the SDP and the Liberals (in an alliance) to make a breakthrough at the elections of 1983 and 1987 meant that Labour was confirmed in its role as the main party of opposition to the Tories. This showed an underlying strength in the Labour Party in these years.

The second half of the 1980s saw a wave of revisionism on the left coming to the fore, epitomised by Neil Kinnock's attempt to reconstruct the Labour Party.[17] Kinnock's historical significance is that, although steeped in the party of Bevan and Foot, he recognised Labour's need to change. To support the victimised, it was necessary to gain the votes of those who were not victimised. As Martin Farr shows in chapter 2 in this volume, Kinnock and the team around him placed increasing emphasis on image and presentation.[18] The left recognised a need to be more in tune with 1980s style, ideas and concepts. This was the age of 'designer socialism' (a term laced with irony). Following Labour's defeat in 1987, the Party's policy review opened up new ideas, including the abandonment of unilateral nuclear disarmament (which, it was clear, the electorate would not accept).[19] More positive noises were made about the value of markets as well as consumerism.[20] Marxist analysis was increasingly critiqued in academic circles for its economic reductionism. Margaret Thatcher's sale of council houses came to seem less heretical and there was an understanding that she had spoken to people's aspirations in a way that the left had not. A notable shift showed that something was changing: it was no longer seen as sufficient to blame reactionary views on 'false consciousness'. The views of ordinary people, even if sometimes unpalatable, had to be taken seriously and not simply dismissed.

John Lloyd took over as editor of the *New Statesman* from 1986–87, which was employed to force new ideas onto the agenda and shift Labour away from the far left.[21] Bryan Gould argued for wider share ownership, although on very different lines from the version promoted by Thatcherism.[22] Roy Hattersley's *Choose Freedom* in 1987 updated Croslandite revisionism and defined democratic socialism in terms of liberty.[23] The 'New Times' project fostered by *Marxism Today* argued that Britain was living in an age of post-Fordism: the shift of manufacturing abroad and the emergence of new technology meant that the economy was no longer defined by the assembly-line techniques of Henry Ford.[24] Such an analysis was Marxist only in its broad-brush economic determinism. What was important about 'New Times' was its attempt to embrace new thinking. It sought to understand a society that was changing and where new kinds of identity were shaping politics. Designer socialism was not, however, sufficient to enable Labour to win in 1992. This proved to be one of the most decisive modern elections, as it revealed the need for an even more fundamental rethink. Out of this would emerge Tony Blair's New Labour.

This volume resists the view that Labour's political and economic thought was moribund during the 1980s. Labour sought to develop dynamic responses to secure growth in an age of increasing globalisation. Eric Shaw's chapter (chapter 1) shows that Labour embraced new views on the role of the state and state intervention in the economy. There was much talk of the development state in the 1980s which would aid economic growth. Linked to this process was the idea of a national investment bank (an idea revived in Labour circles after 2015), which Richard Carr explores in chapter 4. Much of this reflected the success of continental social democracy, which seemed an attractive alternative to Thatcherism. For that reason, Labour abandoned its suspicions of Europe and became committed to the European cause up until the 'Brexit' referendum of 2016.

This volume is an attempt to probe the issues that are at stake in understanding the trajectory of the British left after 1979. In this work we are moving into new territory, as the scholarly literature remains relatively limited. The 1980s left has been covered by sometimes brilliant journalistic accounts but is now coming under the scrutiny of academic historians.[25] What are the paradigms that should shape an exploration of the history of the left in the 1980s? Do historians have any special insights that differ from those of other commentators?

The chief paradigm of modern political history has concerned the relative autonomy of the political.[26] Sociological explanations sometimes have limited value in explaining the trajectory of politics. Why, for example, do workers vote Conservative (which, from one point of view, does not make sense)? There has been a greater emphasis on the contingencies of politics and the role of language and strategy in shaping political appeals. Political parties create constituencies of support at least as much as they reflect them.[27] In chapter 1 Eric Shaw shows how New Labour was dependent upon the rhetorical construction of 'Old Labour', which resisted serious analysis of the historical record.

Building a history of Labour in the 1980s requires an analysis of the ways in which the party responded to social change. The 1992 election showed that its attempts to create a political coalition of voters who were prepared to accept limited tax increases to pay for high-quality public services had failed. One phase of Labour's history came to an end and New Labour filled the void. The left focused on issues around welfare and not on the economy itself, where it tended to become more open to market-based solutions. There were, however, considerable continuities from Old Labour into New Labour (more so than adherents of either grouping often allow).[28]

The remaking of class politics

This section argues that Labour's problems need to be seen in terms of the longer-term challenges that beset the party. The 1980s in some respects merely highlighted these longer-term trends and made them visible.

Any evaluation of Labour politics needs to consider the question of class and organised labour. Following the introduction of universal suffrage for both men and women between 1918 and 1928, the working class by any definition constituted the majority of the voting population. The Labour Party had developed a coherent identity based on the values of the working class in its organised form (through the trade union link) and on socialism (following the introduction of Clause 4 of the Party's constitution of 1918). However, Labour has never enjoyed a total monopoly of working-class people. The Conservatives have always managed to attract large numbers of working-class votes. In 1931 they even (in the form of the National Government) managed to win 55 per cent of the working-class vote.[29] The Labour Party has always had to look beyond its working-class base and appeal particularly to the professional middle classes.[30] In 1945, it managed to fashion a vast cross-class coalition of voters based on workers with also about 30 per cent of the middle-class vote.[31]

Labour was at its electoral high point in the 1940s and 1950s, not least because the Second World War had transformed the bargaining power of organised labour. The 1945 Labour Government introduced the welfare state (including the National Health Service) and a massive programme of nationalisation and secured Indian independence. In 1945, Labour received 47.8 per cent of the popular vote and in 1951 it actually managed to gain 48.8 per cent, a larger proportion of the electorate than the Conservatives, who actually won the election.

Labour's vote thereafter declined (and we should see the party's fate in the 1980s as part of this longer trajectory of electoral failure). There were many reasons for this, but let us note two factors that shaped the party's post-1951 fortunes. The first was the struggle over the direction that the party should take, having accomplished many of its major reforms when Clement Attlee was Prime Minister. The party was divided in the 1950s by the conflict between Bevanites, who demanded a move to the left, and the revisionist approach favoured by Labour leader Hugh Gaitskell and party philosopher Tony Crosland, who suggested that socialism was better secured by economic growth and redistribution than by further nationalisation. The divisions between the two sides helped to keep the party out of power till 1964 but have continued to recur in various ways since then. This was true of Labour in the 1980s and of the party after 2015.

The second factor that damaged Labour was the development of affluence and mass consumerism. Post-war Labour and trade union politicians never quite knew how to react to a society that was simply very different from that of the interwar depression which had shaped their outlook. Even the coming of commercial television was opposed, while pop music and advertising were treated with suspicion by some.[32] Such a society seemed to favour the Conservative Party, which marketed itself as the party of the consumers rather than of the producers (it also presented itself as the natural party of government, which made Labour seem the party of sectional interests). In the 1950s commentators noted the decisive influence of affluence, social mobility and 'embourgeoisement' which softened the edges of class divisions. Working people acquired a level of security that had been denied them in the interwar period.[33] Well before the 1980s, politics was becoming less tribal, as the re-emergence of the Liberal Party as a force in the 1960s and 1970s showed.

Yet it is worth putting this in some perspective. Despite the development of affluence, the Labour vote held up remarkably well in the 1950s (although not enough to win elections). Working-class life remained a struggle against poor living conditions and the snobbish belief that workers were somehow inferior because they did not buy into a middle-class view of the world. It was arguably only in the 1970s that affluence really began to reshape popular attitudes. Thatcherism was in some respects the expression of a new kind of society, increasingly impatient with bureaucracy, inflation and restrictions on consumer demands. While Harold Wilson managed to secure three election victories in the 1960s and 1970s, the fundamental divisions over political strategy and the reaction to affluence dogged not only Labour but left-wing politics in general.

We should therefore view the conflicts of the 1980s in part as the continuation of long-term problems which divided the left in the post-war period. The role of trade unions (integral to the corporatist politics of the 1960s and 1970s) became increasingly controversial.[34] Harold Wilson's and Barbara Castle's trade union reforms (White Paper *In Place of Strife*) had been defeated in 1969. Attempts at industrial partnership and a counter-inflationary incomes policy finally dissolved in the 'winter of discontent' in 1979. To a large extent, the great era of post-war social democracy was destroyed by the paradox that trade unions could bring down a union-backed Labour government. In theory this should have been impossible, given that Labour was meant to be the party of the unions, and yet it happened. A significant number of trade unionists actually voted for Margaret Thatcher in 1979 (further evidence that sociological explanations for political behaviour may be problematic or, at least, reductive). Basic assumptions about the politics of class were being overturned. Labour and the left were associated with the promotion of unaccountable bureaucracies (the nanny state, nationalised industries), vested interests (trade unions) and opposition to individual choice. Many key promoters of Thatcherism (the journalist Paul Johnson, the economists John Vaizey and Alan Walters) were, significantly, people who had been on the left but had had a change of heart as they confronted the challenges of the 1970s and the unprepossessing nature of the Soviet Union. They brought the zeal of the convert to the Thatcherite project. A new kind of populist right-wing politics emerged which the left reacted to in different ways. Could the appeals of class and social solidarity still provide the basis of a mass politics? This is what was at stake in the politics of the 1980s.

Labour's civil war of the early 1980s was to some extent a replay of the divisions between Bevanites and Gaitskellites in the 1950s. In the 1980s case, many of the Gaitskellites, such as Roy Jenkins, opted to leave the party and form the SDP. Both Michael Foot and Neil Kinnock clothed themselves in the mantle of Aneurin Bevan (the political figure who most embodied Labour's idealism). It was obvious that the opposition vote to Thatcherism was divided, allowing the Tories to gain huge majorities in 1983 and 1987. For the first time, the left developed the niggling feeling that the historical momentum was not on its side. Yet the 1980s continued to provide models where solidarity with the struggles of workers could be the cause of mass mobilisation (as Maroula Joannou's chapter 8 on the miners' strike shows). Arguably, the decade proved to be the coda to an era of mass politics led by trade unions that lasted from the 1880s to the mid-1980s.

Another way of understanding the left in this period is to reflect on the way that it made sense of its past. It was heavily divided over the record of the Labour governments in the 1960s and (especially) the 1970s. There had always been a strain on the left which distrusted the parliamentary road to socialism.[35] The Wilson and Callaghan governments between 1974 and 1979 were accused by Tony Benn and others on the left of betraying their own supporters. The 1945 Labour Government was spoken of, however, with increased respect as Thatcherism threatened the achievements of the Attlee governments with its programme of privatisation. Michael Foot and Neil Kinnock continually extolled the way in which Labour had spoken for the nation after the war and changed it. Martin Farr's chapter 2 shows how Michael Foot's frame of reference was continually attached to the past, particularly the 1930s (one reason why Foot came to support the Falklands task force was his long-standing opposition to appeasement and determination to resist dictators). Nostalgia was built into Labour's psyche, making it seem rather backward looking and adrift from a changing society (which explains why New Labour in the 1990s was so uninterested in the party's past).[36]

We should see the 1980s as highlighting conflicts over competing notions of class loyalties, social mobility and individual aspirations that have shaped British politics ever since. These questions were not entirely new but the issues were redefined as it appeared that the notion of the traditional working class was changing.[37] Work itself was taking new forms with the development of service industries and the decline of manufacturing. The signature policy of Thatcherism proved to be the privatisation of state-owned industries and services. Nationalisation had been at the core of the way many on the left defined socialism. By the later 1980s, it was clear that the privatisations of the Thatcher governments would be difficult to reverse. Globalisation, membership of the European Economic Commonity (EEC) and the destruction of Britain's industrial base meant that the idea of socialism in one country was increasingly untenable. The Alternative Economic Strategy floated by Tony Benn in 1976 (which involved import controls, protectionism and a siege economy) was quickly abandoned even by the left. The experience of the 1970s and 1980s suggested that in an international marketplace governments could not control their own destiny. In time, this became a problem for the right (as it began to turn against Europe), but it also meant that the left lacked an economic policy. The chapters by Eric Shaw (chapter 2) and Richard Carr (chapter 4) explore how Labour attempted to fill this void.

Changes in class structure were not the only problem. We should view the experience of the left through the prisms of gender and race (themes in the chapters of Maroula Joannou and Robin Bunce, 8 and 9, respectively). It became apparent that the twentieth-century labour movement had thrived on a view that privileged white, male workers. Yet women had always been part of the labour force although trade unions often had a problematic relationship with them. The spectacle of dock workers supporting Enoch Powell after 1968 challenged the view that working-class people always held progressive views. The mythology of a heroic working class struggling against oppression and embodying the promise of a new society (the essence of the Marxist view) was challenged from within as it became clear how oppressive many of these same workers could be.

Changes in economic structure validated women's roles in the work-force. The experience of labour in the 1980s required an acknowledgement that the labour force was changing and that it was extremely diverse. Left-wing politics ever since has been an attempt to come to terms with this reality. There were demands for there to be black and women's 'sections' within Labour (a move resisted by the party as sectarian). The white working-class no longer seemed like heroic agents of change and in time would be vilified as 'chavs' or the 'underclass' or (in time) as 'left behind' voters who would be as likely to vote for the anti-immigrant United Kingdom Independence Party in the early twenty-first century as to vote Labour.[38]

The global dimension

It is limiting to view this subject purely through a purely British lens. This book is distinctive in its ambition to situate the left within both the national and the global context. The declining fortunes of the British left matched the fortunes of the left in many (but not all) countries and need to be seen in that wider perspective. Socialist and social democratic parties were regularly defeated. In the United States Ronald Reagan and George H. W. Bush began to unpick the New Deal Order that was embodied by the Democratic Party.[39] We need to consider the British left with reference to global politics and the international socialist movement, as both played an important role in defining its ideas and attitudes in the last decade of the Cold War. Labour was opposed to membership of Europe for much of the 1980s, until it discovered the virtues of Jacques Delors's social vision of Europe and considered it a means of circumventing Thatcherism.

At the same time, non-British influences helped to define Labour's ideas and actions at different times in the twentieth century.[40] Global affairs influenced Britain's domestic politics as similar issues to those that defined the 1930s – high unemployment, a new right-wing philosophy and changes in the USSR – again shaped international politics.

The USSR had long been an important international influence on Labour, and it was no less so in the 1980s. The country that supposedly embodied 'actually existing socialism' had exerted a particular hold on sections of the party since 1917, when events in Russia briefly pushed the British labour movement leftwards. There had been much talk of forming soviets and following the revolutionary ways of the country's Marxists.[41] While this did not last, it left an interest in what was happening in the Soviet Union. The presence of a socialist alternative to liberal democracy and Labour's own strand of socialism continued until the end of the Cold War. Many visitors went to the USSR to see socialism supposedly being built, a fact which helped to define Labour's political thought in different ways.[42] The thought and actions of this particular country influenced Labour's ideas and its vision as it further embraced planning and the notion of the state's having a more interventionist role in the socio-economic life of Britain.

Labour was also influenced by less extreme versions of state intervention, including Roosevelt's New Deal in the United States and Swedish social democracy. These tied in with ideas already present in the party, such as the Fabians' 'top down', managerial approach to politics. Between the wars, Labour's ideas concerning the state were shaped by the domestic problems that faced Britain during the Great Depression, by its own traditions, by international revolutionary socialism and by more moderate, although no less international, alternatives to capitalism. After the war, Labour's Foreign Secretary, Ernest Bevin, rejected closer links with the USSR and tied Britain's fortunes to the West and the USA. The Cold War side was picked, but some on the Labour left still saw the USSR and the 'people's democracies' in the Eastern Bloc as worthy of their support. Other alternative forms of socialism and social democracy were also discussed at various times during the Cold War, including Mao's China, Castro's Cuba and Hawke's Australia. Labour was therefore never a 'little Englander' party; nor was the left more generally.

By the 1980s, Labour had to determine where it stood on the decade's big global issues – the end of *détente*, the renewed East–West hostilities and the arms race, challenges to Soviet control in Eastern Europe and changes in the Soviet leadership. In 1984, Labour's leaders met with Mikhail Gorbachev, who told them of the USSR's concerns over Ronald Reagan's 'Star Wars' programme. Gorbachev hoped that there would be a 'demilitarisation' of outer space. Questions about nuclear disarmament had informed debates within the Labour Party since the early peace marches and were again important in this decade. Some rejected the notion of unilateral disarmament, while others embraced the radicalism of the protesters at Greenham Common.

Labour's 'modernisation' process was also influenced by its relations with the wider world. China had once attracted interest as an alternative model of socialism, but in the post-Mao age, Deng Xiaoping's market reforms led the country's economy down a very different path. This was also true in France and Greece, where socialist governments quickly adopted a more neo-liberal approach to the economy. And after Mikhail Gorbachev pursued his restructuring of the Soviet economy – and ultimately Soviet ideology – Labour soon followed suit and Neil Kinnock's policy review in 1987 led to his own *perestroika* of the Labour Party.

Many of these issues are discussed in the chapters by Callaghan (chapter 6) and Davis (chapter 5). Policies pursued by Labour in the 1970s – state ownership and state-directed economic policy, hostility to NATO and the EEC – were discarded in the 1980s not only by Labour but also by other European socialists.[43] And, after 1985, Gorbachev's restructuring of Soviet socialism had a significant impact on Labour's own political thought and helped it to move into a new ideological era. International politics and changing global circumstances thus played as influential a role in defining Labour's understanding of contemporary issues as domestic affairs did.

The left was rather more successful when fighting for human rights abroad. South Africa under apartheid was vilified and the cause of Nelson Mandela championed, while Margaret Thatcher's government appeared to do nothing to challenge the regime. There were mass demonstrations, part of an international cultural offensive that took in pop music ('Free Nelson Mandela'), sport and consumer boycotts. The left made it clear that apartheid South Africa had pariah status, and supported the African National Congress in its struggle with racial injustice. In 1990 Mandela walked free and apartheid crumbled.

To be on the left in the 1980s involved spending a lot of time thinking about Nicaragua, Soviet dissidents and the Middle East. Closer to home, there were demands to withdraw British troops from Northern Ireland. The British left is sometimes criticised for its intellectual insularity.[44] This is true in some respects, but the wider world was central to the way the left viewed itself, from Neil Kinnock's opposition to nuclear weapons to anger about third-world hunger and the mounting level of debt in poorer countries.

Left-wing identities

How did the culture of the left change in the 1980s? Changing attitudes to gender, race and sexuality explain why the decade became increasingly shaped by the politics of identity. This was in some respects the left's response to the right's emphasis on choice. The new emphasis was on diversity rather than simply the collective. In this view, everyone is part of a minority of some kind. Issues about racial and sexual discrimination (neither of which was new in 1980) reached new prominence. The spectacle of women protesting at Greenham Common and the mobilisation of miners' wives during the strike offered examples of what seemed to some to be distinctly female forms of protest not shaped by masculine norms. The ways in which men and women experienced poverty differently became an issue.[45] The use of Section 28 of the Local Government Act in 1988 to prevent the alleged promotion of homosexuality by local authorities and schools caused outrage. The experience of the left in the 1980s suggested a move towards a new kind of politics, based on identity, choice and the individual.

The most enduring achievement of the post-Attlee Labour Party had been in the moral reforms of the 1960s, ending capital punishment, legalising abortion and homosexuality and ending censorship of the arts. In retrospect, the sexual politics of the 1980s left continued this tradition (see Paul Bloomfield's chapter 3).[46] Ken Livingstone's GLC, for example, recognised the competing demands of gays and lesbians for recognition and freedom from discrimination. This in turn triggered a right-wing response about the 'loony left' obsessed about 'political correctness'. Having been in the vanguard of 1960s liberalism and the avant garde, the left was denounced for being allegedly made up of puritans and kill-joys, eager to complain about any statement or form of behaviour that might be sexist or racist or in some way offensive. The Labour MP Clare Short, for example, condemned page 3 of the *Sun* newspaper, which featured photographs of naked women to boost sales. The emphasis on social diversity marked a shift away from the universalist approach of the left in its earlier forms. In retrospect, however, this emphasis on the rights of minorities and the celebration of difference created a politics of inclusiveness which refashioned the social agenda. Economic liberalism in its Thatcherite form shaped modern politics thereafter, but it has since become difficult to succeed in politics without being some kind of social liberal. In retrospect, the final triumph of the 1980s left was the decision by Conservative Prime Minister David Cameron to introduce gay marriage in 2014.

This also explains why the left increasingly turned to arguments about citizenship rather than socialism.[47] The creation of Charter 88 and its promotion by the *New Statesman* under the editorship of Stuart Weir in the later 1980s supported the introduction of a written constitution (to ensure basic civil liberties) and proportional representation as the way forward for the left. There were also calls for a popular front against Thatcherism made up of non-Tory forces from the Liberals through to the far left.

The character of the left was in many respects defined by Thatcherism and the need to oppose Tory legislation. Margaret Thatcher was clear that her aim was to destroy everything that the left stood for. This meant that left-wing politics were combative. Rising unemployment and the reform of trade union rights produced an angry response; so did 'the Cuts' (huge reductions in government spending on public amenities). The decision to accept American cruise missiles led to the revival of CND. Margaret Thatcher's celebration of Victorian values and her claim that there was no such thing as society led to accusations that she was turning the clock back to the era of extreme laissez-faire in the nineteenth century.

At the same time intellectuals such as Stuart Hall argued that Thatcherism was creating a new kind of hegemony and common sense which the left needed to find a way of contesting.[48] There were new strains of thinking that would commence the long task of bringing Labour back to power in 1997. The intellectuals around the think-tank Demos and *Marxism Today*'s 'New Times' project laid the basis for New Labour by documenting how the economy was moving into a post-Fordist mode which rendered previous assumptions about political strategy redundant (although some of these figures subsequently repudiated New Labour). If capitalism was changing, it followed that the left had to change as well.

Another factor that contributed to the changing culture of the left was national identity. The huge popularity of Margaret Thatcher after the victory in the Falklands and the alleged role of the 'Falklands factor' in securing her electoral landslide in 1983 stunned many on the left. Class loyalties had been seen on the left as the important thing; workers possessed a class but not a nation (which was often viewed as a form of false consciousness). However, there was no mistaking the rise of different kinds of nationalist politics in Scotland and Northern Ireland, which had powerful appeal. Some felt that the appeals of patriotism had to be reworked in radical forms.[49] The popularity of the royal family was acknowledged but was also the source of a revived republicanism which argued that Britain's antiquated institutions needed to be transformed in a modern polity.[50] Mass immigration had, in any case, required the notions of what constituted Englishness and Britishness to be fundamentally rethought. Citizens with families who came from other parts of the world, and particularly from Britain's former colonial possessions, sometimes challenged the romanticism about the empire and Britain's imperial past.[51]

Evaluations of the left in the 1980s follow some of the standard paradigms of labour history: the significance of class and movement cultures, the debates about ideology and strategy, the legal status of trade unions, the opportunities taken or missed, the role of riot and resistance, the attempts at alternative forms of living, the role of charismatic leadership. Yet, as this Introduction has shown, the 1980s was a decisive decade which transformed the place of labour in society.

New paradigms will also be necessary to evaluate the fate of the left after 1979. Many workers lost the kind of identity that unions gave them. Deindustrialisation and lack of union membership left them feeling abandoned, exposed to the currents of the global marketplace and doomed to working in a low-wage service economy. The move towards greater equality of incomes that had characterised the post-war decades came to an end in the 1980s and wealth increasingly became skewed towards people at the top.[52] And yet living standards improved for most. Lower inflation and the shift towards reduced rates of income tax created (to quote John Kenneth Galbraith) 'a culture of contentment'.[53] Not much could be done to help the underclass when the majority had never had it so good. Movement politics had less purchase when politics started to become about issues of individual choice and aspiration. New dynamics had come into play.

The print culture of the left needs exploration. The 1980s was notable for the dramatic press onslaught on Labour.[54] Michael Foot and Neil Kinnock were pilloried and caricatured so that many voters could not take them seriously. The majority of the press barons (particularly Rupert Murdoch) supported the Conservatives and promoted a vicious campaign against Labour. Margaret Thatcher's government rarely had to worry about press coverage. Labour was, however, supported by Robert Maxwell's *Daily Mirror* and by the *Guardian* (although the latter was often positive about the SDP). There was also a wider alternative press that included *Militant* (supporters of Militant claimed that it was a newspaper and not a movement), the *New Statesman*, *Tribune*, *Socialist Worker* and *Class War*. There were concerns that the left was at odds with popular culture. The popularity of the *Sun* (with its heady cocktail of page 3 girls, bingo, celebrity gossip and joyous jingoism) suggested that the left had lost touch with what many ordinary voters wanted. When the *News on Sunday* was launched as a left-wing tabloid in 1987, it folded within seven months. It was worthy but dull, failing to find the right tone for a popular newspaper. By the end of the 1980s, the left seemed entirely at odds with popular culture. Historically, this was merely the continuation of an ongoing discomfort that many left-wingers had with popular culture.[55] Keir Hardie on one occasion visited a Manchester theatre and was so shocked by a scene in which a woman sat on a man's lap that he walked out. Trade unionist Ben Tillett once complained: 'If the Labour Party could select a King, he would be a Feminist, a Temperance crank, a Nonconformist charlatan … an anti-sport, an anti-jollity advocate, a teetotaller, as well as a general wet blanket.'[56] There was a discernible shift away from extreme puritanism in the later 1980s, evident in the appeal of alternative comedians such as Ben Elton and Alexei Sayle who showed that the left needed to have a sense of humour if it was to persuade.

The 1980s was the decade in which Labour had to concede that image and presentation mattered. It was symbolised by the decision of the party to adopt the emblem of the red rose (even arguing about how long the stem should be). The alleged control-freakery of the Blair years was founded in a feeling that arguments about policy were seen by the public as evidence that the party was divided and therefore unable to govern. It became increasingly important for Labour to be seen to speak in one voice (a view that contrasted with figures such as Ken Livingstone who believed that Labour should be a parliament of the left, priding itself on its rainbow-like appeal, with different political colours represented). The great literary treatment of 1980s Labour proved to be David Hare's play *The Absence of War* (1993), in which a Labour leader (clearly based on Kinnock) loses his authenticity and integrity when he is taken over by the spin doctors who stress the need to appeal a wider public.

Left-wing politics can fruitfully be analysed through the emerging history of the emotions. Many people on the left presented their politics in rigorously rationalistic form (although less so with reference to Marx as the 1980s went on). Yet politics is also a matter of temperament. We need to think seriously about the way left-wingers performed their politics (although comparable arguments could be made about people on the right). There were emotional responses to the 'boss class' and demands for 'street credibility'. There was the way the trauma and anguish of defeat had to be managed. There was the relish for the demo, the loud hailer and the mass meeting. The identity of the 'activist' was clearly important for some.[57] The language of altruism, compassion and social justice was important for all (with the implication that Tories lacked all of these qualities). Items of clothing could express some of these feelings: the donkey jacket, the 'Cole Not Dole' badge. There was a distinct material culture of the left. Clearly, much of this was also framed by gender and by social location. Labour in the 1990s seemed to have a different emotional vocabulary from the 1980s, where there was less of a knee-jerk desire to attack the leadership. Some of this was no doubt driven by the experience of continual defeat, which made party members look to Tony Blair, a figure who would not have been acceptable to the party ten years earlier.

The left was sometimes presented as humourless. To be on the left requires the view that ideas and strategies should mean something. This in turn leads to claims of betrayal and disputes about minor issues of policy or belief. There was a recognition on the left later in the decade that a joyless approach, looking disdainfully down on people who were not 'ideologically sound' (a vogue term usually employed ironically), was problematic when it came to developing a mass movement. More seriously, it suggested that the left was at odds with popular culture and with many working-class people who were viewed as racist, sexist, homophobic, jingoistic and addicted to the *Sun*.

There are other optics for exploring the left in the 1980s. These would include greater attention to the local and the personal. We need new histories of constituency Labour parties and the ways they operated. Alternative left-wing movements such as the Socialist Workers Party need greater treatment. So too does the history of student radicalism (a subject by no means confined to the 1960s). There were multiple cultures of activism more generally. At the same time, the figure of the activist was often unattractive to many who nevertheless possessed left-of-centre sympathies. This was a problem for the Bennite vision of activists' democracy. The 1980s ended with the emergence of a solid constituency concerned about environmental causes, evident in the 2,299,274 votes for the Green Party in the 1989 European election (although it gained no members of the European Parliament).

Labour's defeat in 1992 was a turning point. While hopes were high for a victory against John Major (who replaced Margaret Thatcher as Conservative Prime Minister in 1990), the defeat of Neil Kinnock's Labour Party suggested that a large part of the south of England would not elect a party that was committed to increasing taxation (even on those able to pay). This had a huge political and psychological impact. It made way for the coming of New Labour which was partly based on the belief that Labour would never win if it was simply associated with high taxation. There was also a psychological and emotional consequence. It seemed that Britain was doomed to permanent Conservative governments, making opposition feel pointless. Many people who had been politically active seemed to check out of politics and look elsewhere for sources of meaning.[58]

Tony Blair argued that Britain changed in the 1980s but Labour failed to come to terms with this. For New Labour, it was important to recognise the motivating force of aspiration in the lives of ordinary people. It is difficult not to view the left of the 1980s in the light of New Labour (which, as Eric Shaw shows in chapter 1, was animated by a particular view of Old Labour). Blair's decision to abandon Clause Four and his relentless pursuit of 'Middle England' was a renunciation of a record of electoral failure under Foot and Kinnock.

At the same time, the election of Jeremy Corbyn as Labour leader in 2015 and again in 2016 prompts some reconsideration of Labour's record, reminding us that there may be a number of alternatives to viewing the 1980s through a New Labour prism. The significance of Corbyn, very much a veteran of

Labour in the 1970s and 1980s, suggests that the left was not totally defeated at the end of the 1980s but went into a kind of hibernation (with the arguable exception of Ken Livingstone's period as Mayor of London). On the other hand, the youthfulness of Corbyn's supporters leads one to argue that they represent a distinctively new formation, rooted in the Iraq War, the 2008 recession, the Occupy movement and dismay about inter-generational theft. The Corbynite view would suggest that Labour in the 1980s abandoned principle and capitulated to neo-liberalism and a Cold War view of the world. The reality is more complex and it is the duty of scholars to tease out some of these complexities. For example, many of the key figures in New Labour had a history on the left which they never formally renounced.[59]

This subject lends itself to exposition in a tragic mode. The labour struggles of the 1980s have provided subject matter for a wave of populist British cinema: *Brassed Off* (1996), *Billy Eliot* (2000), *Pride* (2014). Lacking a name, this genre celebrates the decency of ordinary humanity and evokes a sense of solidarity that appears poignant because it is fast disappearing in contemporary Britain. These films show how far we have come. The 1980s resonates within modern popular culture because it carries the feeling of a world we have lost: the belief that Britain could be a different place and that there might be alternatives to a market economy. This viewpoint was crushed by the events of that decade. A new common sense emerged that differed from post-war Keynesian social democracy. The market was seen as liberating and market-based solutions were the best ones. The institutions of the state with its public services required privatisation or constant reform if they were to survive. The identity of the customer was as important as that of the citizen. Self-fulfilment was what counted.

History should, however, never just be written by the winners. We need more complex histories of the decade that shaped the way we live now. The left of the 1980s was easy to caricature at the time and still is: naive, idealistic, puritanical, hypocritical, given to idle gestures and rhetoric, backward looking (in the way radicals paradoxically so often are), always assuming it knew what was best for other people, so often succumbing to the narcissism of small differences which created splits and distrust. It had remarkably little to say about wealth creation. Yet there was also a serious moral purpose which set the left apart as well as a commitment to social improvement. In its various forms it contributed to the changing landscape of Britain in the 1980s. This volume explores some of the ways in which it did so.

Notes

1 Tony Benn, *Arguments for Socialism* (London: Penguin, 1980).
2 Diane Abbott, Bernie Grant, Paul Boateng and Keith Vaz were elected in the 1987 General Election.
3 E. P. Thompson and Dan Smith, *Protest and Survive* (London: Penguin, 1980).

4 Raphael Samuel, Barbara Bloomfield and Guy Boanas (eds), *The Enemy Within: Pit Villages and the Miners' Strike of 1984–5* (London: Routledge and Kegan Paul, 1986); Diarmaid Kelliher, 'Solidarity and Sexuality: Lesbians and Gays support the Miners', *History Workshop* 77 (2014), 240–62.
5 Ken Livingstone, *If Voting Changed Anything, They'd Abolish It* (London: Collins, 1987).
6 Martin Pugh, *Speak for Britain! A New History of the Labour Party* (London: Bodley Head, 2010).
7 Richard Hill, *The Labour Party and Economic Strategy, 1979–97* (Basingstoke: Palgrave, 2001); James E. Cronin, *New Labour's Pasts: The Labour Party and Its Discontents* (London: Longman, 2004).
8 Tony Judt, *Postwar: A History of Europe since 1945* (London: Heinemann 2010); Geoff Eley, *Forging Democracy: The History of the Left in Europe, 1850–2000* (Oxford: Oxford University Press, 2002).
9 Margot Finn, *After Chartism: Class and Nation in English Radical Politics, 1848–1874* (Cambridge: Cambridge University Press, 1993); Paul Corthorn and Jonathan Davis (eds), *The British Labour Party and the Wider World: Domestic Politics, Internationalism and Foreign Policy* (London: I. B. Tauris, 2012).
10 Stuart Hall and Martin Jacques (eds), *New Times: The Changing Face of Politics in the 1990s* (London: Lawrence and Wishart, 1989).
11 Eric Hobsbawm et al. (eds), *The Forward March of Labour Halted?* (London: NLB, 1981); Eric Hobsbawm, *Politics for a Rational Left: Political Writing, 1977–1988* (London: Verso, 1989).
12 Stuart Hall, *The Hard Road to Renewal: Thatcherism and the Crisis of the Left* (London: Verso, 1988), p. 196.
13 David Kogan and Maurice Kogan, *The Battle for the Labour Party* (London: Kogan Page, 1982); Patrick Seyd, *The Rise and Fall of the Labour Left* (London: Macmillan, 1987).
14 John Shepherd, *Crisis? What Crisis? The Callaghan Government and the British Winter of Discontent* (Manchester: Manchester University Press, 2013).
15 Paul Corthorn, 'Michael Foot as Labour Leader: The Uses of the Past', in Richard Toye and Julie V. Gottlieb (eds), *Making Reputations: Power, Persuasion and the Individual in Modern British Politics* (London: I. B. Tauris, 20005), pp. 151–65; Kenneth O. Morgan, *Michael Foot: A Life* (London: Harper Press 2007); Andrew Scott Crines, *Michael Foot and the Labour Leadership* (Newcastle: Cambridge Scholars, 2011).
16 Nicklaus Thomas-Symonds, 'A Reinterpretation of Michael Foot's Handling of the Militant Tendency', *Contemporary British History* 19 (2005), 27–51.
17 Eric Shaw, *Discipline and Discord in the Labour Party: The Politics of Managerial Control in the Labour Party, 1951–87* (Manchester: Manchester University Press, 1988); Richard Heffernan and Mike Marqusee, *Defeat from the Jaws of Victory: Inside Kinnock's Labour Party* (London: Verso, 1992); Patrick Seyd and Paul Whiteley, *Labour's Grass Roots: The Politics of Party Membership* (Oxford: Clarendon Press, 1992); Eric Shaw, *The Labour Party since 1979* (London: Routledge 1994); Neil Kinnock, 'Reforming the Labour Party', *Contemporary Record* 8 (1994), 535–54; Steven Fielding, 'Neil Kinnock: An Overview of the Labour Party', *Contemporary Record* 8 (1994), 589–601; Tudor Jones, 'Neil Kinnock's Socialist Journey: From Clause Four to the Policy Review', *Contemporary Record* 8 (1994), 567–88; Martin J. Smith, 'Neil Kinnock and the Modernisation of the Labour Party', *Contemporary Record* 8 (1994), 555–66; Eric Shaw, 'The Wilderness Years, 1979–94', in Brian Brivati and Richard Heffernan (eds), *The Labour Party: A Centenary History* (Basingtoke: Macmillan, 2000), pp. 112–42; Martin Westlake, *Kinnock: The Authorised Biography*

(London: Little, Brown, 2001); Thomas Quinn, *Modernising the Labour Party: Organisational Change since 1983* (London: Palgrave Macmillan, 2004).
18 See also Lucy Robinson, '"Sometimes I Like to Stay In and Watch TV...": Kinnock's Labour Party and Media Culture', *Twentieth Century British History* 22 (2011), 354–90.
19 Colin Hughes and Patrick Wintour, *Labour Rebuilt: The New Model Party* (London: Fourth Estate, 1990).
20 David Miller, *Market, State and Community: Theoretical Foundations of Market Socialism* (Oxford: Clarendon Press, 1989).
21 See also John Lloyd, *A Rational Advance for the Labour Party* (London: Chatto and Windus, 1990).
22 Bryan Gould, *A Future for Socialism* (London: Cape, 1989).
23 Roy Hattersley, *Choose Freedom: The Future of Democratic Socialism* (London: Penguin, 1987).
24 Hall and Jacques (eds), *New Times*.
25 Andy McSmith, *Faces of Labour: The Inside Story* (London: Verso, 1996).
26 For an analysis of this trend see Rohan McWilliam, *Popular Politics in Nineteenth Century England* (London: Routledge, 1998), pp. 33–52.
27 Jon Lawrence, *Speaking for the People: Party, Language and Popular Politics in England, 1867–1914* (Cambridge: Cambridge University Press, 1998).
28 Steven Fielding, 'New Labour and the Past', in Duncan Tanner, Pat Thane and Nick Tiratsoo (eds), *Labour's First Century* (Cambridge: Cambridge University Press, 2000), pp. 367–92.
29 Ross McKibbin, *Parties and People: England, 1914–1951* (Oxford: Oxford University Press, 2010), pp. 95–6.
30 Duncan Tanner, 'Class Voting and Radical Politics: The Liberal and Labour Parties, 1910–1931', in Jon Lawrence and Miles Taylor (eds), *Party, State and Society: Electoral Behaviour in Britain since 1820* (London: Scolar, 1987).
31 McKibbin, *Parties and People*, p. 186.
32 Lawrence Black, *The Political Culture of the Left in Britain, 1951–1964: Old Labour, New Britain?* (Basingstoke: Palgrave Macmillan, 2003), esp. pp. 94–123.
33 Selina Todd argues in *The People: The Rise and Fall of the Working Class, 1910–2010* (London: John Murray, 2014) that inequality actually increased in the 1950s (pp. 199–212).
34 Keith Middlemas, *Power, Competition and the State* (Basingstoke: Macmillan, 1986–91), 3 vols.
35 Ralph Miliband, *Parliamentary Socialism: A Study in the Politics of Labour* (London: George Allen and Unwin, 1961).
36 Emily Robinson, *History, Heritage and Tradition in Contemporary British Politics: Past Politics and Present Histories* (Manchester: Manchester University Press, 2012).
37 Andre Gorz, *Farewell to the Working Class: An Essay on Post-Industrial Socialism* (London: Pluto Press, 1980).
38 Michael Collins, *The Likes of Us: A Biography of the White Working Class* (London: Granta, 2004); Owen Jones, *Chavs: The Demonisation of the Working Class* (London: Verso, 2011).
39 Steve Fraser and Gary Gerstle (eds), *The Rise and Fall of the New Deal Order* (Princeton, NJ: Princeton University Press, 1990).
40 The present volume extends the arguments developed in Paul Corthorn and Jonathan Davis (eds), *The British Labour Party and the Wider World: Domestic Politics, Internationalism and Foreign Policy* (London: I. B. Tauris, 2008).
41 Ian Bullock, *Romancing the Revolution: The Myth of Soviet Democracy and the British Left* (Edmonton: Athabasca University Press, 2011); Jonathan Davis, 'A New

Socialist Influence: British Labour and Revolutionary Russia, 1917–1918', *Scottish Labour History* 48 (2013), 158–79.
42 Stephen White, 'British Labour in Soviet Russia, 1920', *English Historical Review* 109 (1994), 621–40; Jonathan Davis, 'Labour's Political Thought: The Soviet Influence in the Interwar Years', in Corthorn and Davis (eds), *The British Labour Party and the Wider World*, pp. 64–85; Jonathan Davis, 'An Outsider Looks In: Walter Citrine's First Visit to the Soviet Union, 1925', *Revolutionary Russia* 26 (2013), 147–63.
43 See Eric Hobsbawm, *Age of Extremes: The Short Twentieth Century 1914–1991* (London: Abbacus, 1995), 433–99; Mark Mazower, *Dark Continent: Europe's Twentieth Century* (London: Penguin Books, 1998), pp. 290–401.
44 Perry Anderson, 'Origins of the Present Crisis', *New Left Review* 23 (1964), 26–54.
45 Beatrix Campbell, *Wigan Pier Revisited: Poverty and Politics in the 1980s* (London: Verso, 1984).
46 Stephen Brooke, *Sexual Politics: Sexuality, Family Planning and the British Left from the 1880s to the Present Day* (Oxford: Oxford University Press, 2011).
47 Geoff Andrews, *Citizenshp* (London: Lawrence and Wishart, 1990).
48 Hall, *The Hard Road to Renewal*.
49 Robert Gray, 'Left Holding the Flag', *Marxism Today* (November 1982), 22–7; Raphael Samuel (eds), *Patriotism: The Making and Unmaking of British Identity* (London: Routledge, 1989), 3 vols.
50 Tom Nairn, *The Enchanted Glass: Britain and its Monarchy* (London: Radius, 1988).
51 Bill Schwarz, *Memories of Empire* (Oxford: Oxford University Press, 2011).
52 Richard Wilkinson and Kate Pickett, *The Spirit Level: Why Equality is Better for Everyone* (London: Penguin, 2010); Thomas Piketty, *Capital in the Twenty First Century* (Cambridge, MA: Harvard University Press, 2014).
53 John Kenneth Galbraith, *The Culture of Contentment* (London: Sinclair-Stevenson, 1992).
54 James Thomas, *Popular Newspapers, The Labour Party and British Politics* (London: Routledge, 2005).
55 Chris Waters, *British Socialists and the Politics of Popular Culture, 1884–1914* (Manchester: Manchester University Press, 1990).
56 Pugh, *Speak for Britain!*, p. 74.
57 The classic Labour activist memoir for the 1980s is John O'Farrell, *Things Can Only Get Better: Eighteen Miserable Years in the Life of a Labour Supporter* (London: Black Swan, 1999 [1998]).
58 Alwyn W. Turner, *Things Can Only Get Bitter: The Lost Generation of 1992* (London: Aurum, 2012 [e-book]); Turner, 'Things Can Only Get Bitter', *New Statesman*, 19 March 2012, pp. 21–7.
59 Geoff Mulgan, 'Trotsky, Blair and the New Politics', *New Statesman*, 16 October 2015, pp. 23–7.

PART I
The crisis of the Labour Party

1
Retrieving or re-imagining the past? The case of 'Old Labour', 1979–94

Eric Shaw

God doth know, so shall the world perceive,
That I have turned away from my former self.
(*Henry 1V Part Two*, Act 5, Scene 5)

Our fundamental tactic of self-protection, self-control, and self-definition is ... telling stories, and more particularly concocting and controlling the story we tell others – and ourselves – about who we are.[1]

For Blair, 'Old Labour' was 'like a restaurant that poisoned its guests ... Think of that restaurant. If you had come home after what you thought was a good meal and had been violently ill for a week, what would make you return?'[2]

He who controls the past controls the future. He who controls the present controls the past.[3]

The origins and meaning of 'Old Labour'

This chapter argues that the concept of 'Old Labour' was essentially a strategic device. Coined in the 1990s by a group within the party, known initially as 'the modernisers' and subsequently as 'New Labour', it was used to refer to the party as it existed prior to Tony Blair's assumption of the leadership in 1994.[4] The concept was widely employed, both inside and outside Labour's ranks, and structured public discourse about the party to such a degree that, as the *Independent* put it, it became 'an effortless part of our vocabulary'.[5] As we shall see, it operated as the central organising concept of a larger, more encompassing narrative which creatively reimagined the party's past in a way that facilitated the New Labour 'project'.

Eric Hobsbawm explains: 'What is officially defined as the "past" clearly is and must be a particular selection from the infinity of what is remembered or capable of being remembered.'[6] Not surprisingly, Labour's history has lent itself to a wide range of such definitions, but these represent scholarly divergences, grounded in evidence and logical reasoning and, hence, legitimately differing versions of the past.[7] The view promulgated by the 'modernisers' amounted to something quite different: not a scholarly contribution but a strategic and rhetorical intervention designed to secure behavioural change by reshaping the popular image of the party.

The significance of the craft of persuasive communication is now widely recognised. Its point of departure is the gap between the social world as it objectively exists and as it is subjectively apprehended. Events in the wider world do not manifest themselves as 'pre-existent entities' whose meaning 'can be read straight from reality'.[8] In order for the raw material of existence to be transmuted into something intelligible, meaning has to be assigned. This applies, in particular, to the political world, where myriad events, mostly outside people's direct experience and frequently of little concern to them, swirl around in a kaleidoscope of bewildering patterns.

Inevitably, in a world of competitive politics, rival political camps seek to mobilise support by gaining assent for their slant on events. Blumler has described this as 'the modern publicity process'; that is, the 'competitive struggle to influence and control popular perceptions of key political events and issues through the mass media'. In this intensely fought struggle what counts is 'getting the *appearance* of things right'.[9] Two techniques increasingly deployed by party communicators to achieve this are the use of *narratives* and *framing devices*. A narrative 'refers to the ways in which we construct disparate facts in our own worlds and weave them together cognitively in order to make sense of our reality'.[10] It helps to organise and steer our understanding of the endless succession of events and messages that relentlessly bombard us. Those who devise and disseminate them have two main purposes: firstly, to supply a conceptual vocabulary to structure the target audience's understanding of the social world and, secondly, by helping to shape these understandings, to affect their behaviour in such a way as to serve the narrators' purposes.[11] This process of narrative dissemination we call *framing*. A frame highlights for public consumption the salient features from an otherwise baffling multitude of events, organising them in such a way that the frame offers both a diagnosis of what is wrong and a prescription of how this can be repaired.[12] Framing lies at the core of persuasive communication, as it seeks to 'assign meaning to and interpret relevant events and conditions in ways that are intended to mobilise potential adherents, to garner bystander support, and to demobilise antagonists'.[13]

The problem for Labour, as the modernising group which emerged in the late 1980s (for example, Tony Blair, Gordon Brown, Peter Mandelson, Philip Gould) understood, was that the frame of reference via which most voters viewed the Labour Party was unremittingly grim. Focus group research in the mid-1980s indicated that, for most voters, the party was identified with positions on such matters as welfare, gender and race that were (in Philip Gould's words) 'beyond what ordinary, decent voters considered reasonable and sensible'.[14] The party was seen as in thrall to trade union 'barons', riven by factionalism and prone to extremism. In the vivid words of the modernisers' principal strategist, Philip Gould:

> To millions of voters Labour became a shiver of fear in the night, something unsafe, buried deep in the psyche, not just for the 1983 election campaign or the period immediately after it but for years to come. Like a freeze-frame in a video, Labour's negative identity became locked in time.[15]

In Lewis Minkin's evocative phrase this constituted 'the burden of history'.[16] The proposition at the core of New Labour's strategic thinking was that Labour as a brand was so sullied that it was beyond redemption. As Philip Gould put it, 'Labour had to modernize completely or eventually it would die'.[17] The voters would regain trust in Labour's capacity to govern, and to govern in their interests, only if they were convinced that a surgical break with the past had occurred. The senior New Labour advisor, Matthew Taylor, recalled that, following the 'gut wrenching defeat in 1992', party modernisers 'took it as read that Labour could not be elected unless they had completely eradicated any connection to the discredited party of the winter of discontent [of 1978–79] and the 1983 manifesto'.[18]

One response may have been to attempt to dislodge, or at least dilute these perceptions as unfair, inaccurate and one sided. But this was not the approach taken (or even seriously contemplated) by the modernisers after 1992, and for three main reasons. Firstly, they believed that these perceptions were, if perhaps a little exaggerated, largely correct. Secondly, they calculated that it would be conducive to the success of the 'New Labour Project' if party members could be induced to accept that they were indeed correct. Thirdly, they were convinced that popular attitudes were so solidly entrenched that the prospect of shifting them was minimal.

It is worth reflecting a little further on these considerations. Firstly, the modernisers largely endorsed the voters' jaundiced view of the party. As Gould's authoritative account – the so-called New Labour bible – stated, on such issues as nationalisation, taxation and industrial relations legislation the party had become 'enslaved by dogma'.[19] It had totally lost touch with ordinary 'decent, hard-working voters', declaring 'political war ... on the values, instincts and ethics of the great majority'. Indeed, so disconnected had it become that it 'appeared to inhabit a parallel universe'.[20] No less important, in its own past actions the party had proved unable to tackle the problems of inflation, low growth and unemployment and had allowed itself to become associated in the public mind with profligate spending, 'penal rates of taxation' and 'the politics of envy'.[21]

Secondly, the modernisers felt that too many members were clinging to a version of the past that precluded them from adapting to the present. A party's collective memory not only affords a sense of shared experience and common purpose but also prescribes the lessons that can be learned from the past.[22] This was particularly the case with Labour. As Drucker has explained, its sense of its own past was so powerful that it not only played 'a crucial role in defining what the party is about to those in it' but also established firm parameters limiting the types of policies deemed by members as desirable and tolerable.[23] From the modernising perspective, this attachment to what the modernisers considered a sentimental, insular and narrow-minded view of the past inhibited party members from appreciating the scale of the changes required.

Thirdly, any doubt that the modernisers may have entertained about challenging the party's myths was removed by the scale and unexpectedness of Labour's 1992 defeat. Despite the policy changes effected by Neil Kinnock, the bleak message of post-election opinion research was that most voters continued to view Labour as 'an old-fashioned party, remote from their concerns and aspirations, wedded to high taxation and extravagant expenditure', dominated by the unions, too closely identified with the interests of the poor and ethnic minorities and simply not competent to run the country.[24] For these three reasons the modernisers concluded that Labour's disavowal of its past had to be unequivocal and irreversible, encompassing a renunciation not of this policy or that but of 'what the party has become, what it now stands for, how it works and who, quite literally, it is'.[25]

It is worth noting here the indebtedness of the modernisers to Thatcherism. The Thatcherites had always operated on a strategic plane, grasping the importance of carefully thought-out ideological formulae and idioms in the bid to forge a new common sense about politics. Labour under Kinnock, the modernisers were correct in noting, had never grasped this. It had never evolved its own project. It had, as Hall and Jacques commented, 'no positive ambition to remould society and no concrete image of what such a Labour-transformed society would be like'.[26] In contrast, Labour modernisers did learn from Thatcherism that 'politics is either conducted *ideologically*, or not at all'.[27] The concept of 'narrative' is crucial here.

As we have seen, narratives constitute structures of meaning, rendering otherwise perplexing events intelligible.[28] This was the aim of the modernising narrative – and it required the coining of Old Labour. The term New Labour was 'deliberately designed to distance the party from its past' – to broadcast the fact that it had sloughed off its old ways.[29] This 'implied a fundamental demarcation between the party's past and present practice, advertising a caesura in the historical continuity of the party's evolution'.[30] New Labour, in turn, logically necessitated Old Labour – its dazzling white contrasting with the tawdry, stained 'brand X' of the old. Old Labour 'had to be created because if one is wanting to be seen slaying a dragon then it is important to make that dragon appear as terrifying and potentially dangerous as possible'.[31] In short, for the party's past to be disowned, it first had to be reinvented. In constructing this Old Labour narrative, the modernisers made extensive use of two rhetorical devices which I call *essentialism* and *stereotyping*.

Essentialism refers to the belief that an *entity* or organisation is constituted by a set of properties which define its essential being and which are therefore a fixed part of its DNA. Further, it implies a deterministic analysis of behaviour, since the properties which define an organisation necessarily impel it to act in a particular way. Thus, for the architects of New Labour, Old Labour's dogged refusal to modernise sprang not from choice or contingency but from impulses deep within 'its character, its ethos, implicit even in its founding moments'.[32] In the vocabulary of contemporary social scientists, Labour's trajectory was, from this perspective, 'path dependent'. Path dependency describes the process by which an initial sequence of events, which may be contingent, establishes norms, institutions and organisational practices that consolidate and impose strict parameters for future behaviour. Mahoney argues that an institutional pattern − once adopted − congeals, making it increasingly difficult for an organisation to change course even if to do so would be beneficial.[33]

Thus, for the modernisers, Labour's orbit was firmly set by the circumstances of its birth and by its early formative experiences. As Blair explained to Labour's 1999 party conference:

> Born in separation from other progressive forces in British politics, out of the visceral need to represent the interests of an exploited workforce, our base, our appeal, our ideology was too narrow … . We were chained by our ideology. We thought we had eternal doctrines.[34]

Although Old Labour's precise properties − its 'eternal doctrines' − were never systematically enumerated, they emerge clearly from frequent New Labour usage. They can be itemised as follows:

- nationalisation as a centrepiece of Labour ideology
- the belief that a strong centralising state was the essential instrument for realising Labour's aims
- a commitment to high rates of taxation and spending
- a pronounced antipathy to business and to the use of market mechanisms
- an insistence on maintaining a close and organic connection with trade unionism.[35]

Philip Gould summarised Old Labour more pithily as a combination of trade union-oriented 'labourism' and Fabian statism, embellished by 'the utopianism of New Jerusalem'.[36] This combination of labourism, statism and utopianism formed the mentality of the party, imposing a rigidity of outlook which rendered it incapable of adapting to the profound social changes – the decay of class solidarities and collectivist mentalities, the new realities of individual aspiration and the consumer culture, the dynamics of a globalised market economy – which had swept away the world in which Labour had been created. Because it was trapped in the web of its own past, and its own mythology, because its parochialism and dogmatism stifled its capacity for renewal, the party, Blair concluded, 'had to be radically transformed … in a manner that changed profoundly its modus operandi, its thinking, its programme and above all its attitudes'.[37]

This essentialist depiction of Labour's character and experiences between 1979 and 1992 – however plausible it may have seemed to voters and the media – is not one that many historians would recognise. This is most notably the case of its portrayal of a fixed and immovable party locked into dogma and unresponsive to social change. As Neil Kinnock pointed out, Labour's ideas and methods 'have always been in a state of progressive flux, of permanent evolution'.[38] As long ago as 1956, Tony Crosland had urged the party to revise its programme and objectives to meet the realities of managed, mixed-economy capitalism and, in practical terms, his repudiation of the centrally planned economy dominated by publicly owned industries shaped the thinking of successive Labour governments in the 1960s and 1970s.[39] Far from a 'stubborn refusal to modernise', Labour's voyage from 1979 to 1994 was a period of ideological struggle and extensive policy modifications, culminating in a period of major policy revisions. In what follows I seek to illustrate this point by a survey of the crucial moment of programmatic innovation, the party's Policy Review at the end of the 1980s.[40]

The Review, instigated in 1988 in the wake of Labour's bruising defeat the previous year, undertook a thorough, systematic and wide-ranging overhaul of all aspects of the party's programme. Consisting of four reports, it concluded with the 1992 election manifesto. Far from displaying a party 'trapped by its past and a prisoner of an outdated ideology', the Policy Review not only exhibited much policy fluidity but also progressively detached the party from some of its founding precepts.[41] In what follows I organise a brief discussion of the Policy Review around two pivotal themes: firstly, the economic functions of the state and the balance between state regulation and the market, and, secondly, macro-economic policy and the efficacy of Keynesian demand management.

The process of programmatic change can be elucidated by distinguishing between three conceptions of the economic role of the state: the planning state, the development state and the enabling state, each of which, for a time, structured Labour's understanding of the relationship between public power and private economic activity. The concept of a 'planning state' built upon and expanded the left's 'alternative economic strategy', which was elaborated in the 1970s and held sway in the brief period of left-wing ascendancy in the early 1980s. It envisaged a much enhanced role for public authority in the management and control of the economy. This took the form of a large and complex apparatus of economic planning (so-called Planning Agreements) which would steer investment, encourage new technology and foster balanced economic growth. Planning was tied to schemes with comprehensive proposals to promote industrial democracy and to extend public ownership. Full employment would be secured by a Keynesian reflationary programme engineered through higher public expenditure, with the balance of payments protected by controls on foreign trade and global capital. A tripartite 'national economic assessment' would involve the unions more deeply in policy making, in return for which, it was anticipated, they would regulate the growth of wages. Overall, this constituted a highly dirigiste approach to economic management.[42]

But this period was in many ways an aberration. The 'alternative economic strategy' assumed, in some not very clearly theorised way, that Labour's mission was to radically reconfigure Britain's mode of economic organisation. This objective had never been mainstream thinking in the Labour Party, certainly not after 1945. For the leadership, the problem had always been to find the most appropriate and effective mechanisms and institutional arrangements to restrain, regulate and domesticate free market capitalism to facilitate the pursuit of Labour's traditional values of equality, social justice and co-operation. Not surprisingly, the reversal of the party's leftward slide saw a rapid disengagement from the planning state: in short the concept, far from defining Old Labour, had a short shelf-life and soon expired.

'Labour's Programme 1982', the high point of the left's influence, had condemned 'the view that the operation of the free market – guided only by the forces of profit, self-interest and greed – can ensure that industry meets the needs of the Community'.[43] The three figures largely responsible for framing economic strategy between 1983 and 1987 – party leader Neil Kinnock, shadow chancellor Roy Hattersley and shadow industry secretary Bryan Gould (no relation to Philip) – all took a more nuanced and positive view of the market.[44] But the years 1983–87 were an interregnum where policy development was hampered by crises both internal (the struggle over the Militant Tendency and over 'looney left' councils) and external (the miners' strike). The main changes were negative. The planning, controls, public ownership projects and bold reflationary schemes envisaged by the alternative economic strategy were abandoned and a more rigorous approach to the control of public expenditure was adopted. Hammering out an alternative programme proved more difficult.[45] This had to await the Policy Review, introduced after Labour's third stinging defeat in 1987.

Bryan Gould, Kinnock and Hattersley all believed that the key question pertaining to the respective roles of the state and market was not (as the left in particular tended to believe) which should have primacy but which tasks were best performed by the one and which by the other.[46] This meant acknowledging – as in practice the party had long since done – that in large areas of economic life the market was irreplaceable. As Bryan Gould, the co-convenor of the Productive and Competitive Economy Policy Review group, put it, the market was 'a more efficient and acceptable allocator and distributor of scarce resources, and a more sensitive means of meeting consumer preferences, than any system of planning could conceivably be'.[47] This view was accepted and incorporated in the second Policy Review report, *Meet the Challenge, Make the Change*:

> In very many areas of the economy the market and competition are essential in meeting the demands of the consumer, promoting efficiency and stimulating innovation, and often the best means of securing the myriad, incremental changes which are needed to take the economy forward.[48]

It was, for Labour, an unprecedented public affirmation of the indispensability of the market. But, if Bryan Gould and his allies on the soft left (then including Robin Cook, John Prescott and David Blunkett) repudiated the *dirigisme* of the planning state, they did not share the enthusiasm for the Anglo-Saxon variant of capitalism soon to be articulated by the modernising proponents of the enabling state, such as Blair and Brown. The soft left had emerged as a result of deep fissures within the left over issues such as the Benn deputy leadership campaign, the expulsion of Militant, membership of the European Community and attitudes to the Kinnock leadership. With a weakened Bennite left (including the young Jeremy Corbyn) opting to play no constructive part in the Policy Review, the debate over issues of contention was principally between the soft left and the centre-right, a debate that concluded with the latter's decisive triumph.

The indispensability of markets was common ground between these two currents of opinion but they adopted different views over the scale of reform that the existing British model of capitalism required, with the soft left's 'development state' and the modernising right's 'enabling state' representing conflicting orientations towards the institutional structure and dynamics of British capitalism.[49] Gould was the most formidable exponent of the former. The centrepiece of his analysis, largely endorsed *by Meet the Challenge*, was that problems that had consistently afflicted the UK economy, notably lagging investment and productivity, resource misallocation and weak export performance, were largely the effects of the excessive power of the City. Gould criticised the propensity of all British governments to give 'absolute priority to the interests of those who hold assets and deal in money, as opposed to those who made and provided goods and services'.[50] The outcome was a City-dominated economy with a 'fixation with the short-term', chronic under-investment, the tardy deployment of new technology and the neglect of research and development and training.[51]

It followed that a Labour government 'should intervene in the market as a matter of conscious policy and for defined purposes', particularly over investment and financial flows.[52] But this did not involve the complex planning structures and enlarged public sector envisaged by the planning state. Instead *Meet the Challenge* proposed a 'medium term industrial strategy' which drew heavily upon the activist industrial policies of the Pacific Rim states (notably Japan and South Korea). The report called for the establishment of two powerful new institutions, a British (or National) Investment Bank and British Technology Enterprise, to provide long-term investment capital, stimulate new technologies and identify and nurture new strategic sectors and enterprises (see chapter 4 by Richard Carr in this volume).

But, almost immediately, the advocates of the development state encountered stiff resistance. Its soft left supporters were in effect recommending a challenge to the neo-liberal drift in economic management that had been underway for a decade and a return to more collectivist and (as we shall see) Keynesian recipes. But the bulk of the party leadership visualised a more accommodationist stance, with the centre right broadly endorsing much of the new neo-liberal consensus. This was for a number of reasons. Firstly, their faith in the state's capacity to steer economic life was palpably dwindling, with Kinnock opining that 'the government has neither the means nor the judgment to make large-scale manufacturing investment'.[53] Secondly, they were increasingly determined to avoid any steps that might alienate the City. Indeed, a major re-orientation in attitudes to the role and contribution of the City was a key, if neglected, aspect of the later stages of the Policy Review. For Gould and his allies, the excessive power and reach of the financial sector was economically highly detrimental; hence his argument that 'the attempt to gain the confidence of the financial establishment is not only futile but is not even desirable'.[54] By 1990 such a stance was deemed to be both economically and financially unwise and politically reckless. Reassuring the City became a strategic priority and, with John Smith launching his so-called 'prawn cocktail offensive', considerable efforts were expended by Labour's economic team to convince financial institutions that they could rest easy with the prospect of a Labour government. This was an important step towards Gordon Brown's later 'light-touch' regulatory regime for the City.

With Bryan Gould's summary removal as industry spokesman in 1989 (replaced by the rapidly rising Gordon Brown), it was plain that the days of the development state were over. Instead, Kinnock, Smith and Brown, the three key players, introduced the concept of the enabling state. This approach conceded important market failures, such as lack of investment in human capital (for example, in training and skills acquisition) and in infrastructure, which the state had to address. This was common ground with the development state.

But it placed much more weight on the capacity of the market and profit-seeking private firms to allocate investment efficiently and was chary of any institutions that sought to second guess the market or channel investment. In short, the proper role of the state was to accomplish those tasks which the market alone tended to neglect while leaving intact the major institutions of the market economy. In consequence the Medium Term Industrial Strategy vanished and much-diminished roles were assigned to the British (or National) Investment Bank and British Technology Enterprise.[55] There was to be no serious questioning of the value of the Anglo-Saxon model of capitalism.

In parallel with disagreements over industrial policy, a split steadily widened between the soft left and the centre-right over macro-economic policy. Between 1979 and 1989 macro-economic policy was strongly Keynesian in orientation, with the party committed to restoring full employment and boosting economic growth through a public-expenditure-driven rise in demand. Inflationary pressures would be combatted through a revamped social contract in which the unions would exchange wage restraint for social concessions and a greater role in public policy formation. This approach was forcefully articulated by Gould – but confronted rising opposition from Kinnock, John Smith, Gordon Brown and their economic advisers. Prefiguring the policy line taken by New Labour after 1994, they expressed doubts about the efficacy of traditional Keynesian techniques, given the UK's mounting exposure to an increasingly globalised and liberalised world economy. They no longer believed in the viability of incomes policy as a method of containing inflationary pressures and feared that, in an ever more globalised and integrated world economy, stimulating demand would fuel an inflationary spiral (as had plagued the 1974–79 Labour government), which would in turn provoke speculation against sterling and capital flight.[56]

An increasingly heated debate came to a head over the issue of membership of the European Community's Exchange Rate Mechanism (ERM) at sterling's existing parity. Perceiving the ERM as anti-Keynesian in tone, purpose and effect, Gould persuaded his policy review group in 1989 to lay down stringent conditions for UK membership, but other key figures in the leadership, notably Kinnock, Smith, Brown and their advisers (such as John Eatwell) were unconvinced. Concurring with the government that ERM membership would operate as the sheet-anchor of price stability, John Smith, for example, reasoned that a fixed exchange rate would depress inflationary expectations by denying employers the option of competitive devaluation if they conceded excessive wage claims, and labour market behaviour would adjust accordingly.[57]

Overriding Gould's strenuous objections, the third Policy Review report, *Looking to the Future* (1990), called for Britain to join the ERM at 'the earliest possible opportunity'.[58] Enthusiasts for ERM membership – who included Gordon Brown until 'Black Wednesday' – were in effect signalling that, in order to demonstrate its dedication to monetary stability, even if the short-term cost was higher unemployment, the party was willing to divest itself of control over exchange and interest rates as instruments of macro-economic strategy. In effect, price stability displaced full employment as the primary explicit objective of Labour's economic policy.

An equally cautious stance was taken over fiscal policy. To reassure the markets and voters that the days of the party's spending 'profligacy' were over, Kinnock and Smith committed themselves to expenditure restraint: despite years of tight Tory spending control, the shadow chancellor envisaged only a 'modest increase' in public spending as a proportion of GDP.[59] High levels of taxation, the party now averred, could be economically detrimental, while too much public borrowing could precipitate a serious loss of market confidence. Hence they promised to borrow only to finance public investment and to fund all current social spending out of tax receipts.

It is true that for Labour's 'modernising' right the policy changes orchestrated by the Policy Review were considered too tame and circumspect. Nonetheless, they represented a major shift away from policies espoused earlier in the decade and formed a platform upon which New Labour could later build.[60] In effect, the shift from Keynesianism to a more market-oriented approach that was to define economic policy making under Brown (until the 2008 crash) unequivocally began *before* Blair's accession to the leadership. Although it suited New Labour's strategic purposes to depict Kinnock's attempts to renew the party between 1983 and 1992 as tepid, superficial and largely ineffectual, in fact, as the National Institute of Economic and Social Research pointed out, the outcome of the Policy Review was that 'the economic policy differences between the two major parties are narrower than they have been for twenty years'.[61] The same pattern unfolds in other policy areas such as employment law, where the party reversed its earlier pledge to repeal most Tory industrial relations legislation: given its draconian character, this showed a remarkable degree of flexibility, especially on the part of the affiliated unions. So, to conclude, as Philip Gould did in the wake of the 1992 defeat, that the party 'was *still* the party of the winter of discontent; union influence; strikes and inflation; disarmament; Benn and Scargill' seems a curious historical judgement.[62]

It is worth noting that soon-to-be leading figures in New Labour, Tony Blair, Gordon Brown and Peter Mandelson, all played major roles in the Policy Review. The speed and alacrity with which the substantial changes it wrought dropped out of their collective memory is remarkable. Perhaps their very victory in shifting policy emboldened them to seek more sweeping reversals of policy than were previously thought politically feasible. But, above all, it did not suit their strategic purposes to acknowledge that the age of a newly refurbished and rejuvenated Labour Party was not ushered in by Blair's election to the leadership.

Stereotypes

The second framing device used by New Labour was that of the stereotype. A stereotype can be defined as 'an oversimplified mental image of … some category of person, institution or event which is shared … by large numbers of people'.[63] Stereotyping is part of the wider social process of social categorisation, which is a mechanism to reduce the complexity and ambiguity of social reality through the attribution of a small number of defining collective traits to particular social groups.[64] Stereotyping takes this a step further by defining a person or group in terms of a handful of simply understood properties and, in so doing, defying or denying the complexity of social and political life. The value of social and political stereotypes, as framing devices, lies in their persuasive efficacy: stereotypical images, particularly those of a more emotive cast, are more easily understood, processed and absorbed than more complex and rational messages and therefore facilitate message transmission. It is in this context that New Labour's use of the concept of Old Labour should be placed.

It is important to distinguish here between the two concepts of 'New Labour' and Old Labour. The former is not a stereotype but a descriptive category because it refers to a phenomenon whose properties can be identified and itemised and which manifested themselves in actual behaviour. Old Labour, in contrast, is a rhetorical invention, devised by New Labour strategists who drew selectively from the historical record to weave together a composite whose resemblance to empirical reality was often tenuous.

Like most stereotypes it was misleading – squeezing and distorting a more complicated reality. Old Labour was depicted as an essentially homogenous entity, with all who composed it, whatever their differences of style, values and priorities, inhabiting a common ideological universe. Cronin describes how 'the essential premise of New Labour's break with the past' was the supposition of the fundamental coherence of Old Labour. Left, right and centre were bound to a common stock of flawed and archaic principles which 'pervaded the entire party and its seemingly diverse and competing tendencies'.[65] As Labour's pre-eminent contemporary historian, Lewis Minkin, commented, the usage of the term Old Labour was 'a broad brush and caricatured repository of what was regarded as the misapplication of values, outdated and extreme attitudes and policies, off-putting images and antiquated organisational forms'.[66]

It was a remarkable interpretation of such a conflict-strewn and disputatious party. We are invited to believe that the issues that divided Michael Foot and Denis Healey, Roy Hattersley and Tony Benn, Bryan Gould and John Smith were all minor matters of tone and detail. In fact, just a brief glance at one issue from 1979–94, the future of public ownership, indicates that this was far from the case. In this period, as in the 1950s and the 1970s, Labour was seriously riven over whether an ambitious programme of nationalisation was a precondition of a more equal and a socially just society or whether (as the 'revisionists' contended) it was one instrument among many, and not a very effective one. During the left-wing surge after 1979 the former view prevailed, but not for very long. In 1986 the party published a major report, jointly authored by the then soft leftist David Blunkett and John Smith, on *Social Ownership* which, while proclaiming boldly that common ownership was 'as relevant today as it has ever been', in effect sounded the retreat.[67] The report attracted some criticism but the course was set and, in the second half of the 1980s, the party disassociated itself ever further from any steps to enlarge the public sector or even to restore to public ownership the many industries and utilities privatised by the Tories. Public ownership as an issue hardly figured in the Policy Review debates.[68] The 1992 election manifesto contained no nationalisation pledges and no longer even called for a reversal of *any* Tory privatisation.[69] Far from representing a defining characteristic of Old Labour (as alleged by the modernisers), public ownership ceased to figure as a goal of public policy several years before the emergence of New Labour. The later revision in 1995 of Clause 4 on Labour's Aims was of real *symbolic* significance, but in substantive terms it merely registered a change that had already occurred.

In truth, Labour's complex political culture has always embraced a wide range of traditions, strands and tendencies – ethical socialism, Fabianism, labourism, Marxism and revisionist social democracy – all with their own distinct understandings of the party's role and purposes.[70] This indeed was never more so than in the 1980s, when an array of different groups – the hard left, the soft left, the traditional right (for example, Roy Hattersley and John Smith) and the 'modernising' right (Blair and Brown) – engaged in a contest, sometimes impassioned, to influence party policy, ideology and strategy. This was manifested on an institutional level in a proliferating world of factional competition, between the Manifesto Group, Labour Solidarity, the Tribune and Campaign Groups, the Labour Co-Ordinating Committee and the Rank and File Mobilising Committee. It is hard to conceive how all could be fitted into the one category – Old Labour. But, as Randall has explained, 'the nature of memory is such that it gains its power from sweeping narrative and abhors nuanced analysis'.[71] The object of the exercise was not dispassionate historical scrutiny but a creative reconstruction of Labour's past which would serve the strategic purposes of what was soon labelled 'the New Labour project'.

Exorcising the past

The fact that their narrative was devised for strategic purposes does not mean that its protagonists did not believe it. For such modernisers as Tony Blair, Gordon Brown, Philip Gould and Peter Mandelson, the fraught 1980s was the formative period of their political lives. It was a decade characterised by vitriolic divisions, unstable leadership, rank and file eruptions and a lurch to the left that culminated in the left-wing 1983 election manifesto and electoral disaster. Equally disconcerting were the furious and acrid clashes over the 1984–85 miners' strike, destructive Militant entryism and the behaviour of so-called 'looney left' councils. 'Common to all modernisers', Blair's speech-writer Peter Hyman reflected, 'were the scars caused by the battles with the Left – including Militant – in the eighties. For this generation, Labour was a party that lost elections, that had a series of unpalatable, extreme, often suicidal policies and that was crucified by the newspapers.'[72] Those who came to form New Labour, in short, were 'obsessed with the battles against the ghosts of yesterday'.[73]

New Labour's recoil from the past was as much psychological and emotional as intellectual, a profound sense of alienation from what the party had stood for and how it had operated. 'Tony', Hyman observed, 'has an allergy to old Labour. It's not just that he finds policies such as nationalisation and high direct taxes barmy. He also hates losers, hates impotence, hates meaningless protest. He breaks out into a rash at the thought of being lumped with the failures of Labour's past.'[74]

The depth and vehemence of the modernisers' 'allergy to Old Labour' imparted energy and conviction to their narrative, but ultimately it was driven by cool-headed strategic considerations. Its essentialist and stereotypical character was part of wider bid to lay the modernisers' imprint on a broader universe of political discussion, to populate this with its own distinctive concepts, imagery and rhetoric.[75] The aim was to reformulate the terms which the party used to think about itself, its past, present and purposes. It was a deliberate attempt by the modernisers to break free from the party's traditional understanding of its own past, to displace what it regarded as its complacent and self-congratulatory tone by a more searching and self-critical spirit.

But there was another strategic calculation at work. There are always multiple frames and narratives, although not always equally accessible. The capacity of a narrative to resonate, its perceived plausibility, will vary according to the extent that it is congruent with the wider culture – the common stock of beliefs, perceptions and understanding that circulate widely and constitute some form of conventional wisdom.[76] Stories about the past and present will seem more authentic and truthful to the extent that they conform to the ingrained contours of common-sense wisdom.[77] Persuading voters (especially floating voters) that their perceptions of the party were often one sided, exaggerated and inaccurate would have been a tough assignment. New Labour strategists opted instead to narrow the cognitive gap between Labour's sense of itself and how it was popularly viewed by remodelling the former so that it more closely corresponded to the latter. By confessing the party's past sins it could more persuasively claim to have paid penance and would be – hopefully – absolved: the sinner that repenteth. The very connectivity of the frames deployed by New Labour with established repertoires of belief meant that it appeared merely to be relaying common sense.

What helped immeasurably here was that the Old Labour narrative was widely shared and indeed echoed and amplified by the media. Delivering messages that fitted comfortably into existing media mindsets facilitated effective communication. Thus, rather than contesting the media portrayal of Old Labour, the leadership effectively endorsed it and in this way, they calculated, achieved a more sympathetic hearing.[78] And, indeed, this approach met with real success, since the extent to which the media bought, uncritically, unthinkingly and unquestioningly, into New Labour rhetoric is quite striking.

New Labour's framing strategy was, then, effective – in the short term. With the advantage of hindsight, we can now see that it was sowing the dragon's teeth. Speaking of earlier generations, Drucker noted how its 'strong sense of its own past' operated as a force of cohesion, pride and confidence, binding its members together.[79] Collective narratives about the past play a major role in fostering party unity, furnishing members with common understandings and interpretations and a shared sense of purpose.[80] The 'modernising' project hinged on expunging Labour's past, depicted as a litany of frustrated hopes and failed endeavours from which little or nothing could be salvaged. Liu and Hilton argue that '[a] group's representation of its history will condition its sense of what it was, is, can and should be, and is thus central to the construction of its identity, norms, and values'.[81] But what happens when a party disowns its own past – when its past becomes the object not of pride but of scorn, shame and ridicule? What are the consequences for its sense of identity and purpose and the implications for its morale? For many of its members and its supporters Labour was a party which, whatever its defects and disappointments, represented their values, aspirations and interests. It was the party responsible for the NHS, the welfare state, equal pay, improved education and much else besides. How would they respond to the message that their efforts had been squandered, themselves deluded?

Not surprisingly, New Labour's rhetoric left a residue of bitterness. Since Old Labour was presented so unflatteringly, it was inevitable that those attached to it would experience a sense of personal disparagement and affront. Many came to see New Labourites as ideological interlopers with scant affiliation to the party's ethos and traditions.

Some left, others pragmatically accepted New Labour because it did have real accomplishments and, after all, presided over an unprecedented three successive general election victories. Others kept their own counsel. But the crucial point is that New Labour never won any ideological hegemony within the party. The appeal of its most substantial ideological innovations, such as the commercialisation of greater competition within the public services, its deregulatory drive and its eager embrace of the City, was limited to a small number of 'true believers'. It deployed astute and energetic party management techniques, coupled with highly skilled media and public relations operations, to stabilise its rule and marginalise its critics. But once its electoral performance began to flag, so did its hold on the party's loyalties. New Labour's 'disarticulation of the party from its past' became a defining feature of its own ethos – but it was one which caused many Labour supporters to wince.[82] Its willingness to play fast and loose with the party's own history came to be seen as a typical example of 'New Labour spin', nurturing the perception of Blair, Mandelson and the rest of the modernisers as masters of manipulation but destitute of probity and integrity.

The resentments and antipathies that had festered over the years, the profound sense of alienation from the whole of the 'New Labour project', eventually exploded in the 2015 leadership election race. This was remarkable not only for Jeremy Corbyn's wholly unexpected and astonishing victory but for the very poor performance of the only unhesitatingly pro-New Labour candidate, Liz Kendall, who mustered less than 5 per cent of the vote. Indeed, the Corbyn insurgency can be seen as a delayed reaction by party members against those who, they felt, had stolen their party.

Conclusion

The concept of Old Labour was the centrepiece of a past that was reconstructed and re-imagined for political purposes. Historical narratives involve the selective appropriation of past happenings, but, for Labour's modernisers, the choice of which version of the past to exhume, so to speak, was driven principally not by any interest in historical accuracy but by strategic considerations. The strategic objective of their distinctive 'mobilisation of memory' was to validate 'New Labour', within both the party and the public at large, by delegitimating Labour's past. Only, so the argument read, by convincing the electorate that Old Labour had been decisively repudiated could the party be fully rehabilitated.

In the short term, this appeared to have worked, with the validity of the 'Old Labour/New Labour' dichotomy taken for granted in public discourse about the party. How successful New Labour rhetoric was in reconfiguring the party's public image is, though, highly questionable. A comparison between polling in 1993 and 2010 indicates an astonishing persistence of often highly adverse perceptions of the party, despite the tremendous alterations that had occurred in ideology, policy and leadership in the intervening years.[83] Indeed, it could be argued that the modernisers' caricatured view of Old Labour legitimated it in the eyes of many voters. An Old Labour which 'only existed in the imaginings of the Labour modernisers and, by osmosis, the media' came to acquire the aura of a more solid reality in the public mind.[84]

Internally, too, the effects of the Old Labour myth could be said to have been, for the modernisers, counter-productive. Their success in marginalising and, indeed, reducing to an impotent rump the hard or Bennite left was reversed with spectacular suddenness. The backlash against 'Blairism' amongst disaffected and estranged party members was so intense, partisan and indiscriminating that New Labour, for many, became as stereotyped and caricatured as Old Labour had been, its achievements either derided or ignored. For the avatars of Corbyn's 'authentic' Labour, 'New Labour' has become the new Old Labour.

Notes

1 David Dennett, quoted in David Lodge, *Consciousness and the Novel* (Harmondsworth: Penguin, 2002), p. 15.
2 Peter Hyman, *One Out of 10: From Downing Street Vision to Classroom Reality* (London: Vintage, 2005), p. 53. Hyman was a senior No. 10 aide.
3 George Orwell, *1984* (Harmondsworth: Penguin, 1949), p. 26.
4 The appropriation of the label of 'modernisers' was in itself a strategic initiative, an attempt to control the terms of the debate within the party: James E. Cronin, *New Labour's Pasts: The Labour Party and its Discontents* (London: Longman, 2004), p. 4. For this reason, throughout the text, I place inverted commas over the word 'modernisers'.
5 *Independent*, 22 July 1995, p. 16.
6 Eric Hobsbawm, 'The Sense of the Past', in Hobsbawm, *On History* (London: Abacus, 1997), p. 27.
7 See, for example, Brian Brivati and Richard Heffernan (eds), *The Labour Party: A Centenary History* (Basingstoke: Macmillan, 2000); David Coates (ed.) *Paving the Third Way* (London: Merlin Press, 2003); Cronin, *New Labour's Pasts*.
8 Ignacio Bresco de Luna, 'Form and Content of Historical Accounts: Studying the (Re)construction of Past Events', *Psychology and Society* 2 (2009), p. 107.
9 Jay G. Blumler, 'Elections, the Media and the Modern Publicity Process', in Marjorie Ferguson (ed.), *Public Communication: The New Imperatives* (London: Sage, 1990), pp. 103, 106. Emphasis in the original.
10 Molly Patterson and Kristen R. Monroe, 'Narrative in Political Science', *Annual Review of Political Science* 1 (1998), 315–31.
11 P. L. Hammack, 'Mind, Story, Society: The Political Psychology of Narrative', in Michael Hanne (ed.), *Warring with Words: Narrative and Metaphor in Domestic and International Politics* (New York: Psychology Press, 2014), pp. 61–2.
12 Donald Schön and Martin Rein, *Frame Reflection* (New York: Basic Books, 1994), p. 26.
13 David A. Snow and Robert D. Benford, 'Ideology, Frame Resonance, and Participant Mobilization', *International Social Movement Research* 1 (1998), 197–217, at 198.
14 Philip Gould, *The Unfinished Revolution* (London: HarperCollins, 1998), p. 50.
15 Gould, *The Unfinished Revolution*, p. 21.
16 Lewis Minkin, *The Blair Supremacy* (Manchester: Manchester University Press, 2014), p. 68.
17 Gould, *The Unfinished Revolution*, p. 161.
18 Matthew Taylor, '"Modernisation" as Labour's Meta-Narrative', Political Economy Research Centre, University of Sheffield, Annual Lecture, 16 May 2002.
19 Gould, *The Unfinished Revolution*, pp. 3–4.
20 Gould, *The Unfinished Revolution*, p. 19.
21 Labour Party Manifesto, *Because Britain Deserves Better* (London: Labour Party, 1997), pp. 1, 3, 12.

22 Phillip. L. Hammack and Andrew Pilecki, 'Narrative as a Root Metaphor for Political Psychology', *Political Psychology* 33 (2012), p. 84.
23 Henry M. Drucker, *Doctrine and Ethos in the Labour Party* (London: Allen & Unwin. 1979), p. 25.
24 Giles Radice and Stephen Pollard, *More Southern Discomfort* (London: Fabian Society, 1993).
25 Cronin, *New Labour's Pasts*, p. 2.
26 Stuart Hall and Martin Jacques, 'March Without Vision', *Marxism Today* (December 1990), pp. 26–31.
27 Stuart Hall, 'Thatcher's Lessons', *Marxism Today* (March 1988), p. 274. Emphasis in the original.
28 Alan Finlayson, 'From Beliefs to Arguments: Interpretive Methodology and Rhetorical Political Analysis', *British Journal of Politics and International Relations* 9 (2007), p. 557.
29 *Independent*, 22 July 1995, p. 16.
30 Nick Randall, 'Time and British Politics: Memory, the Present and Teleology in the Politics of New Labour', *British Politics* 4 (2009), pp. 190–1.
31 Ivor Gaber, 'Slaying the Dragon', in James Curran, Ivor Gaber and Julian Petley, *Culture Wars: The Media and the British Left* (Edinburgh: Edinburgh University Press, 2005), p. 189.
32 Gould, *The Unfinished Revolution*, p. 23.
33 James Mahoney, 'Path Dependence in Historical Sociology', *Theory and Society* 29 (2000), 507–48, p. 508.
34 http://news.bbc.co.uk/1/hi/uk_politics/460009.stm (accessed 20 July 2017).
35 See, for example, Hyman, *One Out of 10*, p. 54.
36 Gould, *The Unfinished Revolution*, p. 25.
37 Tony Blair, *A Journey* (London: Hutchinson 2010), p. 48.
38 Neil Kinnock, 'New? We've Always Been New', *New Statesman*, 28 February 2000, p. 28.
39 C. A. R. Crosland, *The Future of Socialism* (London: Jonathan Cape, 1964 [1956]).
40 For detailed accounts see Eric Shaw, *The Labour Party Since 1979: Crisis and Transformation* (London: Routledge, 1994), pp. 81–107 and Colin Hughes and Patrick Wintour, *Labour Rebuilt* (London: Fourth Estate, 1990).
41 Peter Mandelson and Roger Liddle, *The Blair Revolution* (London: Faber & Faber, 1996), p. ix.
42 Labour Party Manifesto, *New Hope for Britain* (London: Labour Party, 1983).
43 Labour Party, *Labour's Programme 1982* (London: Labour Party, 1982), pp. 8–9.
44 See Neil Kinnock, *Making Our Way* (Oxford: Blackwell, 1986); Roy Hattersley, *Choose Freedom* (London: Penguin 1987); Bryan Gould, *A Future for Socialism* (London: Jonathan Cape, 1989).
45 Richard Hill, *The Labour Party and Economic Strategy, 1979–97* (Basingstoke: Palgrave, 2001), pp. 136, 138.
46 Gould, *A Future for Socialism*, p. 95.
47 Gould, *A Future for Socialism*, pp. 95–6.
48 Labour Party, *Meet the Challenge, Make the Change* (London: Labour Party, 1989), p. 10.
49 John Smith took an intermediate position.
50 Gould, *A Future for Socialism*, p. 22.
51 Labour Party, *Meet the Challenge*, p. 13.
52 Gould, *A Future for Socialism*, p. 108.
53 *Guardian*, 2 May 1990, p. 13.
54 Gould, *A Future for Socialism*, p. 85.

55 Labour Party, *Looking to the Future* (London: Labour Party, 1990), p. 15.
56 Hill, *The Labour Party and Economic Strategy*, p. 147.
57 *Independent on Sunday*, 6 May 1990, p. 1 (and pp. 10–12 in the Business on Sunday supplement to the same issue).
58 Labour Party, *Looking to the Future*, p. 7.
59 *Independent on Sunday*, 6 May 1990 p. 1 (and pp. 10–12 in the Business on Sunday supplement to the same issue
60 Richard Heffernan, 'Labour's Transformation: A Staged Process with No Single Point of Origin' *Politics* 18 (1998), p. 104.
61 National Institute of Economic and Social Research, 'Policy Options under a Labour Government', *National Institute Economic Review* (London: NIESR, 1990), p. 52.
62 Gould, *The Unfinished Revolution*, p. 158.
63 Stallybrass, quoted in Henri Tajfel and Joseph P. Forgas, 'Social Categorisation', in Joseph P. Forgas (ed.), *Social Cognition* (San Diego, CA: Academic Press, 1981), pp. 113–40, p. 129.
64 Tajfel and Forgas, 'Social Categorisation', p. 135.
65 Cronin, *New Labour's Pasts*, pp. 10, 14.
66 Minkin, *Blair Supremacy*, p. 128.
67 Labour Party, *Social Ownership* (London: Labour Party, 1986), pp. 1–2.
68 Shaw, *The Labour Party since 1979*, pp. 47–9, 85–9.
69 Labour Party Manifesto, *It's Time to Get Britain Working Again* (London: Labour Party, 1992).
70 See for example, Nick Ellison, *Egalitarian Thought and Labour Politics* (London: Routledge, 1994); Stephen Meredith, 'New Labour: "The Road Less Travelled"', *Politics* 23 (2003), 163–71.
71 Randall, 'Time and British Politics', p. 197.
72 Hyman, *One Out of 10*, p. 52.
73 Minkin, *The Blair Supremacy*, p. 131.
74 Hyman, *One Out of 10*, p. 11.
75 See Alan Finlayson, *Making Sense of New Labour* (London: Lawrence & Wishart, 2003) and Norman Fairclough, *New Labour, New Language?* (London: Routledge, 2000).
76 Edwin Bacon, 'Public Political Narratives', *Political Studies* 6 (2012), pp. 768–86, p. 782.
77 Snow and Benford, 'Ideology, Frame Resonance', p. 210.
78 Gaber, 'Slaying the Dragon', p. 215.
79 Drucker, *Doctrine and Ethos*, p. 25.
80 Patterson and Monroe, 'Narrative in Political Science', p. 321.
81 James Liu and Denis Hilton, 'How the Past Weighs on the Present: Social Representations of History and their Role in Identity Politics', *British Journal of Social Psychology* 44 (2005), 537–56, p. 537.
82 Randall, 'Time and British Politics', p. 194.
83 Compare the findings of Radice and Pollard, *More Southern Discomfort* and Patrick Diamond and Giles Radice, *Southern Discomfort Again* (London: Policy Network, 2010).
84 Gaber, 'Slaying the Dragon', p. 215.

2
Leading the Labour Party in the 1980s

Martin Farr

Leading the Labour Party in Opposition must be a nightmare.[1]

The period from 4 May 1979 to 18 July 1992, when James Callaghan, Michael Foot and Neil Kinnock led the Labour Party in opposition, was for each, respectively, one of 'unrealistic and often malignant factions', 'self-inflicted lacerations' and 'self-indulgence, vanity, stupidity, introversion'.[2] The party was to spend what would be thirteen years out of power very publicly preoccupied with issues that were both chronic and acute. A week after losing office, with an exasperation borne of familiarity, Callaghan confronted Tony Benn: 'What are these great issues that have to be debated?' 'One of them', Benn replied, 'is the question of the leadership.'[3] It was his contention, and that of many more on the left who felt that the Parliamentary Labour Party had become too far removed from the Labour movement in the country, that there had developed a 'totally independent parliamentary leadership'.[4] With defeat, the left felt that their moment had arrived. For them, the failure of the 1974–79 governments, in both political and electoral terms, held a lesson. As their *de facto* leader put it: 'Leadership there must be, but not all from the top.'[5]

Labour in opposition tends to be defined by its reaction to Labour in power. After 1970, this reaction was cushioned by the party's soon regaining power, albeit precariously; in the 'long 1980s' there was no such distraction. Blame could be apportioned. The person at the top may have been the most prominent, but ought not to be the most significant: 'it doesn't matter who is Leader', Benn maintained, 'if the structure of accountability and the policies are right'.[6] Nevertheless, leaders there were: as many in the 1980s as there had been in the preceding forty years. Callaghan, Foot and Kinnock have each been the subject of, and in varying ways have subjected themselves to, biographical scrutiny.[7] There have been studies of their elections as leader, and of their leaderships, but no comparative assessment of them has been made.[8] In offering one, a clearer sense of what leadership was both possible and desirable might better be seen. Most elemental was the very nature of leadership, which can be assessed by considering the ways in which each one of the three became leader of the Labour Party; once leader, each then sought to establish himself – the annual meeting of the Labour movement, the party conference, being central to this. The actual experience of leadership can be appreciated by considering the leadership characteristics of each one, how they managed the party and whether they were seen as effective leaders when viewed by (or, more accurately, when mediated to) the electorate and by the party, both generally and in the form of formal challenges to their position as leader. Finally, their leaderships can be measured, to some extent objectively through demonstrable electoral results, and more subjectively through their own estimations. There is an inherent imbalance in comparing the three, in that they held the office of leader of the opposition, respectively, for 17, 35 and 102 months. Each nevertheless sought to give direction to a party that was defined by collectivism in a period when solidarity was conspicuous by its absence; there was for Callaghan 'an atmosphere of mistrust and cynicism in which the motives and actions of Party leaders were continually questioned'.[9] For all the legitimate concerns about party structures and processes, it was the leader who commanded attention, both at the time and subsequently. Indeed, the perennial 'best leader who never was', Denis Healey, would likely have found the challenge to be one that went beyond Labour: the 1980s marked the lowest level of satisfaction with the leadership of governing parties in British history.[10] This was one area of national life, at least, where the Labour Party was a full and active contributor.

The nature of leadership

> [F]or all our political lives, the Labour Party has been badly let down by its leaders.[11]

Becoming leader

On becoming leader of the opposition on 4 May 1979, three years, one month and one day after becoming leader of the party, James Callaghan had wanted to stand down. Both of those who turned out to be his immediate successors urged him to stay.[12] The general expectation on the day after the general election was that Denis Healey would become leader; indeed, said a generous Michael Foot, (who in 1976 had been elected deputy, having come second to Callaghan in the previous leadership election) a good one.[13] As it was, Callaghan endured over a year of increasing impotence as leader in opposition until he resigned in October 1980, having, he hoped, taken the 'shine off the ball' for his anointed Healey.[14] The problem was, as one future deputy leader put it, that the anointed 'scared the life out of us'.[15] So it was that an unthreatening Foot was prevailed upon to stand against Healey by, most volubly, Clive Jenkins.[16] But there was another problem. As Foot's campaign manager, Neil Kinnock, put it: 'he didn't want to be leader'.[17] Peter Shore didn't want him to be leader either: he had expected that Foot would support him.[18] Foot's pressganged candidature had multiple significances. A considerable figure in his own right at the beginning of the 1980s, Foot was, more importantly, also not other considerable figures, and not two in particular: in 1980 he was not Healey, and in 1981 he was not Benn. Foot was not only the person most likely to beat either of these two, but was also the candidate most likely to minimise the likelihood of a split, and therefore the leader least likely to be challenged when the electoral college devised for the election of the leader came into being in 1983.[19] The impending prospect of Healey as leader proved to be sufficiently scary that Frank Field could inform Foot that 'a decisive swing has occurred to you over the past few days'.[20] Foot won by ten votes in the closest leadership contest since the first in 1922, yet he was held to be the first leader 'whose candidature was determined by overwhelming popular demand within the party'.[21] Even one reliably histrionic Healey supporter admitted that 'we all verge dangerously near veneration in our regard for you'.[22] Healey became Foot's deputy in what was immediately dubbed the 'coalition leadership' of a 'coalition Labour Party.'[23]

Tony Benn congratulated Foot on 'a historic victory that will put heart back into the party'.[24] The Liberal leader, David Steel, also congratulated Foot: 'I regard your election as possibly helpful to my Party.'[25] The question of whether Healey as leader would have vindicated Steel, and prevented the Social Democrats from leaving the following year is unanswerable, although that has never discouraged its routinely being asked. Roy Jenkins felt that Foot's 'election cleared the mind'.[26] The consciences of some of those who voted for Foot expressly in order to create a reason for themselves thereafter to depart from the party may have been less easily salved.[27] At the age of 67 there was always something of the temporary about Foot in his new position ('an ideal caretaker in a large block of flats on the Earls Court Road'[28]). After Foot led Labour to its worst performance since 1918 his departure, like his arrival, was expedited and his successor was heralded (by the ever-helpful Clive Jenkins), much to Foot's irritation: such pre-emptory activity meant that he was 'instantly deprived of the dignified exit' for which he had hoped.[29]

Foot's successor was a less likely leader still. If Callaghan had been the most ministerially experienced leader of the party – indeed, of any party – then Kinnock was the least experienced. As a party of government, Labour had never had a leader who had not been a minister, even if the Leader had also been a rebel. Kinnock's early-career recusance included his resignation as

Foot's parliamentary private secretary in 1975 and his refusal of office under Callaghan in 1976 in order to remain a backbencher who could be relied upon to rebel. Shore, who in 1983 stood again, to come last again, was briefed on his rival's '[l]ack of experience, lack of any economic or defence background, a continuation by other means of the last four years, lightweight against [the Prime Minister], and even against Steel, or [David] Owen'.[30] But, as Gerald Kaufman put it, Kinnock was also 'checklist soft-left' and had advocated the creation of a 'broader electorate for Leader', a development which, Owen told Roy Hattersley, was 'tailor-made for Kinnock'; Benn went so far as to claim that Kinnock owed him the leadership.[31] 'Your candidature is not relevant', Callaghan told Shore; 'It is Kinnock or Hattersley and I must cast my vote accordingly.'[32] In the event there was no real contest; as Frank Chapple told Kinnock, it was always 'in the bag'.[33] (Such string pulling inspired *Private Eye*'s 'Kinnochio', clattering into life before Clive Jenkins's beaming Geppetto.)[34] After three party leadership elections in seven years, Kinnock commenced the longest period as leader of the opposition in history.

Hattersley, who had come second to Kinnock and became his deputy, had thought that the 1980 contest would effectively elect two generations of leader: Foot to be followed by his protégé Kinnock, or Healey by Hattersley.[35] The Foot campaign was, perforce, a Kinnock campaign. Kinnock–Hattersley was immediately dubbed the 'dream ticket' born of the 'new realism'; the 'balanced ticket' favoured by the 'mainstream'; and, by the august left, 'The NIGHTMARE ticket'.[36] Despite their differences, Callaghan and Foot had demonstrated that an effective and trusting working relationship was possible, and one thing at least that the three leaders had in common was that none of them publicly criticised the others. Quite the contrary: Callaghan was open about the 'bed of nails' he had laid for his successor, a leader inclined to lenience for whom the miserable experience provided a revelation: '[o]ne way or another', Foot stated afterwards, 'full executive power for the party leadership will have to be re-established'.[37]

Conveying the leader

Leadership may not have been sufficient, but it was necessary, and it was central to the left critique of the failure of the Labour Government and to what had to change.[38] Viewed from the responsible right, as Austin Mitchell characterised it, '[t]o lead was to betray'.[39] In 1980 *Tribune* cited 'the Leader's production of his own manifesto' as an example of betrayal, and stated that the demand that 'joint responsibility for both the successes and failures' of the leader would be to his advantage.[40] That, Callaghan doubted: in the USA the virtual exclusion of congressmen and senators from the nomination process had not proved to be to his friend Jimmy Carter's 'advantage'.[41] By chance, speaking to one of Carter's chief tormentors, William F. Buckley Jr, Benn said that he wanted a leader 'accountable to the whole party and not simply to the parliamentary faction' as a means to a party run by the membership rather than the leadership, with much wider consultation between the Parliamentary Labour Party (PLP), whose members would have been subject to reselection, and the National Executive (NEC), which would have authority for a manifesto spared from a leader's veto.[42] 'Gladstone used to say in private that what he meant by practical politics was the next election,' Foot wrote later. 'The NEC had its eyes firmly fixed – on the next conference.'[43] Six party conferences shaped the period.

From the first, there was not merely disagreement but contrariety. 'Nothing in the history of the Labour Party can be compared', Shore recalled, 'in its sheer viciousness, with the Brighton Conference of October 1979.'[44] It was perfectly consistent that Benn thought '[t]he whole conference has been really friendly'.[45] From the platform Frank Allaun, chairman of the conference, and Ron Hayward, general secretary of the party (in a speech that Callaghan thought 'despicable'), condemned the parliamentary leadership for taking 'no notice' of the wider party – a charge that both Foot and Callaghan repudiated.[46] A proposal to establish an electoral college to replace the PLP electorate for the leadership was defeated, but defeat was merely deferral; the direction of travel was clear. Callaghan nevertheless managed to secure a commission of enquiry in order, as Benn put it, to 'delay the democratising process'.[47]

The commission begat its own conference, at Bishop's Stortford in June 1980. To general astonishment, Callaghan had refused to comment on his own position as this 'would mean that I would lose all authority', obviously declining though his authority was by then.[48] He despaired at what transpired. If there was to be an electoral college, Callaghan scribbled in his marginalia, 'then PLP to elect its own leader!'; a 5 per cent threshold for a leadership challenge was 'dangerous'; as to a manifesto 'drawn up annually both when the Party is in opposition and in government', he merely jotted 'Help!' When he was told that the manifesto would merely last until the following year's conference, 'whereupon the whole process would start again', he again jotted 'Help!'[49] Yet this 'contrived democracy' was agreed by the leader at, wrote the *Guardian*'s Peter Jenkins, what 'may have been his Munich'.[50]

If Bishop's Stortford was Callaghan's September 1938, then Brecon was, almost, his September 1939. 'Enough is enough,' he told the All Wales Rally. 'I ... propose to assume my full responsibility as leader of the party and now put my judgement to all the party on the best way to settle these domestic issues.'[51] To gird him, Owen had sent Callaghan a copy of Len Williams's *locum* general secretary's speech to the Scarborough Conference of October 1960 ('Nowhere in the Constitution is authority given to the Party Conference to instruct the Parliamentary Labour Party'). '[I]t has been my bible for the last 20 years,' Callaghan assured him, 'and the wording is engraved on my heart!'[52] At what he described as the 'not exactly pleasant' Blackpool

Conference of October 1980, Callaghan once more sat listening as the leadership was denounced by delegates, one of the most prominent being Patricia Hewitt, for its distance.[53] In an 'apocalyptic speech [which] was wildly cheered' Benn then condemned the leadership and the government in rhetoric that was as oratorically effective as it was factually misleading.[54] The PLP reported, to Callaghan's strong agreement, that 'the over-riding objection [to the college] is that such an arrangement might produce a Leader who could not maintain the confidence of his colleagues'.[55] Mandatory reselection and the principle of the college were agreed, but Callaghan had at least – just – kept control of the manifesto from the NEC. For *Labour Weekly*, 'the score between Left and Right was reckoned roughly a draw'.[56]

'Conference was pretty beastly as you can imagine,' Callaghan confided in Harold Lever afterwards, 'but I do not let it disturb me any more, and I shall take my own decisions.'[57] Seven days later he did exactly this. Callaghan had decided to circumvent conference and to dish the college: by his sudden resignation, it would be the PLP that would elect his successor. Callaghan's decision meant that the party was presented with precisely what it had spent eighteen months trying to avoid: a leadership election at the same time as an unresolved row over the electorate.[58] This led to the historic Wembley Special Conference on 24 January 1981, which determined the specifics of the college; Foot was by then the leader. Though ostensibly of the left, but foremost a parliamentarian, Foot supported neither reselection nor the college: he did not want 'right honourable marionettes'.[59] The least that he could countenance was 50 per cent of the college being reserved for the PLP, yet what Shore described as his 'disastrous misjudgement' in not speaking for this meant that 30 per cent was agreed.[60] Among those who resigned from the party were nine peers, on the grounds, *inter alia*, that the election of the leader should remain in the hands of MPs.[61] The left being thus strengthened within the electoral college, the annual conference at Brighton in September 1981 was free to adopt an Alternative Economic Strategy, to go with what was effectively a Bennite 'Alternative Political Strategy'.

The party that Foot led at least had a memory of power; the 'disastrous and bankrupt' estate that he bequeathed in 1983 could boast barely 200 MPs.[62] Kinnock's motivation as leader was therefore simple: 'the party's first duty is to get elected', to which end 'the hard and loony left', he privately claimed, 'are my only problem'.[63] If leadership of the party was the prerequisite for leadership of the country, the country would be stirred by a Labour leader fighting his own, as Hugh Gaitskell had done in 1960. Kinnock challenged the hard and loony left in the same, most public fashion. The calculated drama of the Bournemouth Conference of October 1985 was such that Kinnock's declamatory moment remained undulled, despite featuring in every television or radio documentary about Britain in the 1980s. Members of Militant heckled. Eric Heffer walked out. 'No Leader in the past', Benn said of the ensuing 'witch-hunt', 'has ever had the determination to remove a complete section of the Party.'[64] The following day Kinnock retrospectively confronted the greatest crisis of his tenure when he attacked the leadership of the miners' strike: 'I really enjoyed myself', Kinnock recalled, 'hammering Scargill', in one of two speeches that ensured the conference would invariably be referred to as a turning point.[65]

The experience of leadership

> I ... feel upset and angry at the way you are sometimes treated as Leader.[66]

Being leader

One issue for the three leaders was age and the traces of age. Callaghan was frequently described as 'avuncular', but that trait was less evident after May 1979 as a certain lassitude compounded the consequences of prolonged high office. Contrary to appearances, Michael Foot was a year younger than Callaghan. He was not the last career rebel to lead the party and, in turn, to hope for discipline; at least in his case, as Callaghan's deputy Foot emphatically had been loyalist rather than a loner. Subsequently, he eloquently expressed how 'Brother Tony' differed from him in this fundamental respect. At the time Benn gave Foot cause both to mollify – supporting him as chair of the Home Policy Committee and his return to the shadow cabinet – and to enjoin – disciplining him over committing the party to nationalisation without compensation.[67] Demonstrations of authority by Foot were temperamentally uncharacteristic. Distinctly unlike the other two leaders' – and the worse for it – Foot's public profile was that of the intellectual, the man of letters, prone to placing events in historical, often apparently first-hand context: the Argentinian Junta as another fascist aggressor; mass unemployment as an echo of the Slump; Lord Hailsham as once 'licking Hitler's jackboots';[68] Militant recalling the Socialist League; the depredations of the scavenger Tory press being those which Clement Attlee and Hugh Gaitskell too had had to endure; the Prime Minister as Neville Chamberlain *redivivus*. This served to convey to the viewer, listener or reader that Foot was a leader marked by senescence. Even the potentially normalising effect of a dog was partially negated by its being named after a nineteenth-century statesman.

Visually, Foot was unkempt; aurally, he was prolix. His discourse ('The sentence he started on *Nationwide* was still going when I switched on *TV Eye* three hours later') was also a political proxy: to avoid causing offence, Foot's nephew Paul said, he became a 'living parenthesis'.[69] Ever conscious of television, Foot's protégé, Kinnock, always appeared immaculate, while retaining the prolixity – and for the same reason. Neil Kinnock could be garrulous and diffuse in the House of Commons, and that mattered, given that he was much more active there than was either of his predecessors (and most of his successors).[70] For fear of upsetting people as changes were being made, Kinnock admitted later, 'I had to flannel'.[71] His director of communications, Peter Mandelson, found that the phrase '"Welsh windbag" occurred disturbingly often in the attitudinal research'.[72] It was a sign of his inexperience that Kinnock accepted the necessity of being groomed for his new role: a cuttings file of post-war leaders of the opposition was prepared for him, their myriad crises underlined in red.[73] His own leadership being constantly audited by polling, Kinnock was told what 'a leader', as distinct from 'a politician', was, and that the quality on which he consistently polled the highest – being 'in touch' with 'ordinary people' – was not typical of them: he was informed as to Prime Minister Thatcher's 'admiration paradox'.[74] Latterly bedecked in ersatz regimental (rather than Transport and General Workers' Union) tie, dark, double-breasted suit and gold-framed spectacles, Kinnock exhibited what even a supportive newspaper described as 'borrowed gravitas'.[75] His difficulty in resisting making a joke had long been noted.[76] 'Prime ministerial, prime ministerial', he was once overheard (possibly jokingly) saying to himself.[77]

The process that Kinnock put himself through culminated in 1990, in the mid-term of his second Parliament as leader. The 'confidential' Project Liberation was a strategy devised by Kinnock's team: to 'neutralise deficiency' against the Prime Minister in regard to his 'ability' and 'strength'; to '[w]in new support by exploiting his strengths', namely pride, empathy and 'bringing together the nation'; to '[l]iberate NK from the shackles of the past'; and to '[g]ive NK necessary support to enable him to do this'. Polling revealed that Kinnock's key weaknesses were that he was thought to be 'too emotional' and that he did not appeal to women aged over forty-five. He was 'constrained by a series of boxes': that of statesman ('has to behave and perform like a PM at all times'), party ('has to use language that ensures continuing Party support') and 'baggage' ('In the past supporting positions and policies he did not necessarily agree with'). Kinnock's core deficiency in ability would be neutralised by demonstrating his effective management of the party and the ejection of 'sectional interests'; secondarily, it required 'clear, crisp language and concepts' and '[a]ppropriate use of managerial language', avoidance of 'the vernacular and colloquial' and of 'overly emotional language and gestures and excessive physical gesticulation'. Peer-group approval ('endorsement of NK's managerial abilities by industrialists, manager[s] and politicians') should be prominent. Kinnock's core deficiency in strength would be neutralised by his espousal of a clear sense of direction for Britain and his taking a stand 'when it mattered'. Neutralising the leader's deficiencies went alongside exploiting his strengths. Core strengths were quality-of-life issues (such as education and health), stirring a sense of pride and patriotism and his appeal as bringing the country together. Alongside 'running a tight ship' and managerialism was his appearance on Terry Wogan's BBC1 television show, which would allow 'the person' to complement 'the politician'.[78] 'NK must give a clear sense that he says what he thinks, does what he wants,' Project Liberation averred: 'That he is his own man'.

Managing the party

On becoming leader of the opposition Callaghan took the opportunity to return some of his colleagues to the backbenches: 'I am trying to give new people a little experience during the coming session.'[79] In the first shadow cabinet elections since 1973, neither Kinnock nor Eric Heffer was among the twelve elected (Denis Healey was top). However, Kinnock did not exhibit Heffer's 'fastidiousness' and accepted a portfolio.[80] Given his lack of frontbench experience and that the portfolio was education, a policy area of particular association with Callaghan since 1976, Kinnock's promotion was trebly significant. It was also soon followed by a threat of the sack when he rebelled in a House of Commons vote on nuclear weapons.[81] Callaghan disabused a protesting Moss Evans of the notion of freedom of speech: 'we must have a united team on the Front Bench'.[82]

Management was harder for Foot, the unity candidate who, from the moment he took over the party leadership, received representations from each side complaining of the other.[83] One colleague told him 'not be too magnanimous to the Right wing for it was this as much as anything which proved the undoing of Harold Wilson'.[84] As if to order, and 'making a last, rather desperate personal gesture' by offering himself at all, Bill Rodgers requested the defence or industry portfolio. Foot offered him neither, to Rodgers's (and John Roper's) frustration.[85] Within three months both had defected to the SDP. The inevitable consequences of reselection and entryism meant that Foot was prevailed upon to defend sitting MPs and disown some prospective ones.[86] *Tribune* drew attention to a leader who had once trumpeted tolerance by reprinting his denunciations of the NEC when it had described the Bevanites as 'a party within a party'.[87] These and other matters provided for interminable NEC meetings at the new party headquarters at Walworth Road (opened by Callaghan in July 1979), bookended by general disorder outside as protestors, pedestrians and journalists scrambled on, and off, the pavement.

Project Liberation acknowledged that Kinnock had been 'running a tight ship'. He sought and acquired control over campaigns and communications, a strong leader's office, a manageable PLP and a majority on the NEC. Supporters were given key positions. All served to increase the power of the leader, which was essential for the policy changes that would thenceforth be sought. The NEC could then be marginalised by the transfer of responsibilities to the shadow cabinet, and then to the leader's office. But the strength of the leader's office led to complaints from senior colleagues.[88] Project Liberation advocated '[b]ringing people who work in the organisation together', but Kinnock's experience was that 'being leader is a lonely job. If you assiduously try to make it less lonely, you will be accused of cronyism.'[89] He set up an 'advisory' Leader's Committee, unknown at first to the NEC or shadow cabinet; when the time came to notify them, he said, 'I want to be able to refer to an established institution.'[90]

Project Liberation proposed that the leadership would be strengthened by greater direct involvement of members, who would dilute the influence of extra-parliamentary organisations. Thus did One Member One Vote – OMOV – appeal: 'My view was that if we got it for the selection of MPs, getting it for the leadership would be a very easy stroll.'[91] Kinnock's defeat on this issue at the Blackpool Conference of October 1984 was held by those who formed the subsequent New Labour project to be the major setback of his leadership.[92] It meant that more 'calculated means' would be required 'to compile majorities', and thereafter Kinnock felt that he 'could not afford to be defeated on any major issue'.[93] From 1985 he had a solid majority in the PLP, shadow cabinet and NEC. Ken Livingstone found himself elected to an NEC that was run increasingly like the shadow cabinet, where Kinnock 'continued to bludgeon us into the ground even after winning vote after vote'.[94] Kinnock had overseen what Hilary Wainwright described as 'conservative centralism', marked by exclusion and 'by the avoidance of risk'.[95] His organisational control was greater than that of any previous Labour leader and meant that he was much more able – and certainly more minded – than Callaghan or Foot to exercise patronage, something else that was abjured by the 'Alternative Political Strategy'.

The drafting of the manifesto was a less contentious affair in 1987 than it had been in 1979 or 1983. Also, unlike that of 1979, in its published form the manifesto had a cover image; and unlike that of 1983, the image was of the leader, and of only the leader, red rose in lapel, left arm raised to an audience.[96] Mandelson admitted that the 'aims of our campaign had been to build up his stock as a new kind of leader, and in effect to camouflage most of the policy prospectus'.[97] The result of the general election was evidence to Kinnock that policy had to take as much notice of the views of the electorate as it did of those of conference, and also that the wider party membership ought to be heard – hence 1988's derided polling exercise, Labour Listens. Kinnock succeeded in convincing conference over public ownership, trade union rights and a somewhat less alternative economic strategy. Defence was predictably the most sensitive issue and, suitably enough, the most opaque.[98] The dilemma was that success in changing the policy – such as unilateralism or Europe – would come at the risk of damaging what reputation for consistency he had, or of being too late to carry any conviction; either way, as Roy Hattersley put it, Kinnock would be unelectable either because of the views he always held or because he had changed them.[99] The 1987 Policy Review took two years and was endorsed at the Brighton Conference of October 1989; by the

Brighton Conference of October 1991 a policy commission had replaced delegate resolutions – with a leader's veto on policy.

Being seen as leader

Much depended on whether the public could imagine each of the three leaders as Prime Minister. This was less of a challenge for Callaghan. It was a greater one for portraitists. Of the three, Callaghan was the most inscrutable, possessing neither a distinctive accent nor physical characteristics other than the outsize spectacles that had a further distancing effect. Nor was he much easier to caricature. Such representations as he attracted were circumstantial rather than personal: political cartoonists portrayed him as a large frame contorted between left and right (Benn and Healey), or as the moderate front concealing threatening figures, Benn prominent. By the standards of the *Sun*, Stanley Franklin's representation of Callaghan as Mr Micawber had hardly been personally damning.

The scholar of Swift, however, was nothing less than a gift: Foot was easy to draw and to imitate, being idiosyncratic in both manner and deportment. Within two days of his election, Foot delivered a gift to satirists by breaking his ankle and spending his early leadership hobbling around with his foot in plaster. Cartoonists depicted a dishevelled pensioner in varying states of discombobulation; ten million *Sun* readers every day saw a dwarfish Foot drawn by cartoonist Stanley Franklin as if he had just been electrocuted. Representations of the leader of the opposition varied from a bonfire guy, to the kindly, demented children's television scarecrow Worzel Gummidge, to a wheelchair-bound geriatric (Nurse: 'If you want to stay on, nod your head.').[100] Yet the ordure was partly self-applied. His appearance – waving a stick while walking a dog named after a nineteenth-century statesman – was not one that other leaders were to imitate. 'I am getting more and more concerned that the media should not be given the opportunity of portraying you in an unfavourable light,' one colleague wrote after Foot's most notorious episode, standing fidgeting and ill-dressed at the Cenotaph on 8 November 1981; the party 'depends to a very considerable extent on the image which you are personally able to present'.[101] The Remembrance Day offence caused to many (until that moment) Labour voters was made clear by his correspondents, among the more moderate of whom was an outerwear manufacturer from Leeds who complained about 'the adverse effect that your scruffy appearance is having on our duffle coat and donkey jacket trade'.[102]

Foot subsequently conceded that he should have paid more attention to 'publicity advisers'.[103] The same could not have been said of his successor, who attributed Labour's failures under his own leadership 'partly [to] the way in which over the years I'd been represented, partly [to] the way I represented myself'.[104] Alone of the three, Kinnock was preoccupied by, and sought to shape, representations and receptions of both himself and the party, yet he offered almost as man-sized a target as Foot had done. On the very day of his election, and having just told an entourage of journalists on Brighton beach 'If you want a real scoop, I'll walk out there, on the water,' Kinnock presented to posterity his own, sodden gift by falling over in the surf in front of television cameras. Cambrian cultural stereotypes – variations on emotionalism and verbosity – predominated. Gingerism became mainstream. Kinnock's leadership coincided with ITV's *Spitting Image*, whose millions of viewers were regaled weekly by a loquacious, freckled opportunist. Kinnock's public lapses in judgement – although none, individually, was comparable with Foot's at the Cenotaph – were cumulatively damaging: his intemperate Falklands comment on BBC's *Question Time*, or calling an MP 'a jerk' in the House of Commons.[105] As to the depredations of the scavenger Tory press that he had to endure, John Major agreed.[106]

Such representations mattered because they mattered to Kinnock. Friends thought him to be increasingly driven by fear of failure more than by hope of success; periods of depression were said to be common.[107] While Callaghan had admitted to a lack of educational and intellectual self-confidence, Kinnock's education and intelligence were questioned even by his supporters.[108] Project Liberation counselled that 'language [and] concepts' were important. Alone of the three leaders, Kinnock published his own statements of political principle. His excursions into ideas were not particularly ideational. He highlighted, as he tended to more generally, the self-consciously sanitising prefix 'democratic' to socialism, but was not seriously revisionist other than in calling for a 'third way' between 'the old social democracy [and] the new ultra-leftism'.[109] Often to the frustration of his office, Kinnock insisted on writing his own speeches, and collected some in a book he entitled *Making Our Way*. '[T]he politics of production' was the theme of a thin, workaday volume.[110]

Unlike his deputy, four years a cabinet minister – during which time 'I had grown some scar tissue' – Kinnock's lack of extensive front-bench experience meant that he was unprepared for the extent of the attention he would receive.[111] After Labour Listens Mandelson urged a tougher *mien*, even through applying PEET: Personal Effectiveness Enhancement Training.[112] The Shadow Communications Agency (SCA) developed a 'writers' group' to 'sharpen up our lines, help provide gags'.[113] Displaying what might have been described as borrowed juvenescence, Kinnock presented the British Rock and Pop Awards, launched a range of T-shirts and appeared in the promotional video for Tracey Ullman's *My Guy*, a 1984 top-twenty hit in the Netherlands. The most vaunted representation was Hugh Hudson's 1987 party election broadcast, known as 'Kinnock: the Movie' and, less commonly but more aptly, 'Chariots of Kinnock'. So much was invested in it that perhaps for the first time a party television broadcast was advertised in the press: 'Neil Kinnock. The Complete

Picture'.¹¹⁴ An unparalleled example of presidential campaigning, over the course of nearly ten minutes it contained no reference at all to the party, but footage from the Bournemouth speech, and much of the leader's parents, wife and children ('Use family as symbol of Quality of Life values', Project Liberation had recommended). SCA activities were set against a background of the party frequently polling ahead of the Conservatives, yet the leader's personal ratings remained worse than those of any other leader of the opposition – with the exception, that is, of his predecessor.

Being challenged

The outcome of these various processes could be determined, although (the 1988 challenge notwithstanding) they were never acted upon: even in the event that electoral defeat was merely likely, Labour leaders had never been unseated, and were almost never challenged. It helped Callaghan that his approval ratings were high – over 60 per cent; Foot's peaked at 49 per cent, but by his last year had slumped to nine.¹¹⁵ In an attempt to arrest the slide, in June 1981 Foot had invited Benn to challenge him as leader. Despite Foot's 'pleadings' Benn had instead stood against Healey as deputy, thereby undermining the leader even more than he could have done by challenging him.¹¹⁶ Subsequent speculation about the leadership prompted Benn to pen an open letter to the shadow cabinet requesting 'each and every member' publicly to state his or her support for Foot.¹¹⁷ Nevertheless, the leader remained unchallenged despite, according to one journalist, there not being an MP 'who believed, privately' that he would be elected Prime Minister.¹¹⁸

The absence of unity was most marked in the public mind by the presence of 'phantom leaders' such as Benn and Scargill.¹¹⁹ 'Presenting Labour in a positive light will be difficult, presenting Kinnock in a positive light much less so,' felt Philip Gould at the SCA.¹²⁰ Bob Worcester, the party's pollster, maintained that 'Kinnock's profile is much more important even than policy.'¹²¹ Kinnock was told that the gains he had made in his first months had been lost during the miners' strike: 'there is considerable scope for strengthening the image', a subject he always took seriously.¹²² Gould recommended repeated, targeted messages established by working groups; Worcester recommended concentrating on, in order: issues, party image and that the 'party's only serious weakness is Kinnock's inability to be perceived as Prime Minister'.¹²³ Kinnock trailed on strength, decisiveness and international reputation, and his encounters with the Prime Minister in the House of Commons were usually mismatches.

London Labour Briefing denounced Kinnock's 'marvellous left preaching, vicious careerist practice'; *Tribune* thought that 'his career shows disturbing signs of following that path well-worn by ambitious Labour politicians'.¹²⁴ For Eric Heffer that was precisely the problem. At least 'Gaitskell was known to be on the right of the Party'; it was Kinnock's 'past left-wing mantle, now used against others on the left, which creates confusion and makes it easier for the witch-hunt to proceed'.[125] Benn always thought that 'Hattersley would be easier to deal with than Kinnock, just as Healey would have been easier to deal with than Foot', because Hattersley (and Healey) 'would appease the left whereas Kinnock would pander to the right'.[126] Discontent culminated in 1988 with the first challenge to a leader since 1961. 'Tilting at Windbags'[127] featured Heffer as Sancho Panza to Benn's Don Quixote, the grounds for whose quest were 'that the leadership is killing the party, diluting policy, centralising power'.[128] Hattersley was worried about Heffer's challenge to him; had he lost, Kinnock would have resigned.[129] By immediately and publicly supporting the deputy, Kinnock implicitly acknowledged his – and Foot's – mistake in not having done so in 1981.[130] Unlike in 1981, Benn's 'alternative' merely served to revive and reaffirm the incumbent (it was an 'extravagant non event', Alan Tuffin told him).[131] Kinnock called it an 'unnecessary distraction', but what had once been a distraction was also a mandate.[132] *Militant* had stated that '[a]t stake is the future of socialism'.[133] Kinnock won 89 per cent of the vote. For *London Labour Briefing* that merely meant that the '1989 Leadership Challenge Starts Now!'[134]

By raising the nominating threshold from 5 to 20 per cent in 1988, Kinnock then made it harder to force a contest in future: '[Benn] delivered himself into my hands.'[135] Without obvious competition, 1989–90 turned out to be the party's brightest year in a sepulchral decade. In the Commons a confident Kinnock was sharper, funnier. In June 1989 the results night of the European Parliament elections provided Kinnock with the 'best hours' of his leadership.[136] Although it was not known at the time, or recognised afterwards, in October 1989 Kinnock precipitated the resignation of the Chancellor of the Exchequer, Nigel Lawson.[137] In December *The Times* named him 'Politician of the Year'.[138] In March 1990 Labour overturned a 14,000-vote Conservative majority in the Mid-Staffordshire by-election. Spirits were high. But the mood was infectious. The Conservative Party was unnerved, and reacted decisively. On 22 November Prime Minister Margaret Thatcher resigned and Kinnock told his office 'we've just lost our greatest electoral asset'.[139] Philip Gould felt this to be the moment that 'the Kinnock project went into decline'.[140] If the public had wanted change, they now had it. The following year, with Labour 5 per cent behind the Conservatives and polls suggesting a 15 per cent boost under a different leader, dissatisfaction had reached the point where senior colleagues encouraged the shadow chancellor, John Smith, to mount a challenge.[141] Less than three years after what was Kinnock's emphatic (and should have been his emboldening) re-election, and within one year of his second general election as party leader, once more, and not in the way intended, 'the Man became the Issue'.[142]

The measure of leadership

> There must be a willingness once again to trust the leadership.[143]

'Who leads the Labour Party?' *Labour Leader* asked in 1985, before concluding that it was not the Labour leader.[144] The starkest measure of leadership for a party leader is the result of a general election. Labour's defeat in 1979 was hard to pin on its leader, who on polling day led his opponent (by almost double) as to 'who would make the better Prime Minister'.[145] When James Callaghan was the party's candidate, Labour emphasised 'leadership'; the Conservatives did so only in 1983 when, in tacit assent, Labour did not. In that year, however, Labour advocated, in nuclear disarmament, a policy about which its unilateralist leader cared most, but which, as he was yoked to an equally vociferous multilateralist deputy, served to undermine his authority in a way that might have been predicted. Then, on 25 May, Callaghan publicly disclaimed the party's defence policy and Jim Mortimer, party general secretary, told the press that the Campaign Committee was 'insistent that Michael Foot is the leader of the party', an insistence that became a headline, since the identity of the leader had rather been assumed.[146]

During the 1983 campaign, in his own public meetings Callaghan noted 'Foot's incapacity as a leader' as being an issue.[147] The leader's natural proclivities were apparent to one observer: 'Foot, although patently a very nice man, handles objects in the real world as if they ought to be books, and a baby can tell when the pair of encircling hands would rather be holding a copy of Hazlitt's *Dramatic Literature of the Age of Elizabeth*.'[148] Foot did not adapt to the requirement that campaigning had to be television orientated. Crafting phrases for television news bulletins was not a new discipline, but without applause lines Foot appeared on television speaking at length to a silent audience. After journalists complained that he did not deliver the speeches his team had distributed, Foot read them out, but as he was unable to use a teleprompt, and had bad eyesight, one of the finest orators in post-war politics delivered his perorations hunched over a script.[149] A former colleague who had lost his seat told Callaghan: 'We were told very clearly on the doorstep and in the factories, and ultimately in the ballot box, that the Party had chosen the wrong leader for the wrong reasons.'[150] Whatever the reason, it was for Foot 'a bloody awful result in every stinking way'.[151]

In the six months before the 1987 election the shadow cabinet, to counterbalance polling about Kinnock being inexperienced and weak, was advised to 'refer whenever [possible] to Neil Kinnock's first rate Ministerial team' and to 'refer regularly' to Kinnock 'to build up his leadership'.[152] Thus was there an explicitly 'Presidential-style campaign'.[153] The Prime Minister herself said that her party had 'got to go for Kinnock', and the Conservative campaign and press made much of fresh 'phantom leaders' such as Ken Livingstone and

Bernie Grant.[154] President Reagan's White House administered a calculated personal humiliation to Kinnock when he went to visit the USA in March.[155] In May, Kinnock virtually wrapped and delivered his own present to critics by offering an elaboration on defence policy that was characterised as being inspired by Hereward the Wake and the Mujahedeen, and by undermining his shadow chancellor in deviating from a carefully constructed and repeated line about Labour's tax policy.[156] 'I am dismayed that we did not do better,' Callaghan told Tony Benn after the election, adding, pointedly, that the 'lesson is that the impressions formed by the electorate over a period of four years cannot be obliterated in four weeks campaigning'.[157]

Five years later, in 1992, Kinnock was the first Labour leader since Harold Wilson to go into a general election with a hope of winning it. Acknowledging that his personal negatives had not even been neutralised by emphasising the leader, Labour's 1992 campaign placed Kinnock as *primus inter pares*. A broadcast in the week before polling day focused on the shadow cabinet, and ended with Kinnock behind a desk rather than up a mountain.[158] The Conservatives remained convinced that he could not win, as he was neither 'credible' nor 'numerate'[159] (not unlike Kinnock's predecessor, who disclosed to him, 'I am in fact one of the leading world experts on financial and economic affairs, but this has not always been recognised in all quarters'[160]). Kinnock's last-minute, confidence-betraying equivocation over electoral reform and coalition did not help[161] In Sheffield on 1 April 1992, at a rally the significance of which became almost as overstated as the event itself, Kinnock's overexcited manner overshadowed a sober speech. It was to be emblematic.

The three leaders had assumed their mantles in contrasting ways: Kinnock on pebbles, Foot on crutches, Callaghan in Downing Street. One was deemed to be too young, two too old (Labour would not have another leader aged over sixty for thirty-five years). Callaghan was criticised for staying; Kinnock for leaving; Foot, almost, for being. Although the principal charge after losing power in 1979 (even more than in 1970 and 2010) was that the party leadership had become separated from the membership, the three thought the problem to be deeper still. Callaghan felt that 'we have failed' in not modernising Labour's philosophy: 'We have neglected [political] education. We have allowed it to fall into the hands of the militant groups.'[162] Kinnock too felt that his major failing was not engaging sufficiently with the 'battle of ideas'.[163] There was more to leadership than party management: Kinnock felt that he had 'to repeat the mantra of basic purpose'.[164] That mantra, like all the best ones, was simple: principles into power. But only the second resounded. Callaghan remained in the House Commons for another parliament before, predictably, going to the House of Lords; Foot remained in the Commons for two parliaments before, equally predictably, becoming the first post-war ex-Labour leader to decline to go to the House of Lords; Kinnock may have felt cause for penitence towards those luminaries whom his younger self had castigated for taking themselves off to the 'House of Lords or European Commissions'.[165]

For someone whose public profile was so abiding, representations by and of Callaghan were wanting. Pain may be inferred in his tellingly ending his 1987 autobiography in May 1979. Far from avoiding the subject, the only memoir that Foot ever wrote was of his leadership of the Labour Party in opposition, and he began it by explaining at length why he had not resigned earlier than he did.[166] After the 1992 defeat, Kinnock ended his term as abruptly as had Foot, deciding, perhaps with Callaghan's unhappy twilight in mind, that 'I couldn't take the risk I'd use up a year or more of time that a new Leader would need to get a grip on public attention'. Days later, he was assailed by doubts that that very abruptness might have been his 'gravest mistake as Labour leader'.[167] On the Monday morning following the general election, Kinnock received the first enquiries from publishers and literary agents about his memoirs.[168] He resisted (just as he did similarly sudden offers to establish Kinnock Foundations).[169] In time, Philip Gould, one of the Project Liberation planners, reflected that the project 'didn't work because his real self had changed, become older, wiser, different'.[170] It was this self-abnegation that Kinnock felt that David Hare, albeit through the best of motives, had definitively misjudged in his *The Absence of War*, the concluding play in a trilogy that railed against the political mores of contemporary Britain.[171] The failure to Liberate was less one of diagnosis, or even prescription, than of timing; the 'golden hour' had passed for the person, rather as the 1980s suggested to some that it might also have done so for the party. Kinnock dated his mid-life crisis as lasting from 2 October 1983 to 18 July 1992.[172] Yet, far from embracing the dispensations of senior citizenship in the years that followed, in public appearances and in interviews, he flayed his 'completely unsatisfying' leadership with an openness and frequency that was almost masochistic.[173]

By any measure, Callaghan's leadership of the opposition was a failure; Foot's was simultaneously catastrophic and blameless; the panacea of the putative Denis Healey leadership overlooks its probable consequences in preference for its possible benefits (one reason, perhaps for both Harold Wilson and Callaghan, after having voted for Healey in the first round, reportedly voting for Foot in the second).[174] Kinnock, by contrast, had either increased the number of seats and vote share in consecutive elections, as only Wilson had done, and increased his party's vote share by more than any leader except Attlee, or merely replaced the votes and seats lost under his predecessor. As Labour leader, in terms of cumulative performance measured by seat change, Kinnock exceeded Wilson, and by vote change exceeded Wilson and Blair; by his own admission, however, 'in the end, it's about winning elections'.[175] Of the three who led the Labour Party, only the latter had the scope to be anything other than reactive, yet the more he made his party electable, the less electable he appeared. After its worst defeat, the party had chosen its youngest, most inexperienced and thereby least tainted leader, but the historical and political context of Labour in the 1980s made his a harder task than that faced by any of his post-war predecessors – or successors. Kinnock was less constrained by the party than they had been, but was more constrained by its past and, in so far as doubts about him existed, its present. None of the major policies that he had supported when he became leader did he support by the time he resigned. For someone once thought of as recklessly spontaneous, Kinnock created a cautious and centralised organisation requiring a leader's office of staffers (one of the most prominent being Patricia Hewitt) who were increasingly praetorian in disposition. Kinnock's reforms were gradually acquired, but acquired they were, through his possessing what the other two leaders had lacked: a solid majority on the NEC. Thereby was an electable party fashioned. Structures were necessary for leadership, after all.

The unrealistic, lacerating and self-indulgent factions of the 1980s that had questioned the pre-eminence of the leader resulted in reforms that served greatly to empower him: the electoral college meant legitimacy, and so authority, and did so by having broadened the basis of his election. That the party thereafter was as disinclined to support its leader as it was to displace him was not the least of the reasons why leading the Labour Party in the 1980s was a nightmare. The party was a collective endeavour, and so there was a suspicion of leaders; but because it was a collective endeavour it would not depose them. Disconnected from the mesmerising effects of office, this tendency was exaggerated (it took the party 110 years to produce a leader who could not maintain the support of his colleagues). The party crises of the 1980s were specific to the 'betrayal' of the 1970s, but then the party crises that attended every loss of office were specific. Those of the 1980s were unique in degree, however, and demonstrated for the first time in Labour's period as a party of government that, even if there were many other reasons, an unconvincing leader could be the biggest reason why a voter would not vote for the party. Anyone able to lead the Labour Party in opposition for nine years might have been thought eminently qualified to lead the country, but an effective leader was one who could be envisaged by it as Prime Minister; thirteen years after the introversion began as to whether it mattered who was leader, a concurrence was reached. On 18 July 1992, with 91 per cent of the vote, the party gave the greatest mandate ever received by any leader to one who appeared finally to be what was required, both of the person and of the party. Experienced, self-assured, 'prime ministerial'; to his Tory opponents an *homme sérieux*; of the right of the party, although on excellent terms with the left; promising a smaller leader's office, a more open regime; OMOV. At the count, the new leader thanked Kinnock. 'Our future victory will be built upon the sure foundations he has laid.' In private, he admitted his admiration for Callaghan, the leader who had promoted him to the cabinet in 1978 to give him experience in preparation for leading the Labour Party. 'He never had the chance for a full term,' lamented John Smith.[176]

Notes

1 Margaret Thatcher, *The Downing Street Years* (London: HarperCollins, 1993), p. 360. The author is grateful to Paul Corthorn, Daniel Larsen, and Andrew Thorpe for comments on earlier drafts of this chapter. Abbreviations: JCP: James Callaghan Papers (Bodleian Library, Oxford); MFP: Michael Foot Papers (People's History Museum, Manchester); NKP: Neil Kinnock Papers (Churchill Archives Centre, Cambridge); PSP: Peter Shore Papers (LSE Archives, London); LPAR: Labour Party Annual Report; HCD: House of Commons Debates; HLD: House of Lords Debates.
2 James Callaghan, *Time and Chance* (London: Collins, 1987), p. 566; Michael Foot, *Another Heart and Other Pulses* (London: Collins, 1984), p. 13; Neil Kinnock, *In Conversation with … Lord Kinnock*, Open University, 21 May 2015.
3 Tony Benn, *Conflicts of Interest: Diaries 1977–80*, ed. Ruth Winstone (London: Hutchinson, 1990), p. 501 [10 May 1979].
4 Tony Benn, *The Wilderness Years: 1*, BBC2, 3 December 1995; Tony Benn, 'The Case for a Constitutional Premiership', *Parliamentary Affairs* 33 (1980), 7–22.
5 Tony Benn, *Arguments for Socialism* (London: Penguin, 1980), pp. 178–9.
6 Benn, *Diaries*, p. 509 [26 May 1979]; cf. *Labour Leader*, August 1983, p. 3.
7 Kenneth O. Morgan, *Callaghan: A Life* (Oxford: Oxford University Press, 1997); Mervyn Jones, *Michael Foot* (London: Gollancz, 1994); Kenneth O. Morgan, *Michael Foot: A Life* (London: Harper Press, 2007); Robert Harris, *The Making of Neil Kinnock* (London: Faber & Faber, 1984); Michael Leapman, *Kinnock* (London: Unwin Hyman, 1987); George Drower, *Kinnock* (South Woodham Ferrers: Publishing Corporation, 1994); Eileen Jones, *Neil Kinnock* (London: Hale, 1994); Martin Westlake, *Kinnock* (London: Little, Brown, 2001); Kenneth O. Morgan, *Labour People* (Oxford: Oxford University Press, 1987, 1992); Callaghan, *Time and Chance*; Foot, *Another Heart*; Neil Kinnock, 'Reforming the Labour Party', *Contemporary Record* 8 (1994), 535–4; *Neil Kinnock: The Lost Leader*, BBC2, 5 December 1992; *Kinnock: The Inside Story*, ITV (*1: The Path to Leadership*, 17 July 1993; *2: The Enemies Within*, 25 July 1993; *3: The Pursuit of Power*, 1 August 1993, *4: Victory Denied*, 8 August 1993); Neil Kinnock, 'Neil Kinnock on Leadership, the Labour Party and Statecraft Theory', in Charles Clarke and Toby S. Jones (eds), *British Labour Leaders* (London: Biteback, 2015), pp. 335–56; Neil Kinnock, *Conversations*, BBC Parliament, 26 July 2016.
8 Of their election: H. M. Drucker, 'Changes in the Labour Party Leadership', *Parliamentary Affairs* 34 (1981), 369–91; 'Intra-Party Democracy in Action: The Election of Leader and Deputy Leader by the Labour Party in 1983', *Parliamentary Affairs* 37 (1984), 283–300; Leonard P. Stark, *Choosing a Leader* (London: Macmillan, 1996); Timothy Heppell, *Choosing the Labour Leader: Labour Leadership Elections from Wilson to Brown* (London: I. B. Tauris, 2010); Tim Heppell and Andrew Crines, 'How Michael Foot Won the Labour Party Leadership', *Political Quarterly* 82 (2011), 81–94. Of their leaderships: Peter Shore, *Leading the Left* (London: Weidenfeld & Nicolson, 1993); Kevin Jefferys (ed.), *Leading Labour from Keir Hardie to Tony Blair* (London: I. B. Tauris, 1999); Martin J. Smith, 'Neil Kinnock and the Modernisation of the Labour Party', *Contemporary Record* 8 (1994), 555–66; Martin Westlake, 'Neil Kinnock: Loyalist Reformer', in Martin Westlake (ed.), *Leaders of Transition* (Basingstoke: Macmillan, 2000), pp. 103–33; Kenneth O.

Morgan 'United Kingdom: a Comparative Case Study of Labour Prime Ministers Attlee, Wilson, Callaghan and Blair', *Journal of Legislative Studies* 10 (2004), 2–3, 38–52; Charles Clarke and Toby S. Jones (eds), *British Labour Leaders* (London: Biteback, 2015); Paul Corthorn, 'Michael Foot as Labour Leader: The Uses of the Past', in Julie Gottlieb and Richard Toye (eds), *Making Reputations: Power, Persuasion and the Individual in Modern British Politics* (London: I. B. Tauris, 2005), pp. 29–42; Andrew Scott Crines, *Michael Foot and the Leadership of the Labour Party* (Newcastle: Cambridge Scholars, 2011).
9 Callaghan, *Time and Chance*, p. 565.
10 Richard Rose, 'A Crisis of Confidence in British Party Leaders?', *Contemporary Record* 9 (1995), 272–93.
11 *Tribune*, 7 October 1983, p. 1.
12 Callaghan, *Time and Chance*, p. 565; *The Times*, 15 October 1980, p. 1; Kinnock, 'Neil Kinnock on Leadership', p. 339.
13 *The Times*, 8 September 1980, p. 3; Benn, *Diaries*, p. 498 [8 May 1979]; Benn, *The End of an Era: Diaries 1980–90*, ed. Ruth Winstone (London: Hutchinson, 1992), p. 23 [31 July 1980].
14 Denis Healey, *The Time of My Life* (London: Michael Joseph, 1989), p. 466.
15 John Prescott, *Prezza* (London: Headline, 2008), pp. 142–3.
16 Clive Jenkins, *All Against the Collar* (London: Methuen, 1990), pp. 188–90.
17 Kinnock, 'Neil Kinnock on Leadership', p. 340.
18 Jack Straw, *Last Man Standing* (London: Macmillan, 2012), pp. 138–9.
19 *Tribune*, 7 November 1980, p. 1; *Labour Weekly*, 14 November 1980, p. 1.
20 Field to Foot, 24 October 1980, MFP/MF/L1.
21 *Labour Weekly*, 24 October 1980, p. 3.
22 Andrew Faulds to Foot, 14 November 1980, MFP/MF/L2.
23 *The Times*, 1 October 1981, p. 4.
24 Benn to Foot, 11 November 1980, MFP/MF/L1.
25 Steel to Foot, 11 November 1980, MFP/MF/L1.
26 Roy Jenkins, *European Diary* (London: Collins, 1989), pp. 532–3, 645 [1 December 1979, 10 November 1980]; *A Life at the Centre* (London: Macmillan, 1991), p. 530.
27 Healey, *The Time of My Life*, p. 477; Roy Hattersley, *Who Goes Home?* (London: Little, Brown, 1995), pp. 225–6.
28 *Private Eye*, 24 October 1980, p. 15.
29 *The Times*, 13 June 1983, p. 1; *Daily Mail*, 13 June 1983, p. 1.
30 [David Cowling], memorandum for Peter Shore, PSP/13/146.
31 Gerald Kaufman, *The Wilderness Years, 3: Enter the Rose*, BBC2, 17 December 1995; Benn, *Diaries*, p. 20 [23 June 1980]; Hattersley, *Who Goes Home?*, p. 221; Benn in *The Hugo Young Papers*, ed. Ion Trewin (London: Allen Lane, 2008), p. 211 [7 June 1985].
32 Callaghan to Shore, 22 September 1983, PSP/13/66.
33 Frank Chapple, *Sparks Fly* (London: Michael Joseph, 1984), p. 191.
34 John Kent, *Private Eye*, 15 July 1983, p. 15.
35 Hattersley, in Stark, *Choosing a Leader*, p. 222 n. 58, pp. 134–5.
36 Forward Labour Press Release, 12 July 1983, PSP/13/66; *Tribune*, 24 June 1983, p. 1.
37 *The Times*, 25 November 1982, p. 1; COHSE Branch Ballot Candidates' Election Statements, 7, PSP/13/66; Callaghan, *Time and Chance*, p. 566; Foot, *Another Heart*, p. 163.
38 Ken Coates (ed.), *What Went Wrong* (Nottingham: Spokesman Books, 1979); David Coates, *Labour in Power?* (London: Longman, 1980).

39 Austin Mitchell, *Four Years in the Death of the Labour Party* (London: Methuen, 1983), p. 35.
40 Submission from the Tribune Group of Labour MPs to the Party Commission of Enquiry, May 1980, 2, JCP/56/1784; Martin Flannery to Callaghan, 9 April 1980, JCP/57.
41 Callaghan to Flannery [copy], 17 April 1980, JCP/57.
42 *The Firing Line*, PBS, 4 September 1980.
43 Foot, *Another Heart*, p. 162.
44 Shore, *Leading the Left*, p. 128.
45 Benn, *Diaries*, p. 546 [4 October 1979].
46 Hattersley, *Who Goes Home?*, p. 221; LPAR 1979, pp. 168–9, 188–90.
47 LPAR 1979, pp. 213, 227–30; Benn, *End of an Era*, p. 497.
48 Callaghan, *Tribune*, 20 June 1980, p. 5; William Rodgers, *Fourth Among Equals* (London: Politico's, 2000), p. 195.
49 Callaghan notes, PLP meeting 18 June 1980; Commission of Enquiry notes, June 1980, JCP/59/1788.
50 *Guardian*, 18 June 1980, p. 15; Campaign for Labour Victory, *The Future of the Labour Party*, February 1980, p. 18.
51 *Observer*, 6 July 1980, p. 3.
52 Owen to Callaghan, 7 February 1980, JCP/55/1782; Callaghan to Owen [copy], 8 February 1980.
53 LPAR 1980, p. 143; BBC TV conference footage.
54 Edna Healey, *Part of the Pattern: Memoirs of a Wife at Westminster* (London: Headline Review, 2006), pp. 223–4; Benn, *Diaries*, p. 32 [10 October 1980]; LPAR 1980, p. 147; note, 'Tony Benn Speech', JCP/73; Michael Cocks report, JCP/148; Hattersley, *Wilderness Years: 1*; Callaghan, *Tribune*, 13 June 1980, p. 6.
55 Second Report of the Working Party of the Parliamentary Labour Party, and notes, JCP/54/1778.
56 *Labour Weekly*, 3 October 1980, p. 1.
57 Callaghan to Harold Lever [copy], 8 October 1980, JCP/305; Callaghan to Reg Crook [copy], 8 October 1980, JCP/305.
58 *Labour Weekly*, 17 October 1980, p. 1.
59 Foot, Parliamentary Committee Meeting Minutes, 3 June 1981, Labour Party Papers, People's History Museum, Manchester.
60 Shore, *Leading the Left*, p. 142.
61 To Foot, 2 March 1981, MFP/MF/L27/10.
62 Shore, *Leading the Left*, p. 137.
63 Kinnock, 25 June 1985, 29 February 1984, in *Young Papers*, ed. Trewin, pp. 214, 201.
64 Benn, *Diaries*, p. 457 [21 May 1986].
65 Kinnock, 10 October 1985, 2 October 1985, LPAR 1985, pp. 120–9, 153–6; Kinnock, *In Conversation*.
66 Michael Meacher to Foot, 21 May 1982, MFP/MF/L31/1/4.
67 Michael Foot, *Loyalists and Loners* (London: Collins, 1986), pp. 107–26; Benn, HCD, 10 November 1981, 12, cols 494–500; Kinnock to R. A. Jones, 30 November 1981, NKP/KNNK/1/3/5.
68 *Daily Telegraph*, 20 May 1983, p. 14.
69 Clive James, *Observer*, 29 May 1983, p. 9; Paul Foot, *Labour's Old Romantic: A Film Portrait of Michael Foot*, BBC2, 19 July 1997.
70 Julian Critchley, *Palace of Varieties* (London: John Murray, 1989), p. 46; Michael Rush, 'Engaging with the Enemy: The Parliamentary Participation of Party Leaders', *Parliamentary Affairs* 67 (2013), 751–66.

71 Neil Kinnock in, *Worst Job in British Politics? The Leader of the Opposition*, BBC4, 25 February 2008.
72 *New Statesman*, 1 April 1988, p. 15.
73 NKP/KNNK/2/1/89.
74 'Leadership and Political Leaders: a Presentation to Neil Kinnock', 18 April 1986, NKP/KNNK/2/1/93.
75 *Independent on Sunday*, 12 April 1992, p. 26.
76 Gerald Kaufman, 25 January 1984, in *Young Papers*, ed. Trewin, p. 200; David Hare, *Asking Around: Background to the David Hare Trilogy* (London: Faber & Faber, 1993), pp. 157–260.
77 *Sunday Times*, 12 April 1992, p. 13.
78 Project 'Liberation' [1990], NKP/KNNK/3/4/1/4.
79 Callaghan to Robert Sheldon [copy], 22 June 1979, JCP/246.
80 *Economist*, 23 June 1979, p. 25; *Daily Mail*, 19 June 1979, p. 2.
81 Callaghan to Kinnock [copy], 25 January 1980; Rodgers to Callaghan, 29 January 1980, JCP/54/1778.
82 Callaghan to Evans, [copy] 19 February 1980, JCP/131.
83 MFP MF/L26/33–43.
84 Roy Hughes to Foot, 11 November 1980, MFP/MF/L1.
85 Rodgers, *Fourth Among Equals*, p. 204; Rodgers to Foot, 27 November 1980, Roper to Foot, 8 December 1980, MFP/MF/L10.
86 MFP/MF/L4; Peter Tatchell, *The Battle for Bermondsey* (London: Heretic, 1983), p. 58; Foot, HCD 3 December 1981, 14, col. 398; [Nigel Bowles] to Callaghan, 3 December 1981, JCP/48; Norman Atkinson et al. to Foot, 25 November 1981, MFP/MF/M10/4/2.
87 *Tribune*, 1 October 1982, p. 1.
88 Robin Cook to Kinnock, 18 July 1985, NKP/KNNK/1/2/3; Hattersley to Kinnock, 17 November 1986, NKP/KNNK/1/2/6; Hattersley to Kinnock, 2 July 1987, NKP/KNNK/1/3/20/1; Clare Short to Kinnock, 3 July 1987, NKP/KNNK/1/2/13.
89 Kinnock, 'Neil Kinnock on Leadership', p. 352.
90 Draft Introductory remarks to Leader's Committee [January 1988], NKP/KNNK/3/2/5; Kinnock to Ron Todd [Copy], 7 January 1987, NKP/KNNK/3/2/5.
91 Kinnock, in Stark, *Choosing a Leader*, p. 59.
92 Philip Gould, *The Unfinished Revolution* (London: Abacus, 2011), p. 40.
93 Kinnock, 'Reforming the Labour Party', p. 538.
94 Ken Livingstone, *You Can't Say That* (London: Faber & Faber, 2011), p. 306.
95 Hilary Wainwright, *Labour: A Tale of Two Parties* (London: Hogarth, 1987), p. 290.
96 *Britain Will Win*, Labour Party Manifesto, June 1987.
97 Peter Mandelson, *The Third Man* (London: HarperPress, 2010), p. 100.
98 Neil Kinnock, in *This Week Next Week*, BBC1, 5 June 1988.
99 John Smith, in *Young Papers*, pp. 377–8 [22 April 1993]; John Cole, *As it Seemed to Me* (London: Weidenfeld & Nicholson, 1995), p. 227; Hattersley, *Wilderness Years: 2*, BBC2, 17 December 1995.
100 *Private Eye*, 11 March 1983, p. 1.
101 Stan Newens to Foot, 21 July 1982, MFP/L31/1/4.
102 R. F. Brown to Foot, 26 November 1981, MFP/L41/1.
103 Foot, *Another Heart*, p. 159.
104 Kinnock, *Lost Leader*.
105 To an audience member who heckled that the Prime Minister 'has got guts', Kinnock replied 'And it is a pity that people had to leave theirs on the ground

at Goose Green in order to prove it': *The Times*, 7 June 1983, p. 1; HCD, 20 November 1991, 199, col. 283.
106 John Major to the Leveson Inquiry, 12 June 2012: *An Inquiry into the Culture, Practices and Ethics of the Press, Report* (2012), House of Commons Reports 780-III, p. 1134.
107 Jan Royall, in *Inside Story, 3*; Gould, *Unfinished Revolution*, pp. 87–9; Andy McSmith, *John Smith* (London: Mandarin, 1994), p. 172; Mandelson, *Third Man*, p. 130; Hattersley, *Who Goes Home?*, p. 260.
108 Callaghan, *Labour's Last Premier*, BBC2, 25 April 1992; *Daily Telegraph*, 7 May 1989, 13.
109 Neil Kinnock, *The Future of Socialism* (London: Fabian Society, 1986), p. 1.
110 Kinnock to John Smith [copy], 9 September 1986, NKP/KNNK/1/213; Neil Kinnock, *Making Our Way* (Oxford: Basil Blackwell, 1986), p. vi; *New Statesman*, 28 November 1986, p. 23.
111 Hattersley, *Who Goes Home?*, pp. 286–7.
112 *New Statesman*, 1 April 1988, p. 15
113 Hewitt to Clarke, 16 November 1986, NKP/KNNK/3/2/5.
114 *Sun*, 21 May 1987, p. 15.
115 *Daily Telegraph*, 22 June 1979, p. 2; 19 August 1982, p. 2; 17 February 1983, p. 6; *Daily Mail*, 14 November 1980, p. 2.
116 Foot, *Loyalists and Loners*, p. 123.
117 Benn to Shadow Cabinet [copy], 25 February 1983, MFP/M13/1 ('We are never going to agree about tactics are we', Kinnock to Benn [copy], 28 February 1983, NKP/KNNK/1/3/5); Giles Radice, *Diaries 1980–2001* (London: Weidenfeld & Nicolson, 2004), 83 [23 February 1983].
118 Anthony Bevins, *The Times*, 11 June 1983, p. 5.
119 'Leadership and Political Leaders: a Presentation to Neil Kinnock', 18 April 1986, NKP/KNNK/2/1/93.
120 Gould, *Unfinished Revolution*, p. 69.
121 Worcester, in *Young Papers*, p. 242 [23 July 1986].
122 Worcester to Kinnock, 24 October 1984, NKP/KNNK/2/1/93; 4 December 1985, NKP/KNNK/2/1/88, Patricia Hewitt to Charles Clarke, December 1985, NKP/KNNK/2/1/89; Gould, *Unfinished Revolution*, p. 59; Kinnock, 29 February 1984, in *Young Papers*, p. 202.
123 Worcester, in *Young Papers*, p. 242 [23 July 1986]; Field to Kinnock, 6 March 1987, NKP/KNNK/1/2/5.
124 *London Labour Briefing*, July 1983, p. 1; *Tribune*, 2 September 1983, p. 1.
125 Eric Heffer, *Labour's Future* (London: Verso, 1986), pp. 75–6.
126 Benn, *Diaries*, p. 350 [16 May 1984]; Livingstone, *You Can't Say That*, p. 269; Healey, *Time of My Life*, p. 216.
127 *ILP Magazine*, Summer 1988, 1.
128 Benn, *Diaries*, p. 540 [23 March 1988]; Vladimir Derer, *Voice of the Unions*, May 1988, p. 1.
129 Mandelson to Clarke [1988], NKP/KNNK/2/1/115/1; Kinnock, *In Conversation*.
130 Hattersley, *Who Goes Home?*, p. 231.
131 Alan Tuffin to Benn [copy], 28 March 1988, Heffer Papers, People's History Museum, Manchester, ESH7/7.
132 Kinnock, 4 October 1988, LPAR 1988, 60; *Tribune*, 7 October 1988, p. 5.
133 *Militant*, 1 April 1988, p. 2.
134 Conference Delegates' Briefing, Friday Blackpool 1988, p. 1.
135 LPAR 1988, pp. 74–6; Kinnock, in Stark, *Choosing a Leader*, p. 60.
136 Kinnock, *In Conversation*.

137 Philip Webster, *Inside Story* (London: William Collins, 2016), pp. 99–100.
138 *The Times*, 21 December 1989, p. 14.
139 Kinnock, *In Conversation*.
140 Gould, *Unfinished Revolution*, p. 94.
141 Tony Blair, *A Journey* (London: Hutchinson, 2010), pp. 49–50; Paddy Ashdown, 14 January 1991, *The Ashdown Diaries Volume 1: 1988–1997* (London: Allen Lane, 2000), pp. 107; Bryan Gould, *Goodbye to All That* (London: Macmillan, 1995), p. 239; Kinnock, 'Neil Kinnock on Leadership, p. 345.
142 *Independent on Sunday*, 22 September 1991, p. 17.
143 Callaghan, *Guardian*, 3 October 1983, p. 25.
144 *Labour Leader*, October 1985, p. 1.
145 *Daily Telegraph*, 3 May 1979, p. 1.
146 *Daily Mail*, 27 May 1983, p. 8; *Tribune*, 10 June 1983, pp. 6–7; J. E. Mortimer, *A Life on the Left* (Lewes: Book Guild, 1998), pp. 384–5.
147 'Election '83 notebook', JCP/82.
148 *Observer*, 29 May 1983, p. 9.
149 *Sunday Times*, 22 May 1983, p. 17.
150 Ken Woolmer to Callaghan, 20 June 1983, JCP/ 82.
151 Foot to George Thomas [copy], 1 July 1983, MFP/ML/10.
152 Hewitt to [Bryan] Gould [copy], 5 December 1986, NKP/KNNK/2/1/89.
153 Hewitt to Clarke, 16 November 1986, NKP/KNNK/3/2/5.
154 David Young, *The Enterprise Years* (London: Headline, 1990), p. 210; Norman Tebbit, *Upwardly Mobile* (London: Weidenfeld & Nicolson, 1988), p. 252.
155 Webster, *Inside Story*, pp. 115–17.
156 In the event of Soviet invasion, Kinnock had advocated resistance, which the Conservative tabloids related to the experience of Afghanistan (even interviewing a member of the Mujahedeen on the feasibility of Kinnock's 'guerrilla plan': *Daily Mail*, 26 May 1987, p. 2) and the eleventh-century resistor to the Normans (*Sun*, 27 May 1987, pp. 6, 8; 29 May 1987, p. 1); Kevin Barron to Kinnock, 26 August 1987, NKP/KNNK/1/2/2.
157 Callaghan to Benn [copy] 16 June 1987, JCP/188.
158 Party Election Broadcast, BBC1, 2 April 1992.
159 Michael Heseltine, *Life in the Jungle* (London: Hodder & Stoughton, 2000), p. 409; Kenneth Baker, *The Turbulent Years* (London: Faber & Faber, 1993), pp. 346–7.
160 Foot to Kinnock, 11 January 1988, NKP/KNNK/1/2/5.
161 Kinnock, 2 April 1992, interview, Robin Day, ... *But With Respect* (London: Weidenfeld & Nicolson, 1993), pp. 273–6; *Daily Mail*, 17 January 1992, p. 9.
162 Callaghan, in conversation with Shirley Williams, BBC1, 1 November 1979, transcript, JCP/136.
163 Kinnock, 'Neil Kinnock on Leadership', pp. 346–9.
164 Kinnock, 'Reforming the Labour Party', p. 540.
165 Kinnock, 'Which Way Should Labour Go?', *Political Quarterly* 51 (1980), 411–23, at 411.
166 Foot, *Another Heart*, pp. 13–21.
167 Kinnock to Ben Pimlott [copy], 14 April 1992, NKP/KNNK/3/4/3/1; *New Statesman*, 17 April 1992, p. 6.
168 NKP/KNNK/3/4/3/5.
169 NKP/KNNK/3/4/3/9.
170 Gould, *Unfinished Revolution*, p. 142.
171 *Financial Times*, 18 February 2006, p. 7. The play starred John Thaw as George Jones/Kinnock, on stage, premiering at the National Theatre in 1993, and on screen, in a 1995 BBC adaptation. Hare defended himself against the charge by

stating that he had only presented what he had been told by Kinnock's team: Hare, *Asking*, pp. 157–250.
172 Kinnock, *Conversations*.
173 Kinnock, in *Kinnock: 3 Pursuit of Power*, ITV, 31 July 1993.
174 *Private Eye*, 5 December 1980, p. 4.
175 Kinnock, 'Neil Kinnock on Leadership', p. 343.
176 *Independent*, 19 July 1992, p. 1; *Economist*, 18 July 1992, p. 34; *Daily Telegraph*, 18 July 1992, p. 6; Callaghan, HLD, 12 May 1994, p. 1651; *The Times*, 18 July 1992, p. 16.

3

Labour's liberalism: gay rights and video nasties

Paul Bloomfield

The social liberal reforms introduced by the Labour Party in the mid-1960s encountered increasingly determined opposition from the Conservative right in the 1980s. In the midst of the turmoil of the 1970s, a section of the Conservative Party aimed to provide an alternative to the post-war liberal consensus on moral questions. It was a contradictory melange of the radical and the reactionary, which the historian of sexuality Jeffrey Weeks described as 'a revival of evangelical moralism, fired by an apprehension of basic changes, but made despairing by the legislative reforms'.[1] This moralism was allied to a stated desire to reverse much of the post-war welfare state legislation which had, allegedly, caused the decay that had afflicted the country since the 1960s. Despite having voted for the decriminalisation of homosexuality and abortion while in opposition in the 1960s, in the 1980s Margaret Thatcher and her government used Private Members' Bills in much the same way as the Labour government had done in the 1960s, this time to put socially conservative legislation on the statute book. Rejection of the permissive society and the adoption of more austere 'Victorian values' were an essential element of the New Right's politics and found backing and succour among the right-wing print media and from the long-standing moral watchdog, Mary Whitehouse.

Espousing the nostrums of family values and an aversion to the promotion of minority rights (most infamously in the case of Section 28 of the 1988 Local Government Act), the Conservative government of the 1980s set out to return Britain to the 1950s. David Marquand described this as revenge for 'the so-called permissive society'. He noted the irony of figures who recoiled at the 'mixture of sexual indulgence, cultural nihilism and half-baked Marxism' of the swinging sixties but who supported market liberalism's belief in individualism:

'in market liberalism, after all, the consumer is king, driven solely by the desire to maximise pleasure and minimise pain'.[2]

Personal morality was the area where Thatcherism arguably failed: it was unable to push back the reforms of the 1960s. At a time when the Conservatives were entrenching their economic philosophy in British society, Labour was to make the winning argument in the area of social policy. This chapter explores Labour's liberalism in the 1980s. For the purpose of the chapter, 'liberalism' is defined as meaning 'social liberalism' or 'moral liberalism': support for individual freedoms and opposition to discrimination and 'prejudice'. It also stands for a degree of moral relativism. Two litmus tests of its liberalism were the party's support for gay and lesbian people and its reaction to the issue of video censorship. The reason why these two issues are selected here is that they demonstrate different aspects of liberalism: the liberty to express one's sexuality and the liberty to watch what one wants in the privacy of one's own home. These two aspects of liberalism were not the same and they were both heavily contested in the decade.

An abiding theme in Labour's politics was its rejection of the Conservative Party's moral puritanism. In spite of pressure to tack away from liberal nostrums that were associated with the 'loony left' and were seemingly unpopular with parts of the electorate, Labour maintained a strong sense of social liberalism, which had long existed within the wider movement. If it is true that the right won the economic argument and the left won the social and cultural argument (see the Introduction to this volume), then Labour's ability to withstand populist pressure from sections of the press and public opinion contributed to a new common sense about minority rights and respect for alternative ways of living. In many ways, the Parliamentary Labour Party reacted to some of these issues because of pressure from external forces such as the Gay Liberation Front, or Mary Whitehouse and her National Viewers' and Listeners' Association promoting censorship. In the 1960s, while Labour's social reforms set the political agenda, there was also public opposition to the abolition of capital punishment. Nevertheless, the party had persisted with its penal policy when it would have been easier to concede for electoral gain. In the same way, in the 1980s Labour continued with its defence of socially liberal policies when, again, it could have abandoned them.

This chapter covers a time when the defence and improvement of the lesbian and gay community was employed as a political stick with which to beat Labour. What follows is not an uncritical analysis; it highlights the tensions and contradictions in Labour's liberalism. The party was prone to stumble over the path that it wished to take in pursuit of a more liberal country. Such missteps reflected the internal battles within the party, some of which were the result of poor decision making. In spite of this, during one of its darkest periods of its history Labour projected a pronounced commitment to minority rights and matters of personal freedom and liberty. Many of these issues about morality were framed in terms of the rights of the individual – the freedom of people to express their sexuality and the freedom of people to watch whatever they wished in the privacy of their own home. In this view, the state did not belong in a person's bedroom, or in the living room where they watched television.

The chapter also highlights how a party which, in the 1950s and 1960s, had facilitated a relaxation of censorship laws in Britain was unsure how to react to the great 'video nasties' furore of the mid-1980s and provided little constructive criticism of the legislation when it was presented. It represents the classic dilemma faced by the Labour Party in having to appeal to both the (perceived) liberal-minded middle classes and the more socially conservative working class which it was set up to serve. Despite the upheaval that was taking place within, the Labour Party was to demonstrate that it could still be a reforming force. Labour was to maintain its commitment to minority rights at a time when such sentiments were viewed with downright hostility, particularly in the eyes of the tabloid newspapers. In spite of the divisions within the party, Labour found unity in the promotion of social liberalism.

Labour and gay rights

Labour's liberal credentials were burnished in the 1960s administrations of Harold Wilson and were closely associated with Roy Jenkins. The reforms ushered in during Jenkins's tenure, such as the 1967 Sexual Offences Act, led to his reputation as 'the most influential Home Secretary of the Twentieth Century'.[3] Jenkins had made the case a decade earlier for what became 1960s social liberalism, as had Tony Crosland in his 1956 book *The Future of Socialism*.[4] Both Jenkins's and Crosland's social liberalism was to influence a later generation of Labour politicians, including the future leader of the Greater London Council (GLC), Ken Livingstone, whose liberal initiatives will feature below.[5] Frank Dobson, however, has contended that while it would be churlish to take too much away from Jenkins, the groundwork for much of the 1960s legislation was laid by others such as Barbara Castle and Lena Jeger. Dobson complained to this author about 'the infantilism of a great deal of political commentary which has got to attribute each topic to a particular individual whereas very little in politics or life is like that'.[6] Labour's approach to social liberalism was complex in any case. Figures such as George Brown, James Callaghan and Harold Wilson were uncomfortable with it. Moreover, David Owen, Leo Abse and even Jenkins himself viewed homosexuality as an affliction, with the latter saying it was 'a very real disability for those who suffer it'.[7] In spite of the 'benevolent condescension' of these and other Labour MPs, homosexuality, if not completely accepted, was brought out of the closet.[8] For the *Daily Mirror*, the move put Britain 'in step with the liberal approach adopted by the Dutch fifty-six years ago'.[9] To quote historian

Stephen Brooke, 'it was Parliament that changed the framework of sexual life in Britain' and it was a Labour government which facilitated it, despite disdain among its own supporters.[10] The Conservative MP Sir Cyril Osborne said that Labour would suffer for putting 'buggery in front of steel nationalisation'. While historian Martin Pugh notes that Labour as a party 'was far from happy about the "permissive society"', 74 per cent of its MPs voted for the decriminalisation of homosexuality.[11]

Dominic Sandbrook argues that the 'permissive society' was not the great cultural revolution that Arthur Marwick believes it to have been; rather, it was 'the result of very different, decades-old pressures'. The development of social liberalism by Jenkins, Crosland and others suggests that he is correct.[12] Brooke notes that Labour's socialism has always included a streak of sexual radicalism and stretched right back, even before the Labour Party was founded, to the radical politics of the early nineteenth century. Radicalism had always gone 'hand in hand with ideas of sexual reform'. For Labour, its social-liberal antecedents can be traced back to the works of Robert Owen, William Morris, Edward Carpenter and Olive Schreiner.[13]

The Sexual Discrimination Act of 1975 saw the establishment of the Equal Opportunities Commission to assist with the outlawing of discrimination on the grounds of gender or marital status. However, while decriminalisation had helped to remove the misconception that homosexuals were criminals, the age of consent for gay men (at twenty-one) remained older than it was for heterosexuals. The slow pace of change to full equality had led to the formation in 1970 of the Gay Liberation Front, which in 1975 tried to exert pressure on Parliament, through the Campaign for Homosexual Reform, to equalise the age of consent (and to enact decriminalisation in Northern Ireland and Scotland, where homosexuality was still illegal).[14] This resulted in the formation in the same year of the Gay Labour Caucus, later to become the Labour Campaign for Lesbian and Gay Rights.[15] If Britain was changing tentatively in some respects and faster in others, this was reflected in the Labour Party. As Roy Hattersley attested, 'if the Wilson government had done nothing else, its existence would have been justified by the opportunity it provided for Parliament to create a more enlightened society'.[16]

It was this society which was challenged by the Conservative Government over a decade later. While the creation of the Social Democratic Party (SDP) in 1981 saw the Labour Party lose members known for their liberal reforming instincts, the party's commitment to social liberalism remained, even though the man most commonly associated with the great reforms of the 1960s, Roy Jenkins, now led the SDP. Labour MP Austin Mitchell observed that the loss of the Social Democrats did not affect the social liberalism of the Labour Party at all. For him, it only reinforced the need to defeat the more militant left and govern from the centre.[17] Paradoxically, voters who identified with the Social Democrats were not necessarily inclined to be socially liberal themselves.

Ivor Crewe and Anthony King noted that, on capital punishment and censorship, SDP supporters were sometimes closer to the Conservatives.[18] While the SDP aspired to govern from the 'radical centre', this was not necessarily the position of some of its voters on moral questions.

Labour's pursuit of racial and sexual equality was continued with added zeal in the 1980s. In 1983 under Michael Foot, and again in 1987 under Neil Kinnock, there were specific commitments to improving gender and racial equality, gay rights and a more humane approach to immigration control. Foot was strongly sympathetic to the cause of gay rights, having been a 'fervent' supporter of the Roy Jenkins reforms, aided and abetted by his wife, Jill Craigie, a strong influence on Foot's social liberalism, particularly his feminism.[19] For his biographer Kenneth O. Morgan, Foot resembled Voltaire. He 'devoted a very long life to the pursuit of the highest ideals of free thought, tolerance and civil liberty'. Foot's libertarianism echoed Crosland's description of the attributes which socialists should demonstrate.[20]

In March 1982 the National Executive Committee published *The Rights of Gay Men and Women*, which raised the issue of discrimination in employment. As the Labour Campaign for Gay Rights activist Peter Purton observed, it was only a discussion paper and yet it received the immediate opprobrium of the pro-Conservative press and failed to become party policy at the 1982 party conference.[21] This commitment to the freedom of the individual was emphasised in *Renewal*, the essay collection written by the shadow cabinet. Labour's shadow solicitor general Peter Archer viewed support for gay rights as intrinsic to Labour's values: 'The socialist is descended from a long line who claimed the right to be different.'[22]

At times, Labour could find itself paralysed by events. This was evident in the confusion over support for the candidacy of Peter Tatchell in the Bermondsey by-election of 24 February 1983. The horrific and unedifying campaigning that took place on the part of an independent candidate, John O'Grady, was made all the more embarrassing in that he was a former Labour Party council leader who had received support from the seat's previous MP, Robert Mellish. An infamous example was O'Grady's riding through the constituency on a horse and cart singing lewd songs referring to Tatchell's sexuality ('Tatchell is an Aussie, he lives in a council flat, He wears his trousers back to front 'cos he doesn't know this from that').[23] Tatchell's (and Labour's) campaign was further undermined by references to his campaigning for gay rights and the SDP–Liberal Alliance's literature which referenced their candidate, Simon Hughes, as 'the straight choice'.[24] Outright homophobia appeared in election pamphlets distributed throughout the constituency, including one which asked 'Which Queen would you vote for?'[25]

While Labour was in the midst of one of its darkest moments following the SDP split and the battle for supremacy between left and right, what was striking was the reservation of the Labour leadership in defending its candidate.

Foot had initially denounced the candidature of Tatchell and subsequently offered only lukewarm endorsement. This was mainly due to Foot's hostility to the kind of extra-parliamentary campaigning championed by Tatchell in *London Labour Briefing* (and later reprinted in the *Guardian*), including one accusatory phrase which must have particularly rankled with Foot: 'we now seem stuck in a rut of legalism and obsessive parliamentarianism'.[26] When asked about this twenty years later by Roy Hattersley, Foot remarked that 'it had been put to me that he was the sort of person who opposes Parliament itself. And I had my duties to the Party which I wanted to keep in one piece. A few days later he came to see me and it became clear that he had a real concern for the Party as well as himself.'[27] Tatchell himself publicly disavowed any links to radical leftism, such as were espoused by Tariq Ali, asserting that his 'source of political inspiration is Alfred Salter and George Lansbury'.[28]

Although this must be viewed through the prism of the internal battles against Militant (Tatchell, while not a member of Militant, was viewed as coming from the radical left, and thus was, erroneously, linked to it), the reluctance of the party leadership to allow Tatchell's sexuality to become a matter of public knowledge underlined the gradualist approach that the Labour Party still had towards the matter of gay rights.[29] Tatchell later told Hattersley that during the campaign he 'clearly believed that the Labour high-command expected that, when asked if he was gay, he should categorically refuse to discuss the subject'.[30] This was perhaps in reaction to what James Curran referred to as the tabloid press's attempt to 'discredit him by whipping up atavistic prejudices against him as a deviant'.[31] As Alwyn Turner notes, as Tatchell had yet to come out publicly as homosexual, the tabloid press resorted to 'innuendo to avoid libel actions, while leaving readers in no doubt about their subtext'.[32] Tatchell himself made a point of trying to separate his own sexuality from his support for gay rights, and in doing so earned criticism from rights activists, to go along with the commentary of the tabloids.[33] While Tatchell tried to emphasise the local nature of the election, his sexuality was raised by others when he tried to keep the matter private.[34]

Foot's performance at this by-election showed that he was, for all of his undoubted compassion, unsuited for a role that required a great deal of nuance and subtlety. While he never once condemned, or commented on, the matter of Tatchell's sexuality, his handling of the affair allowed it to fester. In the face of a relentlessly hostile campaign (not least on the part of the Liberals), Labour and Tatchell lost the Bermondsey by-election by 10,000 votes. Tatchell did not return to fight for the seat a second time at the general election a few months later.

Labour's experience at Bermondsey, with a former Labour councillor attacking the candidate's sexuality, was chastening and perhaps, sadly, not surprising. Attitudes in Britain viewed homosexuality in a negative light. In the same year, 1983, 62 per cent of respondents to a British Social Attitudes Survey viewed homosexuality as always/mostly wrong – and within Labour this too was evident.[35] Even Leo Abse, the man who had championed the decriminalisation of homosexuality, could write, less than twenty years after his Bill had been passed, that, as a result of an increase in one-parent families, 'homosexuality and bisexuality is likely to increase as more boys are brought up with no male roles in which to identify'.[36] Abse further suggested that 'the youngster could lose his way and grow up uncertain in his identity' as a consequence of 'the triumphant liberation of women from their domestic thraldom' causing the roles of parents to become 'smudged'.[37]

While Tatchell's sexuality may have been considered a reason for voters to choose an alternative candidate, this did not deter Labour from making a clear commitment to sexual equality in its 1983 manifesto: 'We are concerned that homosexuals are unfairly treated. We will take steps to ensure that they are not unfairly discriminated against.'[38] This was the first time that such a commitment had been specifically made in relation to the gay and lesbian community, something which was absent from the manifesto of the SDP–Liberal Alliance. Indeed, a former Labour-turned-SDP MP, James Wellbeloved, condemned the Labour-run GLC's spending on 'lavish subsidies to organisations ranging from gay rights to supporters of the IRA bombers'.[39] Such sentiments and dubious couplings were an indicator of how matters would be played out over the rest of the 1980s.

Neil Kinnock became Labour leader after the election defeat in 1983 and, together with his new deputy, Roy Hattersley, attempted to extricate Labour from continued electoral defeat. While Kinnock's energies were used to tackle the matter of Militant and the consequences of the miners' strike, his enthusiasm was at times mercilessly mocked by unsympathetic newspaper columnists, and the satirical TV programme *Spitting Image* suggested that the primary reason for his commitment to minorities was as a means of winning votes. Kinnock's attitude to gay rights has been questioned due to a comment made after the Bermondsey by-election when he was asked if the treatment of Peter Tatchell had amounted to a witch-hunt. His ill-considered reply was 'I'm not in favour of witch hunts, but I do not mistake bloody witches for fairies!'[40] Crass as the comment was, Kinnock supported gay rights; the previous year he had called for a Royal Commission on the gay age of consent.[41]

Between 1983 and 1987, Kinnock's Labour Party contended with criticism both inside Westminster and in the press that it was overly concerned with minority issues. On 9 December 1983 Jo Richardson, a supporter of Tony Benn, presented a Sex Equality Bill which attempted to outlaw discrimination in the workplace on the basis of sexuality.[42] The Bill was defeated by 198 votes to 119, with Kinnock supporting the measure alongside other MPs ranging from new MPs such as Tony Blair and Jeremy Corbyn to veterans like Denis Healey and Michael Foot.[43] Some of the attitudes expressed showed how difficult it would have been to get the Bill passed, with the Conservative MP Ivan Lawrence declaring:

> Clauses 3 and 92 on homosexuality will incur the fury of many of our constituents who do not want their children to be taught by people who parade their homosexuality and think that it is a matter for exhibition and pride. How many Members want their children to be taught by a member of the Paedophile Information Exchange?[44]

In spite of these attacks, Labour MPs were not deterred from defending the efforts of councils to promote equality and, in turn, gay rights. Three years later, during a debate on 5 December 1986, Tony Banks, MP for Newham North-West, asked 'why when a local council tried to do something about discrimination against gay and lesbians was there an enormous reaction from Conservative MPs?'[45] This prompted the shadow local government spokesman, Jack Straw, to suggest that while the Conservative Party was attacking those councils that were helping to promote equality, some of its members were themselves gay and 'they deserve the same tolerance as Labour councillors trying to help gay and lesbian people'. This suggestion provoked a furious response from the government benches. A Conservative spokesman stated that the party chairman, Norman Tebbit, 'knows homosexuals and has a high regard for some of them but that does not mean he would approve of them influencing young children'.[46] Straw's reaction was in contrast to the 1970s episode when he chaired the Further and Higher Education Committee of the GLC and had stopped the funding of a training course for social workers on issues faced by gay people, a training course condemned by Conservative members as 'homosexuality on the rates'.[47]

In its 1987 election manifesto Labour again offered a commitment to improving gay rights, albeit in somewhat diffident terms. It simply stated that it would 'take steps to ensure that homosexuals are not discriminated against'.[48] In some ways, this was still a bold move and, as Purton noted, was a consequence of the 1985 and 1986 conferences, which had supported the commitment to equality in the manifesto. This was in no small part due to the support given to Chris Smith, the first openly gay MP, who had been elected in 1983 for the seat of Islington South and Finsbury and had come out in 1984. For Smith, gay and lesbian rights were a natural cause for Labour: 'some people might regard it as marginal to our concerns as a movement. It is not. It is central to our socialism. It is central because we believe in equality – the equal right of everyone to live their life.'[49] Smith's re-election in 1987 may have been a sign of a more tolerant approach of electors towards homosexuality, but such sentiments were not necessarily held by the wider electorate and, as *Gay Times* noted twenty years later, 'it would be another 13 years and three general elections before another openly gay person was elected'.[50]

The decision to fight for gay rights may have been a factor contributing to Labour's losing votes. Where the British Social Attitudes Survey in 1983 showed that 62 per cent of respondents who identified as Labour voters viewed homosexuality as 'always or mostly wrong', by 1987 this figure had risen to 74 per cent. To put the matter in a coldly political perspective, it was risky to continue supporting gay equality in a decade that was marked by anxiety about sexual difference.[51] This was also a time when fear surrounding the AIDS/HIV epidemic was reaching a crescendo, and the association of the disease with the gay community served only to highlight the heightened suspicion with which it was viewed.[52] However, as Arthur Marwick noted, there was 'no real evidence of a return to pre-sixties morality' during this period and, for all the prudery of the Thatcher Government, its advertising campaigns 'brought an anatomical explicitness, and an open acceptance of the sexual urges of young females as well as males, that would not have been contemplated in the sixties'.[53]

There was, however, a perception that gay men were receiving preferential treatment from local councils. The tabloid press reacted furiously to the decision of Lambeth Council to designate homeless people with AIDS as a priority for housing.[54] Labour's core constituency – white, working-class, socially conservative voters – had been attracted to the Tory message in the late 1970s, particularly in Essex and the South East; voters were turned off by talk of yet more nationalisation, while policies such as the Right to Buy found favour with them. The Conservatives and their allies in Fleet Street had been successful in smearing Labour as the 'loony left'. According to Eric Shaw, this provided an 'invitation to voters to define themselves as white and respectable rather than as working class, to identify with the Conservatives as the Party of whites and the upwardly mobile – and to reject Labour as the Party of minorities and the failures'.[55]

The particular *bête noir* for both the Conservatives and their supporters in Fleet Street was Ken Livingstone and the GLC. Livingstone had pushed successfully since the mid-1970s for financial support for gay pressure groups, sometimes in the face of the objections of fellow Labour councillors.[56] In particular, Livingstone's support for the Gay Teenage Group highlighted the difficulties faced by gay people under the age of twenty-one (at that time still the legal age of male gay consent). Livingstone noted that this particular policy created 'hysteria' and led to furious denunciation by Conservative MPs and an attempted investigation into his private life by newspapers such as the *Sun*.[57] Critics of such policies viewed them as, at best, misguided and, at worst, simply cynical politics, money being spent on such causes in order to recruit 'a sizeable army of politically and racially motivated mercenaries, hostile to the State that supports them'.[58] According to *The Times*, Livingstone had only himself to blame, having spent £5 million on causes such as the Gay Arts Sub Group Festival Babies against the Bomb, Lesbian Line Campaign against

Racist Laws and the Gay London Police Monitoring Group.[59] Such support may have been noble in intent but it added to the perception that Labour councils were determined to spend local taxation on what were deemed niche subjects. Polly Toynbee contended that the cause of gay and lesbian equality, as put forward by Livingstone, was actually counter-productive and provided 'the hounds of the moral right all the meat they needed for a successful red-blooded backlash'.[60]

This strong criticism, while publicly rejected, came to be reflected in Labour Party circles. Following the Greenwich by-election of 26 February 1987 (which Labour lost to the SDP), Patricia Hewitt commented in a memo to Kinnock that the 'gays and lesbians issue is costing us dear'.[61] Conversely, Linda Bellos, leader of Lambeth Council, refused to apologise for policies such as assisting homeless young gay men. She accused the tabloid media of wilful misinterpretation, and a similar accusation was made by the leader of Islington Council, Margaret Hodge, who said that, despite the expenditure on the gay and lesbian community of a mere £1,500 out of a budget of £300 million, 'vindictive newspaper campaigns' had distorted the picture.[62] The chair of the London Labour Party, Glenys Thornton, agreed with Hewitt, saying that while Labour councils should not change their policies, they should be better aware of the adverse or, in some cases, misleading publicity created by the tabloid newspapers.[63] Hewitt's thinking was perhaps borne out by voters such as Mrs Gwendoline Naden, who remarked that she had always voted Labour but was likely not to vote at all: 'all these lesbians, gays, if that's the way then fair enough but we shouldn't have to pay for it'.[64] It was perhaps with these sentiments in mind that even Frances Morrell, a noted Benn supporter and the leader of the Labour-led Inner London Education Authority, called for a scaling-back of the presentation of the gay and lesbian issue because 'it makes Labour unpopular, and it causes us to lose elections', consequently 'damaging the interests of interest groups'.[65]

What became Labour's more avowed commitment to gay rights was exemplified by the party's reaction to the introduction of a piece of legislation which became synonymous with the battles faced by gay rights movements in the 1980s. In her speech to the Conservative Party conference on 9 October 1987, Margaret Thatcher took aim at Labour and, in particular, the councils which until a year previously had been part of the GLC, saying: 'Children who need to be taught to respect traditional moral values are being taught that they have an inalienable right to be gay.'[66]

Here was the throwing down of a moral gauntlet: traditional values as proffered by Thatcher did not permit non-heterosexual forms of identity to be discussed in Britain's schools. From having been a supporter of the Abse Bill in the 1960s, Thatcher was now about to implement the most retrograde legislation in relation to gay rights in twenty years.

The Section 28 amendment to the Local Government Act 1988 stipulated that local authorities could not 'intentionally promote homosexuality or publish material with the intention of promoting homosexuality' nor 'promote the teaching in any maintained school of the acceptability of homosexuality as a pretended family relationship'.[67] While historian Richard Vinen later noted that the measure was vague, this did not detract from the intent of the legislation, which was to specifically discriminate against gay people. If it was an obscure codicil to a wider piece of legislation, why did it provoke the backlash which it did? While the measure could be seen as part of the 'loony left' council issue, the reaction to it transcended the actions of certain Labour-controlled councils.[68] The discriminatory basis of the measure was seen as 'a symbol of the prejudice of the present parliament' and, while it was, according to *Spare Rib*, 'legal gobblygook', the intent was 'intimidatory'.[69] It did not matter that the great irony was that it did not prevent teachers from promoting positive images of gay and lesbian identity in the classroom (as sought by figures like the Conservative MP Jill Knight), but applied only to local authorities. It was designed to marginalise.

Labour's initial reaction to the legislation was to support it, despite the avowed declarations made in the manifesto of both the previous year and 1983 and the opposition of the MP for Tottenham, Bernie Grant.[70] In due course, Labour was to strongly oppose it, with the shadow secretary of state for the environment, Jack Cunningham, declaring that it raised 'fundamental issues of personal liberty and civil rights' and comparing it to the discrimination faced by Jews and immigrants.[71] Labour's stumbling into opposition to the measure did not to endear it to those who were being affected by it.

Labour was therefore not a confident liberal party in the 1980s. It was in a difficult position electorally. While figures like Cunningham criticised the introduction of Section 28, the party was aware that to take too strong a stand was to potentially alienate an electorate that at the last general election had once again rejected it comprehensively. Polling on the issue explains the balancing act that the Labour leadership was trying to achieve. As Brooke noted, it was 'hard to see any other space for the espousal of gay rights at this time, particularly given the Kinnock leadership's desire to move Labour to the centre'.[72] Nevertheless, Kinnock referred to the new legislation as a 'vicious … pink star clause,'[73] and at the party conference in 1988, backed by the leaders of the Transport and General Workers Union and the General, Municipal and Boilermakers Union, voted for the eventual repeal of Section 28.[74] Reckless as it may have seemed from a purely political perspective, Labour under Kinnock included the commitment to repealing Section 28 in its 1992 manifesto. The party was also committed to a free vote on the issue of the equalisation of the age of consent. It was not as strong a statement as that which appeared in the Liberal Democrats' manifesto with its commitment to the equalisation of the age of consent as well as the repeal of Section 28, but it did continue the thread of Labour's commitment to equal rights – something that had been absent from the agendas of other parties in the previous two elections.[75] The social conservatism of the 1980s on the matter of gay rights made Labour's position all the more remarkable. As Stephen Brooke observed, 'it was not simply that the Labour Party took up gay and lesbian rights, it was that the Conservatives politicized the issue'.[76] Despite popular opposition, the party found itself compelled to take a stand.

Labour and the video nasties

In the early 1960s the president of the British Board of Film Censors (BBFC) was the former Labour Home Secretary Herbert Morrison, who was keen to promote both his working-class origins and his disapproval, according to the critic Alexander Walker, of 'homosexuality, of loose living among teenage youth, and of whores and tarts, and his disapproval vented on films which featured these things'.[77] Morrison's opinions would have found support from many on the Conservative benches who were now pressing their government for action on what people were able to watch in their homes. Some Conservative backbenchers sought to reassert what they saw as traditional morality in the heart of society, which had been undermined as a consequence of the 1960s 'permissive society'.[78] They wished to regulate what was available for people to watch on their television screens, particularly with regard to the rapidly developing home video market that was emerging in the 1980s.

The unalloyed zeal of the more censorious Conservative MPs was often given tacit approval, and this was particularly underscored by the Video Recordings Act of 1984. Introduced by the Conservative MP Graham Bright as a means of regulating the home video market (ironically, in view of the rapid deregulation that was taking place elsewhere), the Act emerged from a campaign strongly supported by the *Daily Mail* and by Mary Whitehouse's National Viewers' and Listeners' Association (NVLA). The primary purpose of the Act was to ban or censor films with offensive, violent or obscene content: the so-called 'video nasties', films such as *Driller Killer*, *Cannibal Holocaust* and *I Spit On Your Grave*, the majority of them produced by the low-budget exploitation market in the United States and continental Europe.

The sense of outrage demonstrated by the tabloid media made this a *cause célèbre*. It was intensely felt by MPs, who were directly lobbied to support the legislation by constituents, the NVLA, the tabloid press and even television (the BBC's *Newsnight* and *Nationwide* programmes were less than impartial in the way the issue was reported).[79] The *Daily Express* viewed it clearly as society walking 'the tightrope between good and evil', arguing that the country should 'shake ourselves free of the cretinous "progressive" dogma that if we burn video nasties today we shall be burning books tomorrow'.[80] As far as certain tabloid newspapers were concerned, it was very much a moral crusade. However, there were also objections to such films from progressive voices, on the grounds of the depiction of violence against women; for example, feminists picketed the film *I Spit On Your Grave*.[81]

In the face of legislation which decided what people should be able to watch in the privacy of their own homes, there was a need for a response. The resistance to government intervention in entertainment was taken up by pressure groups outside of Parliament, such as the National Council for Civil Liberties, in a rare attempt to counter-balance censorship. This was the period when Polly Toynbee wrote, 'Common sense and the national opinion polls tell us that most people believe that repeated exposure to violence on television and in films is a bad thing. A generation brought up on a diet of violence is likely to produce more violent people.'[82] Her article was symbolic of much of the discourse which was taking place and which had been adopted by those who saw themselves as social democrats, just as it had been by those who identified as traditionalist Conservatives. While the thrust of Toynbee's argument was against the objectification and the depiction of violence against women, it also justified wider censorship, something which film critic Alexander Walker pointed out already existed within the Obscene Publications Act.[83] Even the National Society for the Prevention of Cruelty to Children's Dr Alan Gilmour, while decrying the access children were able to have to such films, said that 'if an adult wishes to watch it that is presumably their right in a free society'.[84]

Would the Labour Party of the 1960s and 1970s have approved of such legislation? In the 1970s, Labour figures featured strongly in cases where censorship was being pushed for by conservative groups. Ken Livingstone, for instance, was vice-chair of the Film Viewing Board of the GLC, which acted as a body to hear appeals by the makers of films banned by the BBFC. Livingstone said that both he and the chair, Enid Wistrich, 'opposed censorship on principle', and set about trying to 'justify ending film censorship for adults'.[85] Yet by the time Livingstone had become leader of the GLC in 1981 his views on censorship were to be 'changed by feminism and by some disturbing films that celebrated sexual violence against women'.[86] As a result, his attitude hardened and became accepting of censorship in films which featured such content. The feminist criticism of degrading images of women became more vocal in the 1980s. Labour MP Clare Short's attempt to ban the pictures of topless women on page 3 of the *Sun* newspaper is an example. This created, in the words of Clarissa Smith, an 'uneasy alliance … between the forces of the Right and feminist groups', both keen to distance their association with each other, yet overlapping 'in their assertions of pornography's degradation and harm to women and children'.[87]

The video nasties episode showed that there were limits to Labour's liberalism. Opposition to the Video Recordings Act came from civil liberties groups, but in Parliament no such opposition existed, or at least very few felt compelled to comment. Few MPs directly opposed the introduction of tighter home video regulation and censorship and it was left to a Conservative MP, Matthew Parris, to suggest that the Act was at best misplaced.[88] Alwyn Turner notes that 'there had been a time when left-wing intellectuals would have opposed such moves, at least on the grounds that "censorship of art by the state is always to be regretted", yet by the mid-1980s such figures were thin on the ground'.[89] There were no challenges to some of the patronising statements made by supporters of the Bill about working-class viewers. Conservative MP Harry Greenaway claimed that videos 'are often a higher priority in the homes of people who are not particularly articulate, and who do not read books or listen to music very much'.[90] The argument was both anti-intellectual and snobbish. Moreover, while the 1984 legislation was sponsored by a Conservative MP, a previous attempt on 15 December 1982 to bring in a similar Bill had come via the urging of a Labour MP, Gareth Wardell, who went on to castigate the Thatcher Government for inaction and support the Bright legislation in Parliament.[91] Indeed, as Julian Petley notes, it was this first attempt to bring in legislation which had prompted the subsequent *Daily Mail* campaign against the video nasties.[92] It was believed then, as indeed it still is, that what was seen on screen would be replicated by some viewers. Denis Howell, former Labour sports minister, said in the House of Commons that 'when instances of it are shown on television there is an immediate increase in the amount of football hooliganism. Obviously, there is a direct relationship between the showing of such news items and the incidence of football hooliganism.'[93] These certainties were never challenged; the assumptions (made on the basis of questionable research) were not scrutinised by any member of the Labour benches, nor was there any highlighting of how censorship could potentially impact on those whom the Labour movement was meant to help. This latter point was made by the human rights barrister Geoffrey Robertson QC, who asked:

> But (to take an entirely hypothetical example) will they be happy to open their Guardians in a year or so to read an angry article by Polly Toynbee about the collapse of a GLC-funded feminist video-collective, whose award-winning educational films about rape ('human sexual activity'), wife battering ('acts of gross violence'), and child birth ('depiction of human genital organs') have been declared 'unsuitable for showing in the home by the BBFC'.[94]

Robertson's analysis may have been somewhat hard hitting, yet the wider point about the potentially invasive nature of cultural censorship was not highlighted by anyone on the Labour benches. This was a long way from the reforming movements of the 1960s, the pushing of envelopes and the broadening of minds, which, for better or worse, had been facilitated by a Labour government. What is particularly ironic is that the man who in 1955 had objected to the banning of 'horror comics' as 'a thoroughly bad Bill'[95] remained silent throughout the passage of Bright's Bill almost thirty years later. Roy Jenkins, as many others in Parliament, did not vote against the measure. Many supported it, including Neil Kinnock. The tabloid press scolded any MPs who harboured doubts, saying that they would 'be a very unpopular minority'.[96]

Bright's attempt to encourage similar legislation in the European Parliament in November 1983 was not successful, despite his efforts to show edited highlights of certain horror films to MPs and MEPs.[97] Similarly, attempts to include sexually explicit films at the committee stage of the Bill were defeated when Labour, the SDP and six Conservative MPs voted against it by 11 votes to 6.[98] Nevertheless, the Bill was passed unopposed in Parliament and became law in 1984. This was not the end of the matter. On 5 December 1985 the backbencher Ivor Stanbrook asked Thatcher to agree with Norman Tebbit 'that many social evils of our time derive from the permissive society promoted by liberal politicians in the 1960s and 1970s'. He called on the government to 'abandon their posture of neutrality on some issues', which was endangering the 'Christian way of life'. In reply, Thatcher remarked that 'the Government have supported private Members' Bills on issues such as controlling video nasties and indecent displays. I hope that we shall continue to take that attitude.' The 'video nasties' furore continued to be a useful prop for the Conservative Government and they were presented in the media as the cause of various societal ills.[99] The Conservative Government was able to do this with the assistance of the opposition benches. In this instance, Labour was a willing participant in abandoning the liberal notion of questioning censorship. Its reasons for doing so were based on the well-intentioned restriction of what could be viewed in the home by children or of the depiction of violence against women. Thirty years earlier, Anthony Crosland had written that the then-current laws on censorship in the arts were 'intolerable, and should be highly offensive to socialists, in whose blood there should always run a trace of the anarchist and the libertarian'.[100] On this occasion, the Crosland legacy was abandoned.

Labour's liberal tradition?

Alfred North Whitehead once wrote that 'the art of progress is to preserve order amid change and preserve change amid order'.[101] In the 1960s it was good fortune that there was a Labour government in power during a period of considerable social transformation. In the 1980s the Thatcher Government not only put a brake on progress but set about reversing it. During that decade Labour (for the most part) maintained a commitment to social liberalism when it would have been so easy to abandon it. It should be said that the issues of gay rights and video nasties were not high on the list of electors' priorities.

Further, the manner in which Labour reached its eventual position on gay equality caused despair among those who wanted a more decisive and principled approach. One could argue that Labour's halting progress in a country as socially conservative as Britain was perhaps the correct strategy to adopt.

When one considers the programme implemented by Tony Blair's New Labour governments, which included the eventual repeal of Section 28, it was in no small part due to the party's continuing the progressive social liberalism that had survived the tumultuous 1980s. Policies which had been derided by a hostile tabloid media as the crackpot ideas of a few London councils were, in due course, to become the accepted norm and provided a link from the Foot era to the Blair years. (Indeed, so accepted were the notions of gay equality that it was a Conservative-led government that introduced same-sex marriage onto the statute book in 2013.) Yet, unlike in 1992, when Labour clearly stated its intention to repeal Section 28, there was to be no mention of this in the 1997 manifesto. In 1994 acrimony was directed toward some Labour MPs who had abstained or voted against a Bill proposed by Conservative MP Edwina Currie to equalise the age of consent, a measure which was supported by Neil Kinnock (now no longer party leader).[102] Indeed, it was 2003 before the legislation was finally repealed, and then by the mechanism of a free vote. As Simon Mackley observed, this prompted the Labour MP David Cairns to ruefully note that they 'would not dream of allowing a free vote on issues of race discrimination or gender discrimination'.[103] So, while in theory Labour was an agent of social liberalism, the move to repeal Section 28 was tentative: perhaps this was due in part to the need to maintain adherence to 'big tent' politics and thus not wishing to push too fast too soon.[104] Labour wanted to appeal to Conservative and Liberal Democrat voters, but also to its own working-class supporters who were less socially liberal. This linked Blair's leadership in some respect to Callaghan's, in that it showed adherence to a more gradualist approach to achieving stated aims, in the belief that this would ensure longer-term acceptance. Ironically, New Labour's record was that of a government that came to power with socially liberal aims which it promptly met, yet it became identified with the illiberal – damaged by the association with the Iraq War, the pursuit of ninety days' detention of suspects without charge and the attempted introduction of identity cards.

Did social liberalism ultimately come at the cost of alienating the working classes who for so long had supported the Labour Party? At the time of writing (2017) the party's association with liberalism has been one of the drivers of the turn towards UKIP in traditionally strong Labour areas, a turn which reflects the natural social conservatism of the working classes and a rejection of metropolitan thinking. The philosophy of Blue Labour, which combines an emphasis on localism, what is seen as a less wedded approach to the top-down aspects of the welfare state and a more socially conservative approach to issues such as immigration, has been proffered as a means of combating the populist right. But should the party abandon a commitment to equality in order to counter the accusations that it is too bound to 'political correctness'? As Patrick Diamond and Michael Kenny wrote, 'while its diagnosis of Labour's ills was powerful, Blue Labour's remedy may have offered the wrong kind of medicine. Many question the implications of romanticising the social relations of the past, against which women, ethnic minorities, gays and lesbians have rightly rebelled.'[105] Moreover, the suggestion that Labour support remains wedded *en masse* to the ideals of social conservatism was not borne out by polling for the British Social Attitudes Survey in 2012, which found that only 29 per cent of respondents viewed same-sex relationships as always or mostly wrong, reflecting a rapid decline in opposition to the LGBT community from the mid-1990s onwards.[106]

Labour should certainly not take its core white working-class support for granted, for, as John Clarke noted, 'Labour without its traditional voters is the SDP – and look what happened to them. As a rootless elitist Party they evaporated like a thimbleful of sherry in the hard Tuscany sun.'[107] Yet Labour has always been at its most effective when it has challenged the accepted norms even when it seemed politically dangerous to do so. Indeed, it would be more severely damaging to the party were it to water down such commitments in order to accommodate those who might never vote for it. It would lose new converts and long-standing supporters in the process. Frank Dobson argues that voter mistrust is a direct result of parties saying one thing and then implementing another, that you may not win the vote but you may, oddly, win the voters' trust. He adds that 'Consensus is something that is pushed through by people with a real commitment to something and it is gradually accepted.'[108]

In the face of crushing defeat and existential crisis, Labour's social liberalism survived the many problems that the party faced throughout the 1980s. The defection of the liberal-minded Social Democrats in 1981 did not diminish the social-liberal instinct within Labour, and indeed the party continued to fight for equality with an ever louder voice when it would have been easier to downplay it. During the 1980s Labour's socially liberal commitment was maintained; after 1997 its liberalism was implemented. Labour lived up to the declaration made in Harold Wilson's famous call to arms: 'The Labour Party is a moral crusade or it is nothing.'[109]

Notes

1 Jeffrey Weeks, *Sex, Politics and Society: The Regulation of Sexuality since 1800* (London: Longman, 1989), p. 273.
2 David Marquand, 'The Paradoxes of Thatcherism', in Robert Skidelsky (ed.) *Thatcherism* (London: Chatto and Windus, 1988), p. 165.
3 Christopher Bray, *1965: The Year Modern Britain was Born* (New York: Simon and Schuster, 2014), p. 277.

4 John Campbell, *Roy Jenkins: A Well-Rounded Life* (London: Jonathan Cape, 2014), pp. 182–3; Anthony Crosland, *The Future of Socialism* (London: Constable, 2006 [1956]), p. 403.
5 Andy Beckett, *Promised You A Miracle* (London: Penguin, 2016), p. 136.
6 Frank Dobson, interview with author, 4 November 2014.
7 Dominic Sandbrook, *White Heat: A History of Britain in the 1960s* (London: Abacus, 2010), p. 338; Martin Pugh, *Speak for Britain: A New History of the Labour Party* (London: Vintage, 2011), p. 337; Ken Livingstone, *You Can't Say That: Memoirs* (London: Faber &Faber, 2011), p. 119; Roy Jenkins, *A Life at the Centre* (London: Macmillan, 1991), p. 209; Weeks, *Sex, Politics and Society*, p. 267; Stephen Brooke, *Sexual Politics: Sexuality, Family Planning, and the British Left from the 1880s to the Present Day* (Oxford: Oxford University Press 2011), pp. 180–1.
8 Brooke, *Sexual Politics*, p. 180.
9 Brian McConell, 'A Charter for the Outsiders', *Daily Mirror*, 5 July 1967, p. 7.
10 Brooke, *Sexual Politics*, p. 183.
11 See Sandbrook, *White Heat*, p. 341; '57 Votes Carry the Sex Bill', *Daily Express*, 12 February 1966, p. 5; Pugh, *Speak for Britain*, p. 336 and Brooke, *Sexual Politics*, p. 181.
12 Arthur Marwick, *The Sixties* (London: Bloomsbury, 2012), p. 13; Sandbrook, *White Heat*, p. 341.
13 Brooke, *Sexual Politics*, pp. 4 and 15–23.
14 'Gay Libs Seek Law Reform', *Guardian*, 3 July 1975, p. 6.
15 www.lgbtlabour.org.uk/history (accessed 3 October 2016).
16 Roy Hattersley, *Fifty Years On* (London: Brown & Company, 1997), p. 177.
17 Austin Mitchell, interview with author, 4 November 2014.
18 Ivor Crewe and Anthony King, *SDP: The Birth, Life and Death of the Social Democratic Party* (Oxford: Oxford University Press, 1995), p. 296.
19 Kenneth O. Morgan, *Michael Foot: A Life* (London: Harper Perennial, 2007), pp. 245–6.
20 Morgan, *Michael Foot*, p. 494; Crosland, *The Future of Socialism*, p. 403.
21 Peter Purton, *Sodom, Gomorrah and the New Jerusalem* (London: Labour Campaign for Gay Rights, 2006), pp. 42, 46.
22 Gerald Kaufman (ed.), *Renewal: Labour's Britain in the 1980s* (London: Penguin, 1983); Peter Archer, *Socialism, Freedom and the Law* (London: Penguin 1983), p. 167.
23 Lucy Robinson, *Gay Men and the Left in Post-War Britain: How the Personal Got Political* (Manchester: Manchester University Press, 2007), p. 157.
24 Eliot Henderson, 'Was the "Loony Left" Right?', *Labour Uncut*, http://labour-uncut.co.uk/2014/02/20/was-the-loony-left-right/ (accessed 26 October 2014).
25 Laurie Taylor, 'Tatchell Man's First Test', *The Times*, 22 February 1983, p. 8.
26 'What Tatchell Wrote about Extra-parliamentary Protest', *Guardian*, 8 December 1981, p. 4.
27 Roy Hattersley, 'Outraged of Lambeth', *Guardian*, 2 February 2000, p. 7.
28 Taylor, 'Tatchell Man's First Test'.
29 Alwyn W. Turner, *Rejoice! Rejoice! Britain in the 1980s* (London: Aurum Press, 2013), p. 48.
30 Hattersley, 'Outraged of Lambeth'.
31 James Curran, 'Hounds Off Peter Tatchell', *The Times*, 20 October 1982, p. 14.
32 Turner, *Rejoice! Rejoice!*, p. 48.
33 Brooke, *Sexual Politics*, p. 242; 'Tatchell Plea for Respite from Press', *The Times*, 15 January 1983, p. 2; Philip Webster, 'Tatchell Hits at "Smears"', *The Times*, 1 February 1983, p. 2.

34 Brooke, *Sexual Politics*, p. 244.
35 www.bsa-30.natcen.ac.uk/read-the-report/personal-relationships/homosexuality.aspx (accessed 26 October 2014).
36 Leo Abse, 'The Law that Failed to Liberate the Gays', *The Times*, 28 July 1982, p. 8.
37 Abse, 'The Law that Failed to Liberate the Gays'.
38 Labour Party Manifesto, 1983, www.politicsresources.net/area/uk/man/lab83.htm (accessed 7 November 2014).
39 'Manchester Spends a Lot on Rubbish', *The Times*, 24 February 1983, p. 4.
40 Colin Clews, *1981. Politics: The Rights of Gay Men and Women*, www.gayinthe80s.com/2014/03/1981-politics-the-rights-of-gay-men-and-women/ (accessed 17 November 2016); Brooke, *Sexual Politics*, p. 244.
41 Robinson, *Gay Men and the Left in Post-War Britain*, p. 173.
42 Purton, *Sodom, Gomorrah and the New Jerusalem*, p. 44.
43 Sex Equality Bill, House of Commons Debates, 9 December 1983, 50, cols 607–44, http://hansard.millbanksystems.com/commons/1983/dec/09/sex-equality-bill 1#S6CV0050P0_19831209_HOC_149 (accessed 17 November 2016).
44 Sex Equality Bill, House of Commons Debate, 9 December 1983, 50, cols 607–44, http://hansard.millbanksystems.com/commons/1983/dec/09/sex-equality-bill 1#S6CV0050P0_19831209_HOC_149 (accessed 17 November 2016).
45 'MPs Trade Accusations over Councils', *The Times*, 6 December 1986, p. 4.
46 'Commons Row over Gay Slur', *The Times*, 6 December 1986, p. 1.
47 Livingstone, *You Can't Say That*, p. 121.
48 Labour Party Manifesto, *Enhancing Rights, Increasing Freedom*, 1987, p. 1, www.politicsresources.net/area/uk/man/lab87.htm (accessed 7 November 2014).
49 Quoted in Brooke, *Sexual Politics*, p. 246.
50 Benjamin Butterworth 'GT Heroes – Chris Smith', *Gay Times*, 30 December 2015, p. 1, www.gaytimes.co.uk/life/19687/gt-heroes-chris-smith/ (accessed 18 November 2016).
51 www.bsa-30.natcen.ac.uk/read-the-report/personal-relationships/homosexuality.aspx (accessed 26 October 2014).
52 Purton, *Sodom, Gomorrah and the New Jerusalem*, p. 45.
53 Arthur Marwick, *British Society since 1945* (London: Penguin, 1990), pp. 363–4.
54 Matt Cook, 'London, AIDS and the 1980s', in Simon Avery and Katherine M. Graham (eds), *Sex Time and Place: Queer Histories of London, c.1850 to the Present* (London: Bloomsbury Academic, 2016), p. 52.
55 Eric Shaw, *The Labour Party Since 1979: Crisis and Transformation* (London: Routledge, 1994), p. 195.
56 Livingstone, *You Can't Say That*, p. 121.
57 Livingstone, *You Can't Say That*, p. 182.
58 George Gale, 'Whites Have Rights, Too', *Daily Express*, 25 April 1985, p. 8.
59 Ronald Butt, 'After the GLC, a Greek Lesson', *The Times*, 21 July 1983, p. 10.
60 Polly Toynbee, 'Freedom's Roadblock', *Guardian*, 14 January 1988, p. 13 and Brooke, *Sexual Politics*, p. 247.
61 Brooke, *Sexual Politics*, p. 247.
62 Geoff Andrews, 'Activists Deny their Loony Left Label', *Guardian*, 7 March 1987, p. 2.
63 John Carvel, 'London Labour Chief Rejects Policy U-turns', *Guardian*, 13 March 1987, p. 4.
64 Andrew Rawnsley, 'SDP raises Ghost of Traditional Labour Voter', *Guardian*, 6 February 1987, p. 3.
65 Brooke, *Sexual Politics*, p. 249.

66 Margaret Thatcher, Speech to Conservative Party Conference, 9 October 1987, www.margaretthatcher.org/document/106941 (accessed 21 September 2016) and Brooke, *Sexual Politics*, p. 247.
67 www.legislation.gov.uk/ukpga/1988/9/section/28 (accessed 21 September 2016).
68 David Willets, 'The Family', in Denis Kavanagh and Anthony Seldon (eds) *The Thatcher Effect* (Oxford: Oxford University Press, 1989), p. 267.
69 Geoffrey Robertson, 'Fear not Clause 28, Only the Prejudice Behind It', *Guardian*, 1 June 1988, p. 19; Sarah Roelofs, 'Section 28 – What's in a Law', *Spare Rib*, No. 192 (1988), p. 42, https://journalarchives.jisc.ac.uk/britishlibrary/sparerib (accessed 18 August 2016).
70 Martin Fletcher, 'Homosexual Bill Wins Labour Vote', *The Times*, 9 December 1987, p. 3.
71 Simon Mackley, 'The Long Road to Repeal: The Labour Party and Section 28', *New Histories*, 5 July 2012, http://newhistories.group.shef.ac.uk/wordpress/wordpress/the-long-road-to-repeal-the-labour-Party-and-section-28/ (accessed 26 October 2014).
72 Brooke, *Sexual Politics*, p. 251.
73 Brooke, *Sexual Politics*, p. 251.
74 Purton, *Sodom, Gomorrah and the New Jerusalem*, p. 51.
75 www.politicsresources.net/area/uk/man/lab92.htm (accessed 13 October 2016); www.politicsresources.net/area/uk/man/libdem92.htm (accessed 13 October 2016).
76 Brooke, *Sexual Politics*, p. 227.
77 Alexander Walker, quoted in Tom Dewe Mathews, *Censored* (London: Chatto and Windus, 1994), p. 159.
78 Marcus Collins, *The Permissive Society and its Enemies* (London: Rivers Oram Press, 2007), p. 29.
79 See also the documentary, 'Video Nasties: Moral Panic, Censorship and Videotape', by Jake West in the collection, 'Video Nasties: The Definitive Guide', Nucleus Films, 2010.
80 'Express Opinion', *Daily Express*, 10 November 1983, p. 8.
81 Julie Bindel, 'I was Wrong about I Spit On Your Grave', *Guardian*, 19 January 2011, https://www.theguardian.com/commentisfree/2011/jan/19/wrong-about-spit-on-your-grave (accessed 21 December 2016).
82 Polly Toynbee, 'Why Nasty Is as Nasty Does', *Guardian*, 13 March 1984, p. 11.
83 'It's Hard to Find a Video Nasty', Letters, *Observer*, 18 December 1983, p. 24.
84 Shyama Perera, 'NSPCC Seeks Curb on Video "Nasties"', *Guardian*, 12 October 1982, p. 6.
85 Livingstone, *You Can't Say That*, p. 105.
86 Livingstone, *You Can't Say That*, p. 107.
87 Clarissa Smith, 'A Perfectly British Business: Stagnation, Continuities and Change on the Top Shelf', in Lisa Z. Sigel, John Phillips and Maryna Romanet (eds), *International Exposure: Perspectives on Modern European Pornography, 1800–2000* (New Brunswick, NJ: Rutgers University Press, 2005), pp. 154–5.
88 Turner, *Rejoice! Rejoice!*, p. 209, and Martin Barker, 'Nasty Politics or Video Nasties?', in Martin Barker (ed.), *The Video Nasties – Freedom and Censorship in the Media* (London: Pluto Press, 1984), pp. 7–38, p. 37.
89 Turner, *Rejoice! Rejoice!*, p. 210.
90 Julian Petley, 'Us and Them', in Martin Barker and Julian Petley (eds), *Ill Effects – the Media/Violence Debate* (London: Routledge, 2004), p. 179.
91 https://www.theyworkforyou.com/debates/?d=1982-12-15 (accessed 27 November 2016); House of Commons Debates, 11 November 1983, 48, cols 521–80.

92 Julian Petley, 'Are We Insane? The "Video Nasty" Moral Panic', *Recherches sociologiques et anthropologiques* 43 (2012), 35–57.
93 House of Commons Debates, 16 March 1984, 56, cols 629–48.
94 Geoffrey Robertson, 'Chain-saw Censor', *Guardian*, 14 March 1984, p. 23.
95 Campbell, *Roy Jenkins*, p. 183.
96 Norman Luck, 'Maggie Pledges War on Nasties', *Daily Express*, 11 November 1983, p. 2.
97 John Burns, 'Video Horror Show Shocks Europe', *Daily Express*, 17 November 1983, p. 3.
98 'Maggie Loses Porn Curb Bid', *Daily Express*, 2 February 1984, p. 7.
99 www.margaretthatcher.org/document/106191 (accessed 4 November 2014); Barker, 'Nasty Politics or Video Nasties?', p. 29; Staff Reporter, 'No Video Nasties – We're British', *Observer*, 14 October 1984, p. 5.
100 Crosland, *The Future of Socialism*, p. 403.
101 Alfred North Whitehead, *Process and Reality* (New York: The Free Press, 1985 [1929]), p. 339.
102 Patricia Wynn Davies, Colin Brown and Marianne Macdonald, 'Sexual Equality for Gays Rejected: Angry Protests Greet MP's Backing for Consent at 18', *Independent*, 22 February 1994, www.independent.co.uk/news/sexual-equality-for-gays-rejected-angry-protests-greet-mps-backing-for-consent-at-18–1395642.html (accessed 18 November 2016).
103 Mackley, 'The Long Road to Repeal'.
104 Collins, *The Permissive Society and its Enemies*, p. 27.
105 Patrick Diamond and Michael Kenny, 'Comment: Liberalism for the Left', *Guardian*, 13 March 2012, p. 28, https://www.theguardian.com/commentisfree/2012/mar/12/labour-lost-liberal-streak (accessed 10 September 2014).
106 www.bsa.natcen.ac.uk/latest-report/british-social-attitudes-30/personal-relationships/homosexuality.aspx (accessed 26 October 2014).
107 John Clarke, 'The Choice – Support or Dump Labour's Traditional Voters', *Labour List*, 9 August 2014, http://labourlist.org/2014/08/the-choice-support-or-dump-labours-traditional-voters/ (accessed 10 September 2014).
108 Frank Dobson, interview with author, 4 November 2014.
109 Stuart Thornton, *Dictionary of Labour Quotations* (London: Biteback Publishing, 2013), p. 375.

4

Responsible capitalism: Labour's industrial policy and the idea of a National Investment Bank during the long 1980s

Richard Carr

This chapter considers two overlapping issues: Labour's conception of the economy, and its overall electability. As to the first, it is widely asserted in both academic and political circles that 'the absence of economic policy credibility was absolutely central to Labour's failure to regain office until 1997'.[1] This was certainly true of the 1983 general election when, as Colin Hughes and Patrick Wintour remarked, 'even 28 per cent [of the vote], the party's lowest since 1918, seemed more than the party deserved'.[2] By 1987 Giles Radice believed that Labour had 'managed to convince the electorate that its heart was in the right place ... [but they] still doubted whether it had the vision, capacity and competence to shape the future'.[3] Indeed, throughout the 1980s, the British people consistently told pollsters both that they expected the economy *to get worse* over the next 12 months and that the policies of Margaret Thatcher would have a positive effect eventually.[4] All this was not merely 'declinism' writ large. Once unemployment began to recede (and indeed to motor down from 1987), the Conservatives had a powerful top-line argument that unleashing the market had helped to 'clear up Labour's mess', while at the same time the opposition was unable to rebut charges that it would take Britain back to the 'dark days' of the 1970s.

The economy was not the only area where Labour lacked credibility. As Andrew Rawnsley summarises, 'the Labour church has a history of doing the splits. It did so in the 1930s. Again in the 1950s. And again in the 1980s.'[5] After 1979, the Bennite left – anti-Common Market, anti-nuclear weapons and pro-nationalisation – grappled for power with the social democratic centre; the split ran through the Limehouse Declaration and beyond, reaching something of a nadir by the time of Neil Kinnock's anti-Militant speech at the 1985 party conference. Although all within Labour and the broader British left could to some degree unite on being anti-Thatcher, what Labour was a vehicle 'for' remained more difficult to resolve. Navigating the path between principle and the pursuit of power was not easy. As such, Kinnock's ultimate legacy was in many ways to have taken Labour from a party that 63 per cent of the British public believed to be 'divided' in June 1983 to one of which only 24 per cent said similar in March 1992.[6] Labour's path from Foot to Blair was not just about two further election defeats, but a gradual realignment of party values and, in short, something of a recovery.[7]

Given such patterns, this chapter attempts to marry both economic and intra-party analysis through the prism of the pledge to introduce a National Investment Bank (NIB), included in the general election manifestoes of 1983, 1987 and 1992.[8] It considers the intellectual history of this idea, the various machinations regarding the similarly corporatist National Enterprise Board of the 1970s, and how the NIB policy not only survived the fiasco of 1983 but remained a key part of Labour's agenda until 1992. As we will see, this policy serves as an exemplar of the way Kinnock managed the Labour Party – providing just enough meat to left and right and allowing both to read into the NIB what they wished it to be. Here the NIB forms a mirror image of Jim Tomlinson's recent analysis of so-called 'declinism' in 1970s Conservative thought – a term that had been so ambiguous that it allowed 'every political tendency to blame their favourite *bête noire*' for Britain's then malaise.[9] Such linguistic dexterity apart, the fact that the NIB was adopted by Foot, nuanced by Kinnock and summarily ditched by Blair helps us to map Labour as it moved from self-satisfied opposition to the compromises inherent in making a serious bid for office. At this point, it is worth declaring an interest: prior to the resurrection of the policy in Labour's 2015 manifesto, the present author consistently argued for the creation of such an institution – including in a March 2012 report for the think-tank Localis.[10] What follows is not so much about the merits or de-merits of the policy, however, as about what such dialogue said of the party and its electoral fortunes.

In terms of political theory, the case for the NIB fell somewhere between the 'valence' and 'position' designations of voter preference that Donald Stokes articulated in the early 1960s.[11] For clarity, 'valence' issues denote those where there is broad agreement between parties over the end goal. In this case, although their methods clearly differed, both Labour and Conservative parties at least *claimed* to be about delivering a better capitalism which gave more people the opportunity to better their lot. Valence politics, in short, is not about wonkish details but about which party the voters believe has the credibility to *deliver*. Equally, the NIB provides a clear instance of Stokes's 'position' politics. Unlike, say, vague calls for 'a more progressive economy', the NIB policy had a certain set of precise consequences where voters could make a rational choice for or against. The story of this chapter, the NIB per se, and arguably of Labour itself in the 1980s, is of 'valence' politics trumping those of 'position'. The rational argument for a NIB was relatively clear (if not, as we will see, uncontested); the electorate just did not trust Labour to manage the economy. At the same time, however, in helping to reorient Labour, the NIB policy had positive effects over the long run.

This brief study adds to a still developing historiographical picture. Richard Hill's *Long Road Back* ably chronicles the path Labour took from the conception of an economy ruled from the commanding heights to the acceptance of a more Rhenish, social market form of capitalism – shifting the party away from William Beveridge and towards Will Hutton. Colin Hays and Dianne Hayter have likewise extended our understanding of the structural shifts in Labour's economic message and the left–right context in which they were conducted.[12] But while economics and business studies academics have analysed the failure of British banks to provide long-run capital to small business, and the forerunner institutions which attempted to address this in the post-war period, few historical studies have provided much specific comment on Labour's NIB idea of the 1980s.[13] Drawing on both archive material and interviews with key shapers of the policy, this summary intends to redress the balance.[14]

Importantly, such debates are not the sole preserve of history. The balance between state and private sector has long plagued the British left. While New Labour was criticised for being too cosy with multinational corporations, under Jeremy Corbyn the party would struggle to gain any toehold with business whatsoever.[15] The 2010–15 Miliband experiment with European social democracy attempted to strike a balance between these two extremes, with Lord Glasman backing a series of regional investment banks along the lines of the German Sparkassen and Chuka Umunna believing there to be 'deeper cultural and institutional lessons from the German experience which we should draw on as we seek to build a New Economy fit for the future'.[16] In terms of trying to generally retool British capitalism, the Miliband leadership had significant merit. But it had other problems that went beyond the trivia of Miliband's problem in eating a bacon sandwich and proved ultimately unelectable. Resolving the dilemmas outlined in this chapter therefore remains a decisive issue for all considering where Labour goes next.

Closing the Macmillan Gap

The concept of a NIB has a long-term pedigree in Westminster politics. In June 1931 the Macmillan Committee proposed a number of interventions to heal British industry, which was still dealing with the immediate consequences of the Wall Street Crash. Most famously, it identified the so-called 'Macmillan Gap' – the situation where 'great difficulty is experienced by the smaller and medium-sized businesses in raising capital [at acceptable rates]'. To get such credit flowing, the committee proposed the creation of a new 'institution acting as an intermediary between industry and investor ... to provide adequate machinery for raising long-dated capital'.[17] Members of the committee disagreed as to whether this new institution should be publicly owned (Ernest Bevin was very much in favour), but the need for some form of *de facto* bank to bridge the gap between businesses that needed to borrow in order to expand (or even just survive) and the low rates that would encourage them to take on such risk was readily acknowledged. The major commercial institutions simply were not doing the job on their own.

After some wartime discussion back and forth between Treasury and Board of Trade departments, one of the less high-profile achievements of Attlee's New Jerusalem was to create two institutions designed to deliver just this. This was not a trend unique to the UK – the Dutch Nationale Investeringsbank (1945) and German Kreditanstalt für Wiederaufbau (KfW, 1948) were among several European bodies formed to address similar market failures. As for Britain, the new Finance Corporation for Industry (FCI) sought 'to provide finance for large scale long-term investments, aimed at industry wide rationalization'.[18] Medium-term loans were provided where 'finance could not be obtained on reasonable terms elsewhere, and where the "national interest" was served'.[19] By the late 1970s, over £240 million of such loans were in operation. Alongside this larger institution, an Industrial and Commercial Finance Corporation (ICFC) was also set up in 1945 to provide finance for smaller and medium-sized concerns. This latter body was intended to plug a huge gap between the level at which ordinary commercial banks stopped lending to smaller firms and the point at which the big capital markets became seriously interested in providing finance. In the end, the FCI and the ICFC merged in 1973 to form Finance for Industry (FFI, later called 3i), which was eventually privatised in the 1990s.

These institutions performed usefully, but were always ultimately hamstrung. Firstly, they were set up as offshoots of the Bank of England to act as instruments subordinate to the major commercial clearing banks. Indeed, according to Chris Lonsdale, many in the commercial banking sector saw the small business-focused ICFC as but 'a necessary evil to prevent Labour's original hopes for a fully-fledged national investment bank'.[20] Equally, as Richard Coopey notes, the major banks were persuaded to provide funds for the new institution only on the grounds that they could then significantly influence its direction.[21] Relations were scarcely better with the Bank of England, which explicitly opposed the ICFC and FCI being used for any 'political' purposes such as increased investment in the regions. Advances of sorts did come over time – from 1959 the ICFC was able to raise its own capital through bond and stock issues – but these served to solidify the already *de facto* independence from the state. Even before merger and later privatisation, the ICFC was a more or less completely self-directing institution acting in its own commercial interest – which, with the various economic travails seen in the 1970s, nudged it further towards short-term 'wins' and away from its original rationale. By the mid-1980s the then merged 3i was making less than a thousand new loans a year – dwarfed by the over 20,000 such deals then brokered by the German KfW equivalent. In a further twist, by the 1980s 3i would be in the bizarre situation of having some of its limited lending guaranteed by a *European* investment bank on whose board sat a British Chancellor arguing that a *National* Investment Bank was the road to ruin.

The impact of Tony Benn

The truncated FFI/3i was not the only institution which backers of a NIB had to contend with. Despite most commentators acknowledging the presence of a continuing Macmillan Gap holding back British industry (blunting the intended 'white heat' of technological revolution in the 1960s), the recent experience of governments launching arm's-length schemes to suit political ends was not without issue. In 1975 the Wilson government passed an Industry Act mandating the creation of a new, state-owned National Enterprise Board (NEB). As envisaged by its architect, Tony Benn, the aim of the new NEB was to acquire a stake in major manufacturing firms – enabling the government to exercise influence over the said firms' activities and deliver a return to the Exchequer if, as expected, such investments proved profitable. A 1974 Cabinet memorandum made clear the interventionist aim to ameliorate the cyclical effects of capitalism: the NEB should 'secure where necessary large scale sustained investment to offset the effects of the short term pull of market forces ... and [provide] an instrument through which the government operate directly to create employment in areas of high unemployment'.[22]

Had the NEB indeed just been about 'picking winners', its opponents might have had less opportunity to undermine its credibility. But, as Cabinet memoranda spelled out, 'it may on occasion be called on to take over an ailing company which is in danger of collapse but needs to be maintained and restored to a sound economic basis for reasons of regional employment or industrial policy'.[23] In 1975 the Ryder Report 'propose[d] that the Government should be prepared to provide £200m in equity capital now and up to £500m in long term loan capital in stages over the period 1976 to 1978' to one such firm, the automotive giant British Leyland.[24] In bringing British Leyland under state ownership – with a pledge to restore the company to profitability by 1981 – the government had taken on the leading player in an industry, automobile manufacturing, which was to experience mass strikes over the late 1970s. Taxpayer funds, in short, were used (or at least, were seen) to pick a *loser* that government intervention had been unable to turn around. In 1986 Margaret Thatcher continued to remind the public that 'taxpayers' grants and guarantees amount to every family giving £200 in assistance to British

Leyland and, alas, British Leyland is still in a loss-making condition'.[25] The Thatcherite notion of sink or swim did not have much rhetorical use for a state-owned floatation device.

This was important, because it undermined the case for the mixed economy and corporatism per se. From the right, Thatcher was able to claim that government getting out of the way was the only way to turn the British economy around. Looking for cuts going into the 1979 election, the Conservatives pledged to 'reduce government intervention in industry and particularly that of the National Enterprise Board, whose borrowing powers are planned to reach £4.5 billion'.[26] Labour's promise to 'expand the work and finance of the NEB … and ensure that we get an adequate return on our investment' certainly gave the electorate a choice, but it was not one that was about to benefit Prime Minister Callaghan.

Importantly, however, failing to find the answers to British Leyland not only bolstered the right, it also served to blunt moderate Labour. As Tony Blair remembers:

> Jim Callaghan had been Prime Minister. The Labour Party was [then] put out of power by Margaret Thatcher. And the Labour Party persuaded itself that the reason why the country had voted for Margaret Thatcher was because they wanted a really left wing Labour Party. This is what I call the theory that the electorate is stupid.[27]

Blair is clearly being somewhat playful here, but there is an underlying point. Just as Thatcher pulled the Overton window of political acceptability to the right, many were unable to reach a coherent explanation as to why she had been able to do so.[28] Before (at least) the mid-1980s, the moderates had failed to win the internal battle within Labour over what had gone wrong with Britain in the 1970s, and into this space came Stuart Holland and the 'Alternative Economic Strategy' of full employment through borrowing to invest, controls on the international capital market and nationalising the large banks. Not everything about this agenda was wrongheaded, but collectively it saw Labour abdicate the centre ground just as much as the government it pilloried. Some saw no issue with this. In 1980, after the US presidential election, Tony Benn consoled himself with the notion that 'with Thatcher and Reagan in power, the polarisation, and the choice for British electors, will be clearer'.[29] Even after Labour's own electoral catastrophe three years later, the new MP Jeremy Corbyn still 'didn't want a binge of recrimination. The campaign had started well and then everything had been fudged'.[30] Rather than policy errors, there had been 'great incompetence in the Party machine; the leaflets put out were absolutely bland crap'.[31] For many on the left, 'one more push' remained the only option. With Benn later believing that Kinnock had 'reduce[d] public expectations by narrowing the vision of the Party to the single, simple objective of installing Labour ministers in office'[32] – suffice it to say, not exactly a trivial goal – projecting competence was far from easy.

With a chasm in the middle of British politics (at least pre- the SDP), the Tories made much early hay. Indeed, once in power, some such as Nigel Lawson and John Redwood were baying for the ailing NEB's blood.[33] While its elimination did not happen quite as quickly as they may have liked, all government supporters were generally agreed on what any rump NEB should *not* do in the 1980s. Thatcher's Industry Secretary, Keith Joseph, saw 'no public benefit in enabling the NEB to act as a general merchant bank, and its powers to promote businesses, or buy shares in them will be restricted within very clearly defined limits'.[34] Strategic intervention was not to be Thatcher's mission. In 1981 the NEB merged with the National Research Development Corporation to form the British Technology Group, whose aim was to commercialise publicly funded developments. As was the case with 3i, even this truncated body would be fully privatised under Major in the 1990s.

Michael Foot's National Investment Bank

Despite a seemingly disadvantageous political climate, the election of Michael Foot as Labour leader in November 1980 meant that the prospect of a 'Macmillan Gap'-solving National Investment Bank was back on the agenda. For all the New Right attempts to own the economic narrative, this was not without significant political justification. As James Fulcher notes, 'the single most important fact in understanding 1980s Britain is the decline in industrial profitability in the previous two decades. This, as measured by the net profit rate, fell from 17.5 per cent in 1960 to a low of 1.7 per cent in 1981.'[35] Something was going disastrously wrong with British capitalism, and a recalibration was indeed needed. Likewise, the success of the aforementioned analogous institutions to the NIB on the continent was not unknown in Westminster. In late 1980 Nigel Lawson fielded a parliamentary question on the potential for the government to provide preferential interest rates for particular areas of commerce and industry – to help close, in other words, various sectoral Macmillan Gaps. His response acknowledged that 'there are schemes which apply on a country wide basis in four EEC member States: Germany, France, Italy and Belgium'. He told the House of Commons that in the French case total interest rate subsidies for particular industries in 1979 had amounted to about 3.1 billion francs (0.6 per cent of total budget expenditure). Rejecting such a course, however, he noted that 'the Government would inevitably have to subsidise, either directly or indirectly, lower interest rates for industry, thus adding to the public sector borrowing requirement'.[36] In the wake of Labour's going 'cap in hand' to the IMF in 1976, this was no small argument, but the fact was that it had once again become *an* argument.

Crucially, under Foot the NIB policy was driven by the far left of the labour movement. In September 1981 Les Wood, general secretary of the Union of Construction, Allied Trades and Technicians, stated that pension funds should be nationalised if their trustees refused to use them to aid British industry: 'we do not want a national investment bank to become a second cousin of Giro'; instead, 'we want it to provide jobs for people'.[37] Earlier that summer, the left-winger John Silkin had included a proposal for the NIB as a key platform of his (unsuccessful) deputy leadership campaign. And at the Labour Party conference of 1982 the hard left almost succeeded in gaining support for the entire nationalisation of Britain's banking industry – with a conference measure failing only by 3,361,000 votes to 3,131,000.[38] Uncharitably put, perhaps, but with friends like those, the policy did not particularly need Conservative enemies.

With the policy's inclusion in Labour's 1983 election manifesto, however, it soon got them. Since the arguments did not shift much over the decade, it is worth sketching out the Conservative rebuttal. Firstly, the government denied that the problem the NIB was intended to solve existed at all: 'there is no shortage of capital for viable investment projects in industry nor of institutions ready to invest it. Therefore the only point of the National Investment Bank would be to provide ... help for the undeserving.'[39] Nineteen-eighties Britain had no 'Macmillan Gap'. The capital markets were providing worthwhile funding, and thus the whole notion was statist tinkering, at best, and downright harmful if it crowded out private lending, at worst.

Secondly, the NIB idea was linked to Labour's concurrent manifesto threat to nationalise one (or more) of the 'big-four' clearing banks. Such a nationalisation would have involved a significant sum: the then stock exchange value of the Midland exceeded £600 million and that of Barclays £1.5 billion.[40] Though the Tories conceded that the costs of setting up a NIB were 'unquantifiable', the sums involved might well have been higher than even these. People may have been growing gradually more sceptical of bankers, but entrusting their money to Michael Foot instead was a leap too far. By Labour's threatening to nationalise a major bank to make way for the NIB, the NIB became less about facilitating productive capitalism and more about the state encroaching into the private sphere. After the experience of the 1970s this was a big leap of faith for some sections of the electorate to take.

And thirdly, as Conservative literature noted, while 'the market value of [UK] pension funds is about £70 billion – a proportion of this money has been "targeted" by the Labour Party for directed investment through the National Investment Bank'. With '11.6 million employees ... members of occupational pension schemes – over half the working population' – the implication was that Labour was about to raid people's hard-earned pension pots to subsidise another failing British Leyland.[41] And, as the Tories hammered home, 'industrialists, not bureaucrats or committees of "wise men", are best placed to determine which investment opportunities are profitable and will create jobs'.[42] The NIB was an example of Labour not only being about to hit high earners through potentially punitive upper rates of income tax, but getting its myopic cronies to mismanage workers' pensions too.

Kinnock's moderate course

So, how did the idea survive the debacle of 1983? Aside from similar admiration held by many Labour moderates for the Japanese MITI, part of the answer lies in the pro-European direction in which Kinnock took the party.[43] Today, Lord Charles Williams remembers that 'some of us Europhiles were admiring (envious) of the German model, particularly the Landesbanks, and thought we could do the same here. The argument was not to find a way of being nice to capitalists but to show that within the boundaries of Clause IV we could do what the capitalists could not because of "short termism" in the capital markets.'[44] In December 1985 shadow chancellor Roy Hattersley noted, 'it is Labour Party policy to create an industrial bank of the sort that has been successful in Germany, Japan, Sweden, and other Scandinavian countries'.[45] Hattersley was a consistent voice for internationalism, and urged Kinnock not to seem to advocate a 'siege economy' like Foot. As the shadow chancellor admitted, however, the difficulty with 'organis[ing] a new [global] economic order' was that 'Reagan will still be President'.[46]

Yet Europe remained a beacon of possibilities, and not just in terms of individual member states. Between 1980 and 1990 the total level of new financing provided by the European Investment Bank (EIB) in Luxembourg increased from 3.5 billion ECU (European Currency Units) to 13.4 billion ECU.[47] This had clear ramifications in the UK – from £417 million worth of loans being issued to UK projects in 1980, by 1989 the amount was approaching £1.1 billion (the UK was second only behind Italy in terms of investment received).[48] Big-ticket items in the late 1980s included £190 million towards the nuclear fuel reprocessing plant in Sellafield, £50 million for the development of the Airbus A-320 aeroplane, £100 million for British aerospace and £200 million for Scottish communications. Significant EIB money also went towards the Channel Tunnel and the development of Stansted airport.[49] The EIB was certainly not without critics and, as Thatcher attempted to negotiate Britain's rebate from the European Community, any financial loss that Britain made to Europe was heavily scrutinised. Indeed, between 1988 and 1991 the UK's total subscription to the EIB was a sizeable 5.5 billion ECU. But with the collapse of communism this money soon assumed a geopolitical importance – even the Conservative manifesto of 1992 spoke of Britain's being 'at the forefront of investing in the markets of Central and Eastern Europe'.[50] Regardless, throughout the 1980s the UK was increasingly part of a scheme to utilise British taxpayers' money to fund and guarantee lending to small, medium and larger businesses across the European continent (and beyond). This did not stop Tory attacks on Labour's attempts to implement a British version of the EIB, but it blunted them. Subsidised lending was happening, and British businesses and infrastructure projects alike were benefiting from it.

Policy precedent apart, one cannot ignore the internal and very personal dimension for Neil Kinnock. As Richard Hill notes, between his election as leader in 1983 and the conference speech of 1985 where he lambasted the Militant Tendency, Kinnock's room for manoeuvre was limited indeed.[51] His defeat at the 1984 party conference over 'One Member One Vote' was particularly salutary, and policies which advanced his own views but could be cloaked in the language of the left were vital during this period. Crucially, the idea of some form of government-directed (or at least influenced) investment bank could mean different things to different people. For some on the left, after 1983 the major problem with the NIB was that the policy did not go far enough. Presenting a paper to the broadly leftist Campaign for Labour Democracy faction in 1985, the Oxford economist (and Trotskyist) Andrew Glyn argued that 'the National Investment Bank, currently proposed by Labour to be funded from repatriated overseas investments and directed towards small and medium firms could make a contribution, but in no way would it guarantee a major expansion of investment'.[52] This was symbolic, he continued, of 'Labour's leaders hav[ing] retreated from the ideas of planning and controlling investment, towards attempting to encourage it by reassuring the private sector'. Paul Flynn MP (first elected in 1987) recalls that the 'left wing were friendly towards the [NIB] idea more so than the right wing'.[53] Either way, the policy's malleability was one of its chief assets. For those on the right, the bank was about encouraging capital flows to productive capitalism – providing succour, as Flynn states, to the 'give greed a chance' brigade.[54] Concurrently, to those on the left it was about bringing the City to heel, plugging the gaps the big banks were refusing to act on, and bringing industry back under state control.

As Bryan Gould noted to the present author, the NIB question was very much tied to 'the issue as to what to commit a new Labour government to do in respect of the formerly nationalised industries, such as BT, that the Tories had in various ways privatised. The unions … were keen to push for a commitment to re-nationalise, but the PLP members wanted to avoid that commitment'. Much of Gould's time in his shadow economic portfolios in the late 1980s was spent 'persuading the unions to accept a form of partial public ownership, such as – in the case of BT for example – obtaining a majority shareholding. It was in the context of that kind of discussion that the concept of a publicly owned investment bank was developed.'[55] Shifting the Labour Party on industrial policy and nationalisation was about restoring Labour's 'valence' to the electorate – here the NIB formed part of the retail offer as such, but it was also not a policy that existed in a vacuum. Just as the Tories had tied the NIB to nationalisation of the major banks in 1983, so too did it not remain divorced from the remainder of Labour economic policy throughout the 1980s. Indeed, the sheer plethora of promised new institutions in areas from pricing to the regions was not always helpful (particularly a new 'British Enterprise' intended as a de facto resurrection of the 1970s NEB), but within the labour movement they could serve useful purposes with different stakeholders. Gradually moving Labour thought from owning the means of production to facilitating responsible capitalism was a process that took time.

As the party became generally more credible, however, so did Kinnock's version of the NIB – and nuancing the vexed funding issue was key here. In 1986 Kinnock explicitly sent out the signal that his NIB was 'not ... an agency for *channelling all national savings*'.[56] To fund a bank capitalised to the tune of a potential £12 billion, he retained the general principle from 1983 of withdrawing tax privileges from pooled investment schemes which did not limit their overseas portfolio to a given percentage, and from those managed funds which did not allocate a stated proportion of their portfolio to loan stock of the NIB. However, all questions of nationalisation of pension funds, uncooperative banks and so forth were dropped – the policy would rely on incentives and providing nudges for market participants to act in the national interest. And, as a further fudge, the party's commitment to raise additional income tax from those earning over £20,000 was also occasionally dangled as a source of funding for the NIB – particularly as revenue from another potential avenue, North Sea oil, dried up from the mid-1980s.

The trade-off here was again between valence and positional politics. If, as it indeed did, Labour highlighted particular ways to pay for the NIB, this meant highlighting groups who might fear losing out (i.e., pensioners) and thereby gaining new 'positional' enemies.[57] Equally, however, if no source of funds was identified for the NIB, this meant undermining the party's valence with the electorate per se. Although we will never know the outcome of a NIBless 1987, the actual result perhaps vindicates taking what positional hit there was. In the end, in 1987 Labour gained around 4 per cent more voters over the age of fifty-five (those of pensionable or approaching pensionable age) on their 1983 performance – compared to an overall swing of just over 3 per cent between the two elections.[58] Conservative attack-dogs such as Norman Tebbit, sent out to claim that Labour intended to 'rob the pensioners', had limited success.[59] Given that such pension funds would be buying bonds in any NIB (likely providing a higher rate than gilts, too) and not taking an equity stake, the Conservative rebuttal in this regard was always half baked at best.

Funding remained a key question, however, and, interestingly, one advocate of directly hypothecating taxes was Tony Blair. In a private paper he pointed to the success of Walter Mondale in winning the Democratic nomination for US president in 1984. One of the biggest charges facing Labour, Blair contended, was Mondale's question to his then rival, Gary Hart: 'where's the beef?' Although he argued that 'the scope from taking from "the wealthy" and giving to "the poor" is not unlimited', hypothecating taxes was certainly an option. Blair wrote that 'spending on industry, through grants, subsidies, training for industry etc. should again come, as far as is feasible, from raising corporate taxes on industry … [which] are actually low compared with our competitors'.[60] Whether Labour's ambitions were big or small, the important thing was to be seen to be realistically able to pay for them. In 1983 Labour, rather foreshadowing 1992, had been accused of more than £26.5 billion of additional spending commitments where the sums did not yet add up.[61] As Peter Mandelson noted, Labour should be careful that 'when talking of our programme we don't promise more than we can deliver or can afford, distinguish between immediate priorities and longer-term goals, aspire to a 10–15 year horizon, and we declare all this openly'.[62] The NIB fitted into such long-term horizons.

But if tax might be needed to fund its upfront costs, the NIB was a part of a more significant transition towards the 'supply side socialism' advocated by John Eatwell, Kinnock's chief economic advisor. According to Martin Westlake, 'for Eatwell, Britain's key economic problem was the weakness of its productive sector. This imposed long-term constraints on possible rates of growth since, when consumption spending rose, imports inevitably increased and pushed the economy into a Balance of Payments deficit.'[63] As a Labour press briefing put it in 1989, 'we have now moved decisively away from a policy of short-term management of the economy through demand management'.[64] Instead of manipulations of exchange or interest rates, or standard leftist fiscal measures on tax and spend, 'supply side socialism' would seek to fix the structural flaws in the British economy over the medium to long term and grow Britain's way to prosperity. As party advisors told journalists, Labour was now about 'the enabling state … [where] the aim is not to pick winners but to create the conditions in which winners can come through'.[65]

Further intellectual ballast came from the Kaldor Group – a group of academics commissioned by Kinnock to rethink Labour's economic priorities. Headed by Nicholas Kaldor and attended by Meghnad Desai, John Eatwell, Andrew Graham and others, the group was convinced of the pressing Macmillan Gap going into the mid-1980s. Although the group was mostly macro focused, it noted that

> [the] characteristics of the UK capital market militate against … two situations in particular. One is the small/medium size firm needing external finance to grow rapidly. During rapid expansion the investment needs are often equal to, or greater than profits. There is therefore no chance during this period of paying high nominal interest rates or high dividends. The other is the medium/large firm with

outdated capital and low profitability, but with good plans for substantial modernisation on a scale that again requires additional external finance. We envisage cases of these two kinds as being especially suitable for support by the proposed National Investment Bank.[66]

The enemy here was predatory, short-term capitalism. As Bryan Gould told a Cambridge audience, 'as long as economic policy making is dominated by the interests of those who hold assets rather than create wealth we shall continue to suffer from chronic short termism and the high interest rates and uncompetitive currency that reflect and accompany it'.[67] This meant a realignment of capitalism, but not its fundamental replacement. As Kinnock put it, 'we have a particular financial system which in its own terms is successful. And we have an unsuccessful industrial sector. Given the role which finance has in a capitalist economy of mobilizing resources – and must have in any economy fuelling production – there must be some causal relationship between the relative success of one and the relative failure of the other.'[68] Expressed more concisely, Kinnock believed that 'British financial institutions ... should be midwives, instead they are undertakers'.[69] Tactics aside, therefore, getting credit flowing was not merely about internal party management. As John Smith argued in his response to the 1985 budget, 'the Tory party has become the anti-industry party. It is the party of fast food services and of financial services ... [and] the jobs of the future [under a Conservative government] will be not so much low-tech as no-tech'.[70]

John Eatwell concurs with this point. Above and beyond plugging the Macmillan Gap, the NIB was an asset because it could help to address the crucial question of technological development while, at the same time, there was the financial expertise around to staff the operation effectively. As to the first, although British Leyland had previously been something of an albatross around Labour's neck, the innovation seen in car manufacturing throughout the 1980s was evidence to many within Kinnock's office that they 'had to back such highly skilled consultative expertise in the automotive sector'.[71] This was also true of aerospace, where, as Kaveh Pourvand notes, 'various government interventions have been crucial to [its] present day success'.[72] Selling such British expertise to the world was something to be encouraged and, while the Thatcher government had utilised tax incentives to bring in foreign investment (including Nissan in Sunderland), it was felt that far more could be done to capitalise on Britain's competitive advantage in such markets. Equally the NIB could contribute to this, Eatwell remembers, because of the presence of many 'really talented investment bankers who had often been trained, as younger men, at the Wilson era Industrial Reorganisation Committee [which had encouraged mergers to produce a more efficient industrial base]'.[73] These were 'often quite conservative people, who had been given responsibility at a young age and had a real practical expertise that could have been brought in [to the NIB]'.[74] Socialising the financial expertise held within the City was held to be both practical and deliverable.

As such, there were clear wins during this period. In May 1985 Smith was able to seize on a recent speech of Nicholas Edwards, then Welsh Secretary, to Cardiff Business Club. Edwards, no paid-up Wet, had argued that there was a 'physical chasm' between the City of London and Britain's industrial areas. Edwards had also stated that 'among many household names in the financial world, there is at best a failure to comprehend the problem … and at worst a startling arrogance that leads them to conclude that all is well, that nothing calls for reform, and that anyone with a good project can always find backing for it'.[75] Pouring praise on Edwards, Smith contrasted his speech with 'the objections of some Conservative Members [which] arise from the fact that they think the City already provides adequately for the needs of British industry'. Labour's broad diagnosis was not without prominent third-party backing, either. In October 1986 the Confederation of British Industry (CBI) called for £1 billion of new infrastructure investment and criticised the halving of capital expenditure as a percentage of overall government investment between 1980/81 and 1985/86. As the CBI noted, 'unless the government takes the initiative now on certain capital projects we shall have lost our chance and slip further behind in the [global] competitiveness league'.[76] The narrative was not wholly slavishly Thatcherite.

In this light, and with Reaganomics then clearly in the ascendancy, it is also worth revisiting the coverage of the NIB in North American newspapers. In February 1986 the *New York Times*, referencing the British press, noted that 'the new Labor [sic] remedies – lower interest rates, competitive exchange rates, a national investment bank, sponsoring technology – sound so prudent and uncontroversial that *The Daily Telegraph*, a Tory paper, asked ironically whether there was a "convergence" between Labor [sic] and Conservative policies'.[77] In the immediate run-up to the 1987 election, the *Boston Globe* noted that 'Labor [sic] also would … impose a "capital repatriation" program to keep savings and investment from going abroad, coupling that with an industrial investment bank for low-cost business loans. But the party promises to renationalise only the gas and telephone companies in its first parliament of five years. That represents a Kinnock victory over the left in his party.'[78] After Labour's election defeat, Toronto readers of *The Globe and Mail* could read of the policy review then underway which had 'several proposals including an industrial investment bank, a more effective science policy and better retraining programs. But [Labour] resolutely reject heavy intervention in the economy and protectionism.'[79] These are only snapshots, but the threefold picture of a moderate policy bolstering a centrist leader who was about strategic rather than blanket intervention was broadly accurate. In this regard, Labour was making some of the progress envisioned by the Democratic Leadership Council in America – which would eventually deliver the election of President Bill Clinton in 1992.[80]

The road to 1992

If 1983–85 saw Kinnock bob and weave within the party, and 1985–87 witnessed a gradual centrist drift, the two-year period after the election defeat in 1987 cemented the victory of the moderate tendency. According to Labour's communications team considering the latest defeat, it was clear that 'the Conservatives won the election on economic grounds' and there were continuing 'perceptions of Labour's lack of economic competence'. There was a need, these documents continued, not to make the message 'too abstract' and to 'engage the interest of both politicians and the general public'.[81] Slightly ironically, this process began with the ultra-wonkish process of a party policy review. For Westlake, 'the Labour Party's 1987–9 policy review was the most comprehensive and systematic attempt ever undertaken by a political party to reformulate its policies ... in theory, each of the policy review groups operated from a blank sheet – in effect a moderniser's charter – but in reality the reforms that emerged were less radical and more cautious than Kinnock'.[82] This review involved subtly shifting the NIB once again.

Prior to 1987 one important change had already been made – Labour had dropped the previous requirement for all lending from the NIB to be subject to firms providing a 'business plan agreed between Government, management, and work-force'. This had helped to blunt charges that 'what [Hattersley] wants to do is bully financial institutions'.[83] But in the wake of the 1987 defeat the bank's remit was again changed. By March 1989 Kinnock was able to state that the NIB would 'back investment that captures markets ... it will be a creative force that invests, builds, and then moves on'.[84] Ken Livingstone and others on the left were opposed to this recalibration of aims.[85] Yet, for revisionists like Giles Radice, 'if it is to be serious about winning ... [Labour] cannot afford to be primarily a class party ... Labour should be, and be seen to be, a broad based national party, concerned with national solutions for national problems'.[86] The evolving NIB was a significant part of this.

By placing the NIB on a more strategic footing, Labour could be more confident going into 1992. Taking two sometimes sceptical newspapers as indicative – *The Times* (1983–87: three critical headlines; 1987–92: zero) and *Glasgow Herald* (1983–87: six critical headlines; 1987–92: zero) – both calmed their ire with regard to Labour's NIB proposal. By 1991 shadow chancellor John Smith was even taking criticisms head on. When speaking in the City he was asked by a representative of the then ailing Prudential insurance fund whether it was wise to create a NIB, since 'governments have a rather poor track record in selecting profitable areas for investment'. Smith jovially countered that 'the private sector has made its share of dodgy decisions, too. D'you know, hard though this is to believe, I understand that a substantial British insurance company went headlong into the property market not so long ago.' *The Times* even drily headlined the account of this incident, 'Prudent Silence'.[87] Smith had good reason to be bullish. Earlier that year the influential National Institute of Economic and Social Research (NIESR) had argued that 'the provision of long time finance through a national investment bank' within Labour's programme could, alongside other measures, help to bring growth of over 3 per cent and maintain inflation at a stable 2 per cent.[88] And the global picture was also moving to the policy's advantage. By January 1992 the unemployment rates of European states operating institutions closest to the proposed NIB were 6 per cent in Germany, 5.6 per cent in the Netherlands and 4.3 per cent in Sweden.[89] These low figures were no doubt largely due to macro-economic factors above and beyond any domestic NIBs, but with a UK unemployment rate of 9.3 per cent (and climbing) Tory charges about the evils of Rhenish capitalism could be batted off.

By February 1992, NOP polling showed that Labour's broad suite of industrial policies, of which the NIB was a big part, had been effectively drawn. Labour was viewed as the party best at 'getting the economy out of recession' (29 per cent to 24 per cent), reducing unemployment (37 per cent to 11 per cent), helping the manufacturing industry (49 per cent to 21 per cent) and was neck and neck as to 'which party will run the economy well' (45 per cent to 45 per cent).[90] Yet 'supply side socialism' was not everything, and it was roughly at this point that the Conservative message regarding 'Labour's tax bombshell' began to filter through. With Tory posters proclaiming an additional £1,250 on the tax bill of every British taxpayer in the wake of a Labour victory, the subtleties of retooling British capitalism through a NIB were not able to push Kinnock to victory. A fourth election on the bounce (the third with a pledge to introduce a NIB) was duly lost.

Conclusion

The case of the NIB is informative in three overlapping regards. Firstly, it helps us understand how Labour talked to itself. The NIB's long-term rationale, after all, was to fix a particular flaw in capitalist systems: the Macmillan Gap of banks not lending to the right places. To fund such beneficial activity one could either take a confiscatory approach – raid major investment funds for the capital necessary to fund this greater good – or incentivise such funds to act in a more responsible manner. Until the 1983 general election the unions' advocacy and a leftist leadership collectively ensured that Labour took the former approach, while after that election Hattersley, Gould, Eatwell and others nudged the party towards the latter. Even if it would not figure in the New Labour platform, the NIB's role in the transition of the party – away from 'national' solutions and towards ones where it was prepared to talk to 'investment banks' – renders it as a significant juncture in the party's history.

Secondly, the NIB tells us much about Labour's outward electability. The 1980s saw Labour gradually shift from the perception that they were blinkered statist blunderers to one where people could see them as semi-credible managers of the public purse. To return to Stokes, in 1983 Labour's advocacy of the NIB suffered both a 'valence' and a 'positional' problem: few thought that it could govern effectively, and there was the direct (if exaggerated) prospect for some pensioners that they would see their future returns hit. Kinnock gradually restored a semblance of 'valence' to Labour on the economy and thus its ability to deliver an effective NIB. Positional attacks from the Conservatives and their sympathetic allies in the press cut through somewhat between 1985–87, but thereafter, partially due to Labour's shift towards supply-side socialism and the strategic state generally (allied to the declining fortunes of the government itself), the NIB was both a viable and a beneficial part of the Kinnock platform. The shifting nuances in the policy also provided a dog-whistle of sorts for the fact that the party had changed from 1983: no bad thing, and certainly something not universally achieved with regard to tax and spend. Had the party won in 1992 the trick would have been for the NIB to avoid the fate of 3i, and to keep an independent NIB focused on national priorities rather than its own bottom line. But with the appointment of a sympathetic top team (the *Spectator* speculated that Charles Williams might be in line to lead the NIB), day-to-day independence while keeping an eye on overarching national priorities was not beyond the realms of possibility.[91] The Bank of England essentially walks such a line today.

Lastly, the NIB is also instructive regarding the birth of New Labour. As noted, through its intellectual roots in 1970s Tony Benn and the Foot leadership, backing the NIB after 1983 helped Kinnock to move Labour towards the centre. And, importantly, the modernisers were watching intently for opportunities to shift the discourse further. They may not all have bought the NIB wholesale (although Blair and Prescott backed it publicly), but they benefitted from its shifting the political terrain in their favour.[92] By 1994 Labour had found the revisionist leader that Giles Radice demanded, one willing to 'accept the market but uphold the case for selective state intervention'.[93] In pledging that 'the war on inflation is a Labour war', and later not to raise the top rate of income tax, New Labour broadly got the economic mood music right in opposition.[94] But one unfortunate casualty of the belief that 'the era of the corporatist state intervention is over' was the relatively moderate NIB.[95] In a sense, for Tony Blair, in changing the party the NIB idea had served its purpose. And as a man about ends rather than means, he chose other means to change the country.

Notes

1 Richard Hill, *The Labour Party and Economic Strategy 1979–97: The Long Road Back* (London: Palgrave, 2001), p. 4.
2 Colin Hughes and Patrick Wintour, *Labour Rebuilt: The New Model Party* (London: Fourth Estate, 1990), p. 6.
3 Giles Radice, *Labour's Path to Power: The New Revisionism* (Basingstoke: Macmillan, 1989), p. 57.
4 See, for example, Ipsos MORI's 'Economic Optimism Index'.
5 *Guardian*, 2 August 2015, https://www.theguardian.com/commentisfree/2015/aug/02/labour-split-corbyn-blairites (accessed 14 January 2017).
6 Ipsos MORI, 'Polls on Labour Party's Image', 1983–92.
7 To contextualise the success of Kinnock, see Charles Clarke, 'Measuring the Success or Failure of Labour Leaders: The General Election Test', in Charles Clarke and Toby S. James (eds), *British Labour Leaders* (London: Palgrave, 2015), pp. 33–52.
8 A note is necessary on the nomenclature: in the 1987 manifesto this institution was called a 'British Industrial Investment Bank'. To further complicate matters, in his 1986 *Making Our Way: Investing in Britain's Future* (London: Basil Blackwell), Kinnock referred to it as the 'British Investment Bank'.
9 Jim Tomlinson, 'Thatcherism, Monetarism and the Politics of Inflation', in Ben Jackson and Robert Saunders (eds), *Making Thatcher's Britain* (Cambridge: Cambridge University Press, 2012), pp. 62–77, at p. 70.
10 Richard Carr, *Credit Where Credit's Due: Investing in Local Infrastructure to Get Britain Growing* (London: Localis, 2012). See also Nick Tott, *The Case for a British Investment Bank: A Report of Labour's Policy Review* (London: Labour Party, 2012), and, utilising a different funding model, Richard Carr, 'Tackling the "Money Octopus": The Financial Sector and the One Nation Tradition', *Renewal* 23 (2015), 30–43.
11 Donald E. Stokes, 'Spatial Models of Party Competition', *American Political Science Review* 57 (1963), 368–77.
12 Colin Hays, *The Political Economy of New Labour: Labouring under False Pretences?* (Manchester: Manchester University Press, 1999); Dianne Hayter, *Fightback! Labour's Traditional Right in the 1970s and 1980s* (Manchester: Manchester University Press, 2005).
13 From an economic standpoint, see Richard Coopey, 'The First Venture Capitalist: Financing Development in Britain After 1945: The Case of ICFC/3i', *Business and Economic History* 23 (1994), 262–71.
14 Thanks are due to Lords John Eatwell and Charles Williams, Paul Flynn MP and Bryan Gould for their comments.
15 Given the extent to which it is repeated, it is worth laying out in full Peter Mandelson's famous quote. New Labour was indeed 'intensely relaxed about people getting filthy rich'. However, this was always 'as long as they pay their taxes'.
16 See *Guardian*, 14 March 2013, https://www.theguardian.com/politics/2013/mar/14/ed-miliband-network-local-banks and *Daily Telegraph*, 23 February 2012, www.telegraph.co.uk/finance/comment/9101672/If-we-want-the-UK-to-grow-we-should-take-lessons-from-Germany.html (both accessed 14 January 2017).
17 Committee on Finance and Industry Report, June 1931, The National Archives (TNA), London, T/200/7.
18 Coopey, 'The First Venture Capitalist', p. 264.
19 William A. Thomas, *The Finance of British Industry, 1918–1976* (London: Methuen, 1979), p. 334.
20 Chris Lonsdale, *The UK Equity Gap: The Failure of Government Policy since 1945* (Farnham: Ashgate, 1997), p. 40.

21 Coopey, 'The First Venture Capitalist', p. 264.
22 Planning Agreement and the National Enterprise Board, 1 August 1974, TNA, CAB/129/178/13.
23 Planning Agreement and the National Enterprise Board, 1 August 1974, TNA, CAB/129/178/13.
24 'British Leyland: The Ryder Report', 23 April 1975, TNA, CAB/129/183/3.
25 House of Commons Debates, 20 February 1986, 92, col. 477.
26 Conservative Party Manifesto, 1979.
27 Tony Blair in conversation with Matt Forde, 22 July 2015, available at www.progressonline.org.uk (accessed 14 January 2017).
28 The Overton window defines the window of policy options which the public will accept. As defined in Owen Jones, *The Establishment: And How They Get Away With It* (London: Penguin, 2014), Foreword.
29 Tony Benn, *The End of An Era: Diaries 1980–90* (London: Hutchinson, 1992), p. 44 [5 November 1980].
30 Benn, *The End of An Era*, p. 296 [12 June 1983].
31 Benn, *The End of An Era*, p. 296 [12 June 1983].
32 Benn, *The End of an Era*, p. xi.
33 Nigel Lawson, *The View from No. 11: Memoirs of a Tory Radical* (London: Bantam, 1992), p. 90; Michael Grylls and John Redwood, *National Enterprise Board: A Case for Euthanasia* (London: Centre for Policy Studies, 1980).
34 Keith Joseph statement draft, 18 July 1979, TNA, PREM/19/260 f114.
35 James Fulcher, 'British Capitalism in the 1980s: Old Times or New Times?', *British Journal of Sociology* 46 (1995), 326–38.
36 House of Commons Debates, 13 November 1980, 992, cols 445–7.
37 *Glasgow Herald*, 11 September 1981, p. 9.
38 *Glasgow Herald*, 29 September 1982, p. 6.
39 Conservative Research Department Confidential Note, 16 May 1983, Churchill Archives Centre (CAC), THCR 2/7/3/10 f5.
40 'Costing Labour's Manifesto Promises', 25 May 1983, CAC, THCR 2/7/3/15 f9.
41 Conservative Research Department Confidential Note, 16 May 1983, CAC, THCR 2/7/3/10 f5.
42 Conservative Research Department Confidential Note, 16 May 1983, CAC, THCR 2/7/3/10 f5.
43 The Japanese Ministry of International Trade and Technology (MITI) was much admired in the West. See, e.g., Chalmers Johnson, *MITI and the Japanese Miracle: The Growth of Industrial Policy, 1925–1975*, (Stanford: Stanford University Press, 1982), passim.
44 Charles Williams to the author, 11 December 2015. In 1987, Lord Williams authored the influential Fabian Society pamphlet, *An Investment Bank for the UK*.
45 House of Commons Debates, 12 December 1985, 88, col. 1093.
46 Hattersley to Kinnock, 24 October 1985, CAC, KNNK/6/1/7.
47 European Investment Bank Annual Reports, 1980 and 1990.
48 House of Commons Debates, 13 March 1990, 169, cols 160–1.
49 House of Commons Debates, 20 April 1990, 170, cols 1047–50.
50 Conservative Manifesto, 1992.
51 Hill, *The Labour Party and Economic Strategy 1979–97*, p. 28.
52 Andrew Glynn, 'A Million Jobs for a Year: The Case for Planning Full Employment', 3 September 1985 draft, CAC, TADA 4/10/1.
53 Paul Flynn to the author, 9 December 2015.
54 Paul Flynn to the author, 9 December 2015.
55 Bryan Gould to the author, 6 December 2015.

56 Kinnock, *Making Our Way*, p. 186. My italics.
57 Albeit balanced against positional friends such as small business and, potentially, the unemployed.
58 Ipsos MORI, 'How Britain Voted since October 1974'.
59 *Glasgow Herald*, 17 September 1985, p. 7.
60 Tony Blair note on 'Public Expenditure', CAC, KNNK/6/1/17
61 'Costing Labour's Manifesto Promises', 25 May 1983, CAC, THCR 2/7/3/15 f9.
62 Mandelson memorandum on General Election Strategy, 27 October 1986, CAC, KNNK/3/2/4.
63 Martin Westlake, *Kinnock: The Authorised Biography* (London: Little, Brown, 2001), p. 434.
64 'Economic Policy after the Review', 22 June 1989, CAC, KNNK/6/2/13.
65 'Economic Policy after the Review'.
66 First Report of a Labour Party Economic Policy, July 1986, King's College, Cambridge, NK/11/10.
67 Bryan Gould speech in Cambridge, 17 May 1987, CAC, BRAY Acc. 870, Box 10.
68 Kinnock, *Making Our Way*, p. 111.
69 Kinnock, *Making Our Way*, p. 111.
70 House of Commons Debates, 11 March 1985, 75, cols 105–6.
71 Lord Eatwell to the author, 8 January 2016.
72 Kaveh Pourvand, *Picking Winners: How UK Industrial Policy Ensured the Success of the Aerospace and Automobile Industries* (London: Civitas, 2013), p. 33.
73 Lord Eatwell to the author, 8 January 2016.
74 Lord Eatwell to the author, 8 January 2016.
75 House of Commons Debates, 15 May 1985, 79, col. 334.
76 See press cuttings in CAC, KNNK/6/2/1.
77 *New York Times*, 18 February 1986, www.nytimes.com/1986/02/18/world/after-thatcher-kinnock-doesn-t-spring-to-mind.html?pagewanted=1 (accessed 14 January 2017).
78 *Boston Globe*, 20 May 1987, p. 5.
79 *Toronto Globe and Mail*, 12 May 1988, p. 8.
80 See Al From, *The New Democrats and the Return to Power* (London: Palgrave Macmillan, 2013).
81 'Developing a Communication Strategy', June 1988, CAC, KNNK/6/2/1.
82 Westlake, *Kinnock*, pp. 425, 427.
83 *Glasgow Herald*, 20 September 1985, p. 6.
84 *Glasgow Herald*, 20 March 1989, p. 4.
85 *Glasgow Herald*, 20 March 1989, p. 4.
86 Radice, *Labour's Path to Power*, pp. 200–1.
87 *The Times*, 18 July 1991, p. 27.
88 Economic briefing, 14 January 1991, CAC, KNNK/6/2/15.
89 Via the European Commission's Eurostat service at http://ec.europa.eu/eurostat
90 David Butler and Dennis Kavanagh, *The British General Election of 1992* (Basingstoke: Macmillan, 1992), p. 98.
91 *Spectator*, 14 December 1991, p. 18.
92 Such as House of Commons Debates, 9 July 1985, 82, col. 1043 and 20 March 1986, 94, col. 445. Prescott as something of a more 'traditional' moderniser, admittedly.
93 Radice, *Labour's Path to Power*, p. 209.
94 Gordon Brown lecture, 17 May 1995, CAC, BRAY 97/097.
95 Bray to Blair, July 1994, CAC, BRAY 97/097.

PART II
The British left in a global context

5

Neil Kinnock's *perestroika*: Labour and the Soviet influence

Jonathan Davis

The 1980s witnessed a fundamental restructuring of socialism as it had been understood and practised in Europe for decades. The various ideas which shaped twentieth-century left-wing ideology underwent a dramatic transformation in the face of significant new challenges, not least the rise and establishment of the New Right philosophy in the guise of Thatcherism in Britain and, more globally and in a Cold War context, Reaganism. Over time, this led to the victory of free markets and liberal democracy over social justice and social democracy. Globalisation began in the 1980s, and how the left dealt with it would define domestic and international politics for decades.

For the Labour Party, these changes were made all the more serious because of what was happening inside the Soviet Union, a country which had informed its political thought since the Russian revolutions and the Stalinist era, although for some this influence stretched into the Cold War years, continuing until the fall of the Berlin Wall in 1989.[1] Neil Kinnock, who replaced Michael Foot as leader in 1983 after Labour's defeat in that year's general election, began to reform the party, and his changes coincided with those made by Mikhail Gorbachev, the last leader of the Soviet Union. Gorbachev's reforms initially changed the structure of the Soviet economy, but ultimately altered the very basis of Soviet socialism. The views and approaches of both leaders encouraged different ways of thinking about their strands of socialism, and the word used by Gorbachev to describe this process of change was *perestroika* (restructuring). This applied as much to what Kinnock was doing to Labour's ideology as it did to Gorbachev's efforts in the Communist Party of the Soviet Union (CPSU), not least because reflecting upon the apparent success of Gorbachev's reforms encouraged a feeling of 'if the Soviets can do it, then so can we'. *Perestroika* in the USSR reinforced the ideological *perestroika* in the Labour Party and helped to smooth the way for Kinnock's reforms as he challenged well-worn and comfortable ideological shibboleths. Alex Pravda and Peter Duncan correctly assert that the 'ascendency of reform within the CPSU ... accelerate[d] a trend ... towards a more positive assessment of reformism within the Labour Party'.[2]

This chapter will consider the Kinnock era and the changes made to Labour's ideology by placing them within the wider context of Gorbachev's reforms, because as they developed, a convergence between Eastern and Western European versions of socialism became evident. This was most apparent as both parties accepted that market-based ideas would need to be a part of their economic policies – a realisation which set in most noticeably after 1987. Although Kinnock's restructuring process began before Gorbachev's, the general election defeat of 1987 was an important turning point which saw Kinnock reconsider further aspects of Labour's political thought as he reinterpreted socialism as the party understood it. And although Gorbachev's turn towards *perestroika* in the same year may have been coincidental, he too introduced a new form of socialism which allowed a convergence of democratic and Soviet socialism to begin. By the time that Margaret Thatcher resigned and the Soviet Union fell, Labour had accepted that the free market should play a greater part in its economic plans, had made the role of the individual a more central feature in its programme and had abandoned unilateralism; in the USSR, the Soviet economy had a private sector, Soviet citizens had the freedom to openly debate and discuss the nation's issues and Soviet socialism no longer had communism as its ultimate aim.

The changing international environment in the 1980s allowed for improved relations between Western European socialist/social democratic parties of the Second International and the CPSU of the Third International. When Kinnock met with Gorbachev in 1989, he sought to discuss what he referred to as a 'Convergence of ideology'. The agenda for their meeting outlined 'the idea of joint ideological discussions ... with a view to increasing understanding between the outlooks of the Second and Third Internationals'.[3] This took on an especially important meaning in that year, as a seminar was held in Moscow to mark the one hundredth anniversary of the formation of the Second International. The historian Ben Pimlott represented the Labour Party and he recalled that the 'most significant thing' about the seminar 'is that it took place at all'. He suggested that it was 'a sign of the times' that this meeting 'was deemed worthy of celebration by the Soviet Institute of Social Sciences and Institute of Marxism-Leninism'.[4] The seminar came a year after the CPSU was invited, for the first time, to send representatives to a meeting of the Council of the Socialist International in Madrid. Aleksandr Veber and Aleksandr Zotov, Advisers with the International Department of the CPSU Central Committee, attended the meeting.[5] Given the history of animosity between the two Internationals, these meetings should be seen as important moments in socialist relations.

The path of convergence was partly laid as Gorbachev's reforms 'social-democratised Bolshevism'.[6] Archie Brown argues that this meant that, by 1991, 'the draft program which Gorbachev espoused and presented to the Central Committee had much more in common with social democracy than with anything remotely like traditional Soviet Communism'. He also notes that the 'the sentiments expressed in his July 1991 speech would have been perfectly acceptable to the leadership of the British Labour Party, the German Social Democrats, or the French or Spanish Socialists'.[7] This was a consequence of Gorbachev's 'New Thinking', not just in foreign policy but also in ideological, political and economic ideas, and his thinking 'acquired a certain Social Democratic coloring'.[8] It could therefore be argued that, had the Soviet Union not collapsed in 1991, then Gorbachev might have successfully 'social-democratised' the Russian republic and a new strand of socialism would have emerged, allowing for a very different set of left-wing ideas to develop in the 1990s.

The international impact of the New Right will also be considered in this chapter, as different socialist ideas were defined by early globalisation. In different ways, it encouraged Kinnock and Gorbachev to reconsider their ideological frameworks. In Britain, Thatcher created a new socio-economic and political environment which warranted an ideological response from Labour, and Kinnock's *perestroika* of the Labour Party was that response. As we shall see, the consolidation of the New Right also inspired changes in the communist left in Britain which emphasised the need for reform inside the USSR and facilitated the changes made by Gorbachev.

This international backdrop was important, as it tied Kinnock's reforms to the wider reappraisals of socialism that were taking place in the socialist movement. The global freeing of markets and deregulation of industries in capitalist and non-capitalist countries alike forced parties on the left to reconsider certain state-led assumptions. Kinnock's ideological restructuring should be considered within this context, as Labour was not only part of a wider internationalist movement, but also was influenced by its internationalism. This was as true in the 1980s as it was in the 1930s when Soviet socialism, social democracy in Sweden and the New Deal in Roosevelt's America all inspired Labour in different ways. Kinnock's restructuring of Labour tied in with the wind of change that was blowing through the socialist movement. For example, French socialists saw President François Mitterrand reverse his Keynesian economic policy to introduce a pro-monetarist *tournant de la rigueur* (austerity turn), and in China, Deng Xiaoping encouraged the Chinese Communist Party to open the country up to the outside world by adopting a more market-based approach to the country's economics. The market-forces approach also helped to define the discussions in the Labour Party and the Soviet Union, facilitating the convergence between democratic and Soviet socialism.

Both Labour and the CPSU showed that they had the capacity to change radically in the 1980s, even if the change came about slowly at times and within specific parameters. This ability to consider different paths and alternative visions allowed for the convergence of socialist ideas which took place in this decade. However, this convergence was not given time to develop within the old ideological environment as, by the end of 1989, the Berlin Wall had fallen and Eastern Europe had freed itself from the Kremlin's rule. This could have presented Kinnock with a chance to offer a renewed version of socialism, devoid of any Stalinist context. Instead, it acted as a reminder that socialism was being rejected by millions of citizens in the 'People's Democracies' who turned to capitalism for answers, and the left's challenge became even more complicated. But until this, and the collapse of the USSR two years later, there seemed to be a genuine possibility of the worlds of the Second and Third International, of democratic socialism and Soviet socialism, converging and creating a new ideological interpretation of socialism for the twenty-first century.

Kinnock, socialism and the USSR before Gorbachev

The transformation of socialism in its various forms throughout the 1980s was dramatic, given where Labour and the CPSU began the decade. They both claimed socialism as their ideological framework, although how this was interpreted differed greatly. For example, by the early 1980s the USSR's questionable grasp of the concept of socialism had gone through a new stage known as 'Developed Socialism', although Marxism-Leninism was still the official ideology. Unlike the Labour Party, the CPSU did not have to consider such things as changes of government or alternative political philosophies. Soviet leaders' understanding of socialism was based on an interpretation of Marxism handed down to them by previous generations of class warriors. It allowed no democratic freedom for its citizens or party members, factions inside the party had been banned since 1921, the party's word was law and the leader's position was, on the whole, incontestable.

In contrast, Labour participated in elections in order to gain power, and it allowed different groups and factions to openly debate and discuss policy even if, at times, they argued fiercely and publicly for or against alternative viewpoints and proposals. In the Kinnock era, Labour was defined as a democratic socialist party, as this ensured that it could differentiate itself from revolutionary socialists (such as the Trotskyists of Militant or the Socialist Workers Party) and the pro-Soviets in the Communist Party of Great Britain (CPGB). Labour had a more values-led approach as opposed to following a rigid philosophy based on a specific set of ideas. It also had to contend with the social democrats who had left the party to form the Social Democratic Party (SDP), meaning that challenges from left and right helped to define Kinnock's thoughts on ideology in the 1980s. In 1985, he declared that 'Democratic socialism is under attack from the right because it is socialism; from the ultra-left because it is democratic. That combined assault requires us to examine and re-examine truths which we have held to be self-evident, to look again at the variety and form of democratic socialism and our prescriptions for the future.'[9]

The broader parameters of the discussion about the nature of democratic socialism were reflected upon in the 1983 pamphlet *Labour's Choices*. This contained essays from the three candidates in the party's leadership election, and the left-winger Eric Heffer outlined here what democratic socialism had achieved by the early 1980s. It was 'of great importance', he said, 'that we explain what we mean by democratic socialism, particularly in the British context. Democratic socialists were responsible for the creation of the welfare state. They have, through Labour governments, pushed forward the frontiers of socialism, creating a number of important socialist outposts such as the National Health Service.' Listing other key aspects, including good living and working conditions, he concluded that democratic socialism 'stands for a fundamental change in society'.[10] He also noted the opportunities that were open for democratic socialism in Europe. These opportunities were greater than they had been for a long time, as some European communist parties were 'developing democratic socialist positions and moving away from Soviet concepts and distancing themselves from Soviet policy'. This opened up the possibility of a socialist Europe which rejected both the 'bureaucratic, totalitarian system of the Soviet Union and the unbridled "free" capitalist system of the USA'.[11] For Heffer's leadership opponent, Neil Kinnock, 'individual liberty and giving people greater control over their destiny' was a key part of democratic socialism, and 'individual freedom' was 'the objective past, present and future of democratic socialism'.[12] Both views highlight the debates that shaped the discussions within the Labour Party in the 1980s, and the direction in which Kinnock began to take the party after he became leader.

There were similarities between Labour and the CPSU as well, particularly where the role of the state was concerned. The two shared a similar outlook on the power of the state, basing their ideas on the economy and social relations on the belief that the central control of nationalised industries – either in part or total – was the best way to deliver the services that people used and needed. In May 1980, Labour adopted the policy document *Peace, Jobs, Freedom*, which talked about extending nationalisation, and a state-led approach still characterised much of Labour's thinking in this period. However, Labour had always accepted that the private sector had a role to play in the national economy, and even at the high point of Labour's nationalisation programme it believed in a mixed economy and a role for the individual. In the USSR, a much more extreme version of state ownership meant that Soviet citizens could not engage, legally at least, in activities that would allow them to show any individual creativity outside of official boundaries. But, despite their differences on this issue, both parties believed, one way or another, that the state should be there to look after the people from cradle to grave.

Labour and the CPSU also shared concerns about nuclear issues, but again the two parties took up different positions. Despite the continuing Cold War, Labour saw the threat of nuclear weapons and the destruction they could bring as greater than the one posed by the Kremlin. It was committed to unilateralism and had close links with the Campaign for Nuclear Disarmament (CND), and when Michael Foot went to Moscow in 1980 he explained to Leonid Brezhnev that the West's Cruise and Pershing missiles, and the Soviets' SS-20s, were a great problem for Labour. The USSR had retained a massive stockpile of nuclear weapons, amassed during the arms race with the USA, although the SALT I treaty had seen positive negotiations between the two sides help to reduce the numbers of weapons on both sides. However, the end of *détente*, after the Soviet invasion of Afghanistan and the election of Ronald Reagan in the US, created an environment in which the world would come the closest it had come to a nuclear conflict since the Cuban Missile Crisis in 1962. By 1983, the West appeared to be hardening its stance as Reagan pushed his Strategic Defence Initiative programme (popularly referred to as 'Star Wars') and labelled the USSR an 'Evil Empire'.[13] This was also the year when a Soviet Sukhoi SU-15 interceptor shot down Korean Airlines flight KAL 007 (killing all 269 on board) and when the NATO war game exercise, Operation Able Archer, appeared so real to the Kremlin that it feared the West was preparing a surprise first strike at Soviet positions in the East.

However, all this changed over the next few years. Mikhail Gorbachev identified nuclear war as one of the greatest threats to the world and took great steps to do something to reduce the possibility of a nuclear conflict. Prior to this, when Neil Kinnock visited the USSR in 1984, he discussed the issue with the CPSU General Secretary Konstantin Chernenko. Among those who accompanied Kinnock to Moscow were his Chief of Staff Charles Clarke, his press secretary Patricia Hewitt, and Labour's shadow foreign secretary Denis Healey who went with Foot three years earlier. Healey returned to the USSR in 1985 alongside George Robertson, Labour's frontbench spokesman on foreign affairs, to attend the Victory in Europe Day fortieth anniversary celebrations in Moscow.

Kinnock and his colleagues were greeted warmly when they met with the Soviets, and they were 'taken very seriously', according to Bowker and Shearman, as Labour was 'courted to a much greater degree than hitherto'.[14] The visit was covered in the main newspapers, and a photograph of Kinnock and Healey took centre stage on the front pages of *Pravda*, *Izvestiya* and *Trud*. The photo and article even relegated a similar story about Austria's Social Democratic Federal Chancellor Alfred Sinowatz ('Fred Zinovats'), who was also visiting Moscow at this time, to a lower place on the pages of these papers.[15] The newspapers carried articles that painted Labour–Soviet relations in a favourable light and, after the delegates returned, Lev Parshin in the Soviet Embassy in London sent Charles Clarke a press release which broadly reflected the content of the articles. It stated that the Politburo 'fully approved the results of the talks between Konstantin Chernenko and Neil Kinnock ... In so doing, it pointed out the considerable role played by the Labour Party in Britain's political life and the importance of contacts with the party for a positive development of Soviet–British relations.'[16]

The delegation sought to emphasise and explain 'as clearly as possible the current position of the Labour Party, in particular seeking to remove any preconceptions that the Soviets may have about our commitment to NATO, our preparedness to increase Spending etc.' and to 'get the earliest possible indication of any flexibility that there may be in the Soviet positions'. This flexibility could have been referring to ideology, as Kinnock and Healey held a string of meetings with Boris Ponomarev from the International Department, and on the back of the official agenda Kinnock wrote: 'Ponomarev visit of particular importance.' This was possibly because he was involved in determining the ideological direction of the CPSU, having been close to chief ideologist Mikhail Suslov, one of Gorbachev's patrons. Kinnock's notes show Gorbachev was already on Labour's radar, as comments include 'apparently Gorbachov [sic] is out of Moscow during this period' and that 'Gorbachev is the next most senior Party Secretary under Chernenko'. The delegation also scheduled a visit to the Institute of American Studies, where they would meet with Institute Head Georgy Arbatov. He was often involved in arms talks between the USSR and USA, and, more importantly here, he was influential in paving the way for Gorbachev's reforms and had 'generally been associated with the less dogmatic "moderate" line in Soviet affairs'.[17]

Healey also met with Vadim Zagladin, a key member of the CPSU's International Department and Ponomarev's deputy. Healey was deeply impressed with Zagladin and found him 'friendly, open and intelligent'.[18] It is clear that meeting with Zagladin at this time was important for the Labour delegation, as he was a worldly-wise politician who travelled abroad and was friends with Western European socialist leaders such as François Mitterrand and Willy Brandt. According to the briefing notes given to Kinnock before the meeting, Zagladin had a 'benign and scholarly manner'.[19] Perhaps more importantly, though, he was an important influence on Mikhail Gorbachev and played a key part in the *perestroika* process. Considering the kind of people Kinnock and other delegates either hoped to meet or did indeed spend time with while they were in Moscow, it is fair to say that identifying like-minded reformers with whom they could discuss ideological questions was a central part of what they wanted to achieve there.

Kinnock and Healey discussed a range of issues when they met with Chernenko. The agenda included defence, human rights, Labour's attitudes to the European peace movement and CPSU–Labour relations. Given that the Cold War was heating up again, it is not surprising that defence and nuclear weapons issues were important parts of the talks. A 'special emphasis' was given to 'considerations expressed by Konstantin Chernenko in connection with the Labour Party programme of defence and security issues', as this 'provides for building a defence system on a non-nuclear basis with the withdrawal of nuclear weapons of every type from Britain's territory'. It was declared that, should 'such a programme be implemented, the USSR would commit itself not to use nuclear weapons against Britain and would be ready to reduce and scrap such a part of its medium-range missiles in the European part of the USSR, that would correspond to the number of nuclear missiles scrapped by the British side'.[20]

Ronald Reagan's Star Wars programme was also covered. Chernenko told Kinnock that 'the problem of outer space is of paramount importance, it is one of the most urgent problems of our time'.[21] Gorbachev brought this up again when he met with Kinnock and other key Labour figures, including Healey, Robertson and Robin Cook, in London in December, noting that 'we attach great importance to the problem of the demilitarisation of outer space'. Gorbachev also mentioned that the Soviet position on unilateralism was clear. He said that 'we do not demand that Great Britain should unilaterally reduce its nuclear forces regardless of whether the Soviet Union will respond or not'.[22] Although Labour was still tied to the policy of unilateralism, the sentiment in this statement from the soon-to-be Soviet leader came to underpin Kinnock's future move away from his unilateralist stance. Over time, this allowed a convergence in foreign policy to develop. Bowker and Shearman note that 'if one compares the Labour's Party programme for the 1987 election, *Modern Britain in a Modern World*, with many of Gorbachev's speeches on foreign affairs, the two parties share a number of complementary policy goals'.[23] In some ways, these were a reaction to the ways in which Thatcherism and the New Right were reshaping the world.

New Right thinking and the left's response

The consolidation and growth of New Right politics laid the foundations of globalisation and encouraged both Labour and the CPSU to rethink their economic and ideological understanding of the world. For Kinnock, Thatcherism was one more factor which led to a wider questioning of the relevance of Labour's traditional class-orientated politics as it had been practised. Henry Pelling considered this in relation to the 'modern', more affluent, Wilson era, asking whether Labour's 'class basis' and 'close ties with the unions' made it 'obsolete in new Britain'.[24] This was as much an issue for Labour in the 1980s as it was the 1960s, although by then there were new concerns, as the former Labour MP Austen Mitchell points out. The political discussions were even more complex in the 1980s as Labour, which 'had grown up in a world of class blocs', had to cope with 'the new consumer democracy of a pluralistic society', and the '"us versus them" politics was less important than a plethora of 'single issues"'.[25] Kinnock acknowledged this as well as the consumerism of the new decade. In 1985 he wrote that Labour had to relate to and draw support from the modern working classes, which were both 'increasingly fragmentary' and enjoying 'upward social mobility, increased expectations and extended horizons'.[26]

Kinnock recognised that British society was changing, and the working class adopted a different outlook as Thatcherism continued to tear down some of the central features of social democracy that Labour had built since 1945. Thatcherism in Britain, and neo-liberalism globally, was winning the political and economic argument (even if it did so with a case built on spin, propaganda and personal debt which would cause great problems in the future) and the left had to respond in an equally radical way. Some continued to fight using the old ideological tools, some used those tools to analyse the problem in new ways and some, like Kinnock's Labour, looked at the consumerism of the new era and tried to adapt the party's principles accordingly. This was not so much an abandoning of Labour's central beliefs (although it appeared like that to some on the left) but, rather, an acceptance that times were changing and that Labour had to change too in order to survive. Class was still important, but so too was a sense of being affluent and able to join in with the growth of consumerism. New interests and new values rivalled the old ones, and Labour had to find a way to appeal to a new generation of (possible) Labour voters while holding on to the old (actual) party supporters. Socialism could not therefore be dropped, as that could alienate those who had struggled for it in the past, but it had to be redefined, arguably to make it relevant in a more materialistic age.

Mikhail Gorbachev had similar issues to deal with in the USSR. Soviet society had changed considerably from the way it was in the early Brezhnev years. It had become more highly educated and more consumer orientated by the early 1980s, but there were now growing problems where delivering people's rising expectations was concerned. There were not enough of the types of jobs that this more educated population expected, and the economy was slowing down, which made it difficult to keep up with society's needs. The drift towards crisis in the USSR demanded a radical response, and Gorbachev was the politician to consider this seriously. He was from a different generation of Soviet leaders, taking over from the seventy-three-year-old Chernenko when he was a comparatively young fifty-four, and had a more global outlook, having travelled widely before he took over in the Kremlin. He visited Britain (where he addressed Parliament in 1984), Canada, Italy and Czechoslovakia, and he was a great admirer of the Czechoslovakian reformist communist leader Alexander Dubček, so much so that in 1987, when asked what the difference was between *perestroika* and the 1968 Prague Spring, Soviet Foreign Ministry spokesman Gennady Gerasimov stated: 'Nineteen years'.[27] All of these experiences influenced his thinking and contributed to his reformist views.

Gorbachev's ascent to power was a turning point which facilitated a convergence of certain aspects of British and Soviet socialism, but in domestic politics where Kinnock was concerned, social issues and economic questions were driven by the new attitudes of the working class, which were, in the 1980s, partly a product of Thatcherism. The domestic challenges that Kinnock faced, together with the changes in the USSR appeared to heightened the need for change in the Labour Party.

This was not just true for Labour, though, as there was a serious difference of opinions in the communist movement as well, and this reflected the various strands of thought in the Kremlin. The Eurocommunists and the thinkers and writers in the *Marxism Today* group were examining different issues and exploring alternative ideas to those put forward by the (still pro-Soviet) *Morning Star* communists. The rebranding of *Marxism Today* made the break with the old *Morning Star* wing of British communism very clear, and this was partly based in what Charles Clarke calls *Marxism Today*'s promotion of 'diversity of thought'. In these new times, it 'resisted unequivocally the centralised and conservative thinking which had dominated much of the left both in the Communist Party, which was *Marxism Today*'s main concern, and in the wider labour movement, notably the trade unions and the Labour Party'. The 'most important target', according to Clarke, was the world communist movement, 'riven as it was between the "Eurocommunism" of Italy and Spain and the hard-line Soviet version which controlled Russia and eastern Europe until the rise of Mikhail Gorbachev and the collapse of the Soviet empire'.[28] These divisions were also noted by Mikhail Gorbachev's foreign policy advisor, Anatoly Chernyaev, from the CPSU's International Department, who said:

> The Eurocommunists have absolutely defeated the faithful, i.e. the people faithful to us. This is a demonstration of the fact that in countries like England there is no need for a Communist Party; the Communist Movement has become obsolete … They do not need us, the CPSU … They see in us neither a model, nor an example, ideal, brother, trusted friend, not even someone who would save them from a nuclear catastrophe. Alas! Many Communist Parties are on this path.[29]

There was an acceptance that things were changing in the socialist and communist worlds, and also that, as the New Right consolidated its power and position, a more nuanced understanding of society, politics and economics was needed. This certainly did not need to mean a rejection of socialism as a philosophy, but as Thatcher's time in office lengthened and as Thatcherism entrenched itself further, it became clear that, for Labour, a different approach to socialism was needed. As Martin Westlake notes, Kinnock and the Labour Party discovered that 'socialism was to prove a blunt and rusted weapon to wield against the dragon of Thatcherism, one which had the propensity to rebound upon the user, for as it was to evolve over the next thirteen years,

Thatcherism became much more than a sequence of policy changes. It became, rather, a systemic change which completely altered the basic framework of any political analysis.'[30]

Colin Leys suggests that this was especially relevant after the 1987 election defeat, with the advent of Kinnock's Policy Review. He notes that by this time 'what was at stake was how far the party should go in accepting the legacy of Thatcherism as a new "settlement", as the Conservatives had accepted that of 1945–51'.[31] Tudor Jones argues that the Policy Review formed a central part of the attempt to widen the party's appeal as it rejected polices recognised as being unpopular with voters – nationalisation, unilateralism and high taxation. It was 'prompted by the electoral success of Thatcherism and by its impact on British politics, evident both in its reshaping of the political agenda and in the institutional and political changes that it had brought about'.[32]

José Harris widens the debate by considering this within the context of the rise of New Labour and of the party's being out of power for a very long time, as the more elections Labour lost, the more time it had to plan changes, implement reforms and alter the party in such ways as to make it a remarkably different entity by the time Kinnock resigned as leader in 1992. Harris asked how far the intellectual roots of New Labour were a 'reflex to Thatcherism, the collapse of Soviet Communism and impatience with prolonged exclusion from office'.[33] However, as our concern is assessing the role of the Soviet Union in the changes that took place in the Labour Party during the 1980s, this question can be modified slightly to focus less on the *collapse* of Soviet communism and more on the changes that were taking place in the Soviet Union itself *during* this period. Considering these, together with the backdrop of Thatcherism, allows for a more complete understanding of the forces which contributed to Kinnock's *perestroika*.

1987 and beyond: new socialisms – affluent and humane

The convergence between Eastern and Western socialism gathered pace from 1987 onwards. It was in this year that Kinnock and Gorbachev turned their parties further towards the free market and accepted that market forces would need to be incorporated into their programmes in order for them to achieve their aims. Over the next few years, new strands of socialism emerged. Kinnock discussed affluent socialism and Gorbachev's ideas developed into Humane Democratic Socialism. These will be discussed so as to consider how two different socialist traditions drew closer as the forces of globalisation continued to grow. For Labour, the 1987 election defeat – its third successive loss to the Tories – forced it to rethink its ideological basis and the more modern society in which it was functioning. For the CPSU, the economic reforms that were central to Gorbachev's *perestroika* highlighted the USSR's turn towards the market.

In some ways, Kinnock's starting point was to consider how Labour should deal with the changing nature of its working-class support and the new desires of the wider population. The new consumerism of the 1980s raised important questions which needed urgent answers. It was at this time that the notion of affluent socialism was discussed by Kinnock, and he did so by raising a question asked by Ron Todd, the Transport and General Workers Union General Secretary. At the party's 1987 conference, Kinnock noted that Todd had asked what to say to a docker earning £400 a week with his own house, a new car, a microwave, video and 'a small place in Marbella'. The answer was not 'let me take you out of your misery, brother'. Kinnock said that Todd 'was not suggesting that we trail in the wake of something called popular capitalism – he was facing a fundamental question for our party with admirable candour that I would recommend universally. It is a question which we must all face if we are going to have an effective response to the changes taking place in our society.'[34] It was also 'not really a very new question', as Kinnock said that he had first faced it 'after the 1959 election'.[35]

The idea of affluent workers and their relationship with the Labour Party led Kinnock to consider what this meant for Labour both in electoral and in ideological terms, and affluent socialism become a more central part of the discussions. Kinnock argued that democratic socialism had to be 'as attractive, as beckoning and as useful to the relatively affluent and the relatively secure as it is to the less fortunate in our society who are frequently referred to … as our "natural vote"'.[36] He rejected the idea that there was 'collision between affluence and socialism', and recalled that he had been to see 'an old socialist in Tredegar, Oliver Jones', who said that there was no collision and that he had been 'striving for both all my life … The point is … that if socialism has got to wait for want, then socialism will wait for a very long time. And it will be right for socialism to wait for a very long time: because if it needs misery to give it a majority, God forbid we have the misery.'[37] The belief was that Labour could achieve power and could reconstruct society only when capitalism faltered had to end, not least because it was evident that this new strand of capitalism was not going to falter in the near future.

Kinnock had to adapt to the more consumer-orientated times of the 1980s, and the 1987 Policy Review was a central part of the process that saw Labour work out what to do next. It became clear that more market-based economics would need to play more of a role in Labour's thinking, although the details took time to be settled upon. Despite the obvious uneasy feelings that such an approach provoked, embracing a market philosophy was seen as a way to re-engage with the electorate and show voters that Labour once again had a credible economic vision. But this had to be done in a way that allowed the party to fulfil its core purpose. In 1988, Kinnock's Policy Review Group discussed 'our vision and our values as democratic socialists' and highlighted

Labour's 'belief in the potential and equal worth of individuals as well as the importance of strong communities and democracy'.[38]

By the late 1980s, democratic socialism meant 'the attainment and development of that balance of markets and non-market forces which pursues the objectives of greater material well-being, greater equality and greater choice'. It would build on the idea that the 'real choice is not between the unregulated market and the bureaucratic allocation of Soviet socialism – both are socially inefficient. Democratic socialists believe in the attainment and development of that balance of markets and non-market forces which pursues the objectives of greater material well-being, greater equality and greater choice'.[39] Kinnock expanded on this idea in his speech to Labour members in Blackpool after he won the leadership battle against Tony Benn in 1988.

He addressed the fact that some saw adopting a market approach as giving into individualism and competition, and that once words like these were used, alongside competitiveness, it was 'not long before we hear people in the movement saying that we are proposing "to run the capitalist economy better than the Tories"'. He said that, while 'the day may come when … this movement, is faced with a choice of socialist economies … until that day comes' and that choice is presented, 'the kind of economy that we will be faced with when we win the election will be a market economy. That is what we have to deal with and we will have to make it work better than the Tories do.' The market economy would continue to exist for some time, but Labour would use it differently and have different priorities, such as funding the National Health Service. But there was 'no "slide to the right" and 'no "concession to Thatcherism"'.[40]

Flexibility in the party's economic models became an important consideration. Kinnock believed that the 'attainment of social efficiency … demands a flexible approach to forms of social ownership, and to the balance of market and non-markets organisation', as one 'particular form and one particular balance will not be appropriate for all time'. Economic structures should be able to 'adapt to the changing needs of the economy and the community'.[41] How much state intervention was desirable in the operation of markets was raised by the Policy Review Group. Markets were accepted as 'an efficient means of guiding and restructuring production, and of enhancing the community of interest between producer and consumer. The market can be a powerful creative force, providing a competitive stimulus to innovation and to provision of variety and choice.' However, 'markets also impose very short-term pressures which result in the immediate waste or even destruction of resources and which seriously jeopardise long-run efficiency'. It was stated that 'we must use markets boldly, opening up new avenues of competition where the very high levels of concentration and market control prevalent in Britain are limiting consumer choice and product innovation. Equally, we must design more efficient means of decisive intervention in the market place.'[42] The type of mixed economy that Labour still believed in was being forced to change by events beyond its control, and it became clear that the market would be a more central part of Labour's economic programme.

The debates about what this turn to the market would mean continued long after Kinnock stopped being Labour leader, but it is clear that by the late 1980s many saw it as an important aspect of how Labour would approach economic questions. Eric Shaw notes that there was a 'fulsome approval for the market' by 1989, and Tudor Jones states that this 'unambiguous acknowledgment of the merits of a market economy' was 'unprecedented in the history of the Labour Party'.[43] Labour was not only dropping its commitment to renationalise old industries which had been privatised by the Tories, but also dropping its commitment to nationalisation as a whole. The economic changes fed into Kinnock's ideological reforms and they show how Labour began to understand and interpret the world in different ways, despite the fact that this meant it had to jettison what some regarded as the party's core beliefs.

A similar turn to the market was taking place at the same time in the USSR. Gorbachev found that a younger generation of Soviet citizens wanted more than just what the older generation had struggled for, and that their hopes went beyond achieving job security and subsidised housing, and the state defining their future. The consumerism of the Brezhnev years had raised expectations, but the economic problems associated with that era meant that a new approach was needed and Gorbachev thought about resolving the USSR's problems in different ways. The late Brezhnev era had seen an unofficial civil society take hold, with citizens organising political activity outside of the remits of the state. Gorbachev responded to this and identified various issues to focus on, largely based on universal 'common human values' and the interdependent nature of the world. It was 'based on a recognition of the diversity of interests and goals of the world's different societies and of the international community as a whole'.[44]

Gorbachev made his 'New Thinking' and the idea of a 'common European home' a central part of his foreign policy. This was his way of dealing with what he saw as two great global problems – the environment (in the post-Chernobyl/acid rain era) and the nuclear threat. For Gorbachev, these crossed class and national barriers and warranted a collective response. Where his domestic policies were concerned, Gorbachev was moving the USSR towards more openness (*glasnost'*) in society and was beginning to inject a market-based approach into the planned economy.

The introduction of a new Law on State Enterprise (1987) and Law on Co-operatives (1988) allowed for more freedom in the economy and a reduction in the role of the state. The first law ensured that as long as enterprises fulfilled state orders, they could dispose of the remaining output as they saw fit. Gorbachev even talked about economic independence and profit-and-loss accounting. The second law allowed for private ownership of enterprises, and individual ownership was now allowed as he encouraged different forms of ownership. Gorbachev was pursuing a social democratic line and introducing a mixed economy into Soviet life for the first time since the 1920s. He was also turning Soviet socialism towards the Western European strand. The changes that he introduced meant that, when *perestroika* ended, Gorbachev's 'political beliefs were closer to those of Eduard Bernstein … or of a German social democrat of more recent vintage, Willy Brandt, than to those of the founder of the Soviet state'.[45] For Archie Brown, the changes in the USSR turned Gorbachev into a social democrat.[46] For Mark Sandle, Gorbachev 'social-democratised Bolshevism' because the 'core values' of Humane Democratic Socialism 'were those of humanism, democracy and freedom, symbolizing the triumph of ethical socialism over its scientific predecessor'.[47]

It was here that the parties of the Western European left played an important part in Gorbachev's thinking, as his ideological reforms fundamentally altered the nature of Soviet socialism to the point that the CPSU began to look like the socialist parties on the other side of the Berlin Wall. These were, in some ways, his model for change. At a time when he was looking to widen democratic engagement in the Soviet Union, Gorbachev enthusiastically declared to a Politburo meeting in April 1988 that 120 million people in Western Europe voted for these parties. This also meant that their support for *perestroika* was an important part of the process.[48]

He certainly received support from Kinnock, who wrote the introduction to the 1988 book *Perestroika: Global Challenge, Our Common Future: A Statement by Mikhail Gorbachev*. The Labour leader wrote that he was 'not surprised by the direction' that Gorbachev wanted to pursue, but 'the pace and the audacity with which he has moved … has been unexpected'. Kinnock was fulsome in his praise for the Soviet leader's 'ability' and his 'capacity to employ a breadth of vision and ambition'[49] was not to be doubted. He also highlighted the possibilities which *perestroika* opened up between East and West, which included 'co-operation rather than confrontation' and 'for welfare rather than warfare'.[50] And when Kinnock met with Gorbachev in London a year later, he congratulated the Soviet leader on *perestroika*, which he called 'an immense tribute' to Gorbachev's socialism and to his imagination. The two leaders had 'a very constructive and friendly meeting' where they discussed a range of issues including the nuclear question, and Gorbachev 'touched upon some ideological points', making it 'very clear that he considered that the right for people to make real choices was basic to his view of socialism in all of its applications'.[51]

The importance of giving people choice was not only a consideration of Gorbachev's. As Labour's Policy Review came to an end, *Meet the Challenge, Make the Change* declared that the 'true purpose of socialism is the creation of a genuinely free society in which a more equal distribution of power and wealth extends the rights and choices of the whole community. That society offers more than the chance to take better advantage of traditional liberties.'[52] Choice and the new role of the individual was a central part of Kinnock's Labour Party as both took on a new meaning in Thatcher's Britain. Kinnock recognised this and sought to reconcile it with his views on democratic socialism, just as Gorbachev was also moving his party further away from the state-led approach to socialism. Labour's affluent socialism may have been a little less pronounced than Gorbachev's Humane Democratic Socialism, but it was no less important, as it laid the foundations for the even greater changes made to the party's ideas by Tony Blair in the 1990s.

The course on which Gorbachev set the CPSU strengthened the hand of the reformers inside the Labour Party, as the Soviet Union's political system 'appeared to have a distinctly "westernized" look'.[53] His fundamental restructuring of Soviet socialism allowed Kinnock to identify with Gorbachev in a way that no other Labour leader had ever been able to identify with a Soviet leader, and this encouraged the reformers to continue along their chosen path. After all, if the General Secretary of the CPSU's reinterpretation of socialism could follow a more social democratic line and establish a mixed economy, then the Labour Party – which was already on this path – could further open itself up to new ways of thinking. This facilitated the convergence of ideas between the Western European and Moscow routes to socialism, and was a powerful driving force in Neil Kinnock's *perestroika* of the Labour Party.

Conclusion

Neil Kinnock had to deal with numerous pressures and almost irresistible forces in the 1980s, and these contributed to his reforms. The new socio-economic and political realities of the decade meant that change was necessary, and Thatcherism and globalisation encouraged Labour to rethink its understanding of socialism. Kinnock was aided in this process by the reformist mood evident in Mikhail Gorbachev's CPSU. As the USSR turned towards the free market, Kinnock's Labour also embraced market-based ideas more than ever, and both parties wrestled with ways to reconcile the role of the state and the role of the individual in the modern world.

Kinnock's changes coincided with Gorbachev's reforms, and the reconstruction of both leaders' ideological frameworks allowed for a convergence of socialist ideas. This in turn created an environment where the Second and Third Internationals could come together in Moscow in a new spirit of comradeship. Of course, the troubled relationship of the past would take time to get over, but the reforms introduced by Kinnock and Gorbachev, in different ways, helped to initiate a new understanding on the left. This contributed to a realignment of Europe's reformist, ethical socialists – like those in the Labour Party – and the Moscow school of socialism, and the convergence of these two strands of socialism, given time, could have developed a coherent challenge to globalisation. That they did not have the time meant that this was a great missed opportunity for the left. The collapse of communism halted this realignment, and it became more difficult to convince people that they should turn to socialism just as millions across Eastern Europe were overthrowing the Kremlin-backed dictatorships which had posed as socialism for more than forty years.

The fall of the Berlin Wall and the collapse of the Soviet Union were greeted by many on the left as a new start for socialism, as they believed that it would be more popular now that it was free from any Stalinist connotations. However, this momentous change instead appeared to discredit the old ideology even more in the minds of many. The general mood seemed to be defined by an implied question: 'why vote for socialism when half a continent is rejecting it?' This facilitated the reformers' rush to embrace the market even further and the post-communist socialist movement became something very different to what it was before 1989, being more concerned with the consumer society and market economics. While social justice and social democracy were not jettisoned completely, they had to sit alongside the pursuit of profit, which became a more central part of the Labour project than it had ever been. But the end of Soviet socialism and Labour's turn towards the individual and the market were consequences of the *perestroika* process of both Kinnock and Gorbachev and, more than a quarter of a century on, the left is still coming to terms with the legacies of both.

Notes

1 See Jonathan Davis 'Labour's Political Thought: The Soviet Influence in the Interwar Years', in Paul Corthorn and Jonathan Davis (eds), *The Labour Party and the Wider World: Domestic Politics, Internationalism and Foreign Policy* (London: I. B. Tauris, 2008); Jonathan Davis, 'An Outsider Looks In: Walter Citrine's First Visit to the Soviet Union, 1925', *Revolutionary Russia* 26 (2013), 147–63; Darren Lilleker, *Against the Cold War: The History and Political Traditions of Pro-Sovietism in the British Labour Party, 1945–89* (London: I. B. Tauris, 2004); Andrew Williams, *Labour and Russia: The Attitude of the Labour Party to the USSR, 1924–1934* (Manchester: Manchester University Press, 1989).
2 Alex Pravda and Peter Duncan (eds), *Soviet–British Relations since the 1970s* (Cambridge: Cambridge University Press, 1990), p. 235.
3 Kinnock Papers, KNNK 10/1/7 (File 1) Churchill Archives Centre, Churchill College.
4 KNNK 10/1/7 (File 1), Ben Pimlott, correspondence with Mike Gapes, 8 June 1989.
5 Aleksandr Veber, 'Perestroika and International Social Democracy', in *Breakthrough To Freedom. Perestroika: A Critical Analysis* (Moscow: R. Valent, 2009), p. 100.
6 Mark Sandle, *A Short History of Soviet Socialism* (London: UCL Press, 1999), p. 418.
7 Archie Brown, 'Gorbachev, Lenin, and the Break with Leninism', *Demokratizatsiya* 15 (2007), 236. Mark Sandle elaborates on this in Sandle, 'The Final Word: The

Draft Party Programme of July/August 1991', *Europe–Asia Studies* 48 (1996), 1131–50.
8 Veber, 'Perestroika and International Social Democracy', p. 99.
9 Neil Kinnock, *The Future of Socialism* (London: Fabian Society, 1985), p. 9, http://lib-161.lse.ac.uk/archives/fabian_tracts/509.pdf.
10 Roy Hattersley, Eric Heffer, Neil Kinnock and Peter Shore, *Labour's Choices* (London: Fabian Society, 1983), p. 7, http://digital.library.lse.ac.uk/objects/lse:qav749qag/read/single#page/1/mode/2up.
11 Hattersley et al., *Labour's Choices*, p. 7.
12 Kinnock, *The Future of Socialism*, p. 3.
13 Ronald Reagan, speech to the National Association of Evangelicals, 8 March 1983, http://voicesofdemocracy.umd.edu/reagan-evil-empire-speech-text/.
14 Mike Bowker and Peter Shearman, 'The Soviet Union and the Left in Britain', in Alex Pravda and Peter Duncan, *Soviet–British Relations since the 1970s* (Cambridge: Cambridge University Press, 1990), pp. 147–67, p. 151.
15 See 'Priyem K. U. Chernenko N. Kinnoka', in *Pravda*, *Izvestiya* and *Trud*, 27 November 1984, p. 1.
16 Press Release from Novosti News Agency, KNNK 10/1/7 (File 2).
17 KNNK 19/2/10.
18 Bowker and Shearman, 'The Soviet Union and the Left in Britain', p. 151.
19 KNNK, 19/2/10.
20 KNNK 10/1/7 (File 2), Neil Kinnock meeting with Konstantin Chernenko, 27 November 1984.
21 KNNK 10/1/7 (File 3), Neil Kinnock meeting with Konstantin Chernenko, 27 November 1984.
22 KNNK 10/1/7 (File 2), Neil Kinnock meeting with Mikhail Gorbachev, 19 December 1984.
23 Bowker and Shearman, 'The Soviet Union and the Left in Britain', p. 152.
24 Henry Pelling, *A Short History of the Labour Party* (Basingstoke: Palgrave Macmillan, 1982), p. 120.
25 Austen Mitchell, 'The Old Right', in Matt Beech, Kevin Hickson and Raymond Plant (eds), *The Struggle for Labour's Soul: Understanding Labour's Political Thought* (London: Routledge, 2004), pp. 261–7, p. 265. Mitchell includes in these 'single issues' feminism, unilateralism, ethnicity and greenism.
26 Kinnock, *The Future of Socialism*, p. 2.
27 Cited in Raymond L. Gartoff, *The Great Transition: American–Soviet Relations and the End of the Cold War* (Washington D.C.: The Brookings Institute, 1994), p. 575.
28 Charles Clarke, 'Learning the Lessons of Marxism Today', 20 December 2011, www.ippr.org/juncture/learning-the-lessons-of-marxism-today.
29 Anatoly Chernyaev, *The Diary of Anatoly S. Chernyaev* (Washington, D.C.: National Security Archive, 2006), p. 54 [22 May 1985], http://www2.gwu.edu/~nsarchiv/NSAEBB/NSAEBB192/Chernyaev_Diary_translation_1985.pdf.
30 Martin Westlake, *Kinnock: The Authorised Biography* (London: Little, Brown, 2001), p. 131.
31 Colin Leys, 'The British Labour Party's Transition from Socialism to Capitalism', *Socialist Register* 32 (1996), 1–26.
32 Tudor Jones, *Remaking the Labour Party: From Gaitskell to Blair* (London: Routledge, 1996), p. 120.
33 José Harris, 'Labour's Political and Social Thought', in Duncan Tanner, Pat Thane and Nick Tiratsoo (eds), *Labour's First Century* (Cambridge: Cambridge University Press, 2000), pp. 8–45, p. 38.

34 Neil Kinnock, *Thorns and Roses: Speeches 1983–1991*, ed. Peter Kellner (London: Hutchinson, 1992), p. 130.
35 Kinnock, *Thorns and Roses*, p. 132.
36 Kinnock, *Thorns and Roses*, p. 132.
37 Kinnock, *Thorns and Roses*, p. 132.
38 KNNK 2/2/14, Policy Review Group meeting 16 November 1988, p. 1.
39 Kinnock, *Thorns and Roses*, p. 5.
40 Neil Kinnock, 'Leader's Speech', Blackpool, 1988, www.britishpoliticalspeech.org/speech-archive.htm?speech=194.
41 KNNK 2/2/14, Kinnock, 'Socialism and Production', p. 5.
42 KNNK 2/2/14, Policy Review Group meeting, pp. 4–5.
43 Eric Shaw, *The Labour Party since 1979: Crisis and Transformation* (London: Routledge, 1994), p. 86; Jones, *Remaking the Labour Party*, p. 153.
44 W. Smirnov, cited in Sandle, *Short History*, p. 383.
45 Sandle, *Short History*, p. 237.
46 Archie Brown, 'Did Gorbachev as General Secretary Become a Social Democrat?', *Europe–Asia Studies* 65 (2013), 198–220.
47 Sandle, *Short History*, p. 418.
48 Brown, 'Gorbachev, Lenin', p. 242.
49 Neil Kinnock, 'Introduction', in Mikhail Gorbachev, *Perestroika: Global Challenge, Our Common Future*, edited by Ken Coates (Nottingham: Spokesman, 1988), pp. 7–13, p. 8.
50 Kinnock, 'Introduction', p. 12.
51 Neil Kinnock meeting with Mikhail Gorbachev, 6 April 1989, KNNK 10/1/7 (File 1).
52 Labour Party, *Meet the Challenge, Make the Change: A New Agenda for Britain: Final Report of Labour's Policy Review for the 1990s* (London: Labour Party, 1989), p. 55.
53 Sandle, *Short History*, p. 379.

6

The international context: end of an era

John Callaghan

Introduction

The main purpose of this chapter is to establish how certain international developments of the 1980s were interpreted by the British left as they were happening. Towards the end of the chapter I will also establish what is considered to be of lasting significance in these developments today, at the time of writing. A general ideological retreat of the left could not have been forecast in the 1970s. There was evidence of mounting problems for the social democratic parties, but there were also signs of ideological renewal and more radical ambitions than had characterised the 1950s and 1960s in many countries. The evidence was contradictory, but persuasive interpretations of the political scene included those that focused on the unfolding crisis of liberal capitalism, sometimes theorised as a fiscal crisis of the state or a crisis of 'overload', 'ungovernability' and legitimation.[1]

The turn to more radical versions of social democracy occurred as the order based on Bretton Woods and the Keynesian welfare state began to break down. In Britain the socialist Alternative Economic Strategy (AES) dominated Labour Party economic thinking in the decade after 1973. In France there was the Union of the Left of 1972, bringing the socialists and communists together behind a Common Programme. In Portugal there were revolutionary events in 1974–75, when the authoritarian Estada Novo regime was overthrown and the left – much of it Marxist – emerged as the strongest political tendency in the country. In Spain, as another dictatorial system began to disintegrate, signs of socialist renewal were visible, especially after the death of General Franco in 1975.[2] In Greece the rise of the Pan-Hellenic Socialist Movement (PASOK) after the collapse of the military junta in 1974 was a feature of another southern

European country in transition to democracy in the second half of the decade. Even in established social democratic strongholds there was an appetite for radical change within the left. In Sweden the turn towards stronger measures promoting economic equality, such as the Meidner Plan, can be traced to the late 1960s, but it also lay behind a raft of social legislation produced in the first half of the 1970s. In West Germany the Social Democratic Party (SPD) government embarked upon a wide range of reforms in education, health and social policy in the early 1970s which greatly expanded the welfare state. Yet the party membership remained well to the left of its leaders at the decade's close.

Reasons for optimism on the left were not confined to social democracy. The big communist parties of Italy, France and Spain seemed to be emerging from aspects of the hidebound thinking which had prevented them from taking liberal democracy seriously. 'Eurocommunism' was the term coined to convey this apparent evolution, with the Communist Party of Italy (PCI) leading the way in both innovative thinking and practical politics – its share of the vote in national elections rising to 34.4 per cent in 1976. Communist parties, however, had long since lost their monopoly of Marxism and revolutionary thought in Western countries. New radical thinking on the left, associated with the so-called 'new social movements', had appeared in the 1960s and was expected to revitalise the old left and possibly produce a new socialist synthesis informed by feminism, ecology, direct democracy and identity politics. Capitalism was very much under scrutiny again and the left was also trying to find answers to the problems posed by stagflation, unemployment, poverty and inequality in an age of multinational corporations operating beyond the Keynesian controls adopted in the 1950s by social democrats and their mainstream rivals. In addition, avowedly Marxist regimes were on the increase in Asia, Africa and Latin America, and the Cold War view of the world depicted by the propaganda of Washington DC since 1946–47 was under increasing attack in the wake of the Vietnam War.

Long-term electoral trends showed that socialist parties had established themselves as the main government party in a majority of fifteen western European states by the mid-1970s, producing 54 per cent of cabinet ministers in the period 1945–75, on the strength of an average of no more than 31 per cent of the vote.[3] However, since the mid-1970s the socialist position had been eroded, partly because of declining electoral support and defeat in general elections (as in Sweden 1976, Britain 1979, Norway 1981) but also because the parties concerned sometimes refused to join coalitions, as in both Sweden and Norway. There was evidence that social democratic parties moving to the left could find themselves isolated, like the Dutch Labour Party (PvdA), or confined to opposition, like the British Labour Party (1979) and the Belgian Socialists (since 1981). In West Germany, only Helmut Schmidt's prestige kept the SPD in coalition with the Free Democratic Party; much of the SPD was demanding left-wing policies which the Free Democrats would not accept, and it was widely predicted at the start of the 1980s that the Christian Democrats under Helmut Kohl would be the beneficiaries of this growing alienation. In October 1982 Kohl became Chancellor, and he held that position for the next sixteen years. There was also a long history of right-wing splits from socialist parties moving to the left, as had happened in Britain when the Social Democratic Party (SDP) was formed in March 1981 by a handful of former Labour Party leaders and MPs, but here the evidence was not encouraging for the right. Splitters calling themselves 'social democrats' had not thrived in Italy or Japan in the 1950s, or in Australia, France (1972–78), Luxemburg (1974) and Denmark (1973).[4] It was the British general election of 1983 which demonstrated the damage caused to Labour by the formation of the SDP. The splitters took 11.5 per cent of the vote and made a major contribution to dividing the opposition to Prime Minister Margaret Thatcher, returning a Conservative government with a massive 144-seat majority on just 42.4 per cent of the vote.

Fading alternatives

The left's prospects at the start of the 1980s were as difficult to interpret as those of the previous decade; by 1990, after years of domination by Thatcher, Kohl and President Ronald Reagan, the picture was much clearer. There was evidence of left-wing strength and vitality in the early 1980s and contemporary events suggested that voters were not automatically lost when parties advanced stronger left-wing policies to deal with national problems. In May 1981 François Mitterand became the first socialist to be elected president of France, after campaigning on the *110 Propositions For France*, the programme of the Socialist Party, variously calling for the creation of public sector jobs, a wide-ranging policy of public ownership, workers' control, a 35-hour working week and measures of decentralisation to the regions. A landslide victory for the Socialist Party followed in the legislative elections, producing the first-ever socialist majority in the Fifth Republic and a reforming government, with four communists included at cabinet level, which proceeded to nationalise banks, insurance and defence companies and to implement many other aspects of the left's Common Programme.

In October of the same year PASOK (the Panhellenic Socialist Movement) won a landslide majority in Greece, forming the first socialist government in that country since 1924. The rhetoric of its leader, Andreas Papandreou, suggested that PASOK was just as radical as the French Socialists. A year later, in October 1982, the Socialist Party (PSOE) in Spain formed its first government since the civil war. The question in Spain was about the survival of democracy and whether a democratically elected government would be allowed to remain in office, not whether socialist reforms were on the immediate agenda. Even so, the PSOE leader, Felipe Gonzalez, who had been unable to obtain a formal repudiation of the party's Marxist programme without a protracted fight (up to 1979), had to be content with a large internal faction continuing to reject the party's alleged 'modernisation' under his leadership.[5]

In short, it was possible to survey the European left at the end of 1981 and perceive 'a period of strength' and even 'a high point for European labour' in terms of electoral results and government office since the late 1960s for Austria, France, Italy, West Germany and even Britain (in respect of years in government). In most of Europe this relative political success was accompanied by a decline in the confessional vote, a vote which generally favoured the right, and an increase in trade unionisation up to the end of the 1970s, which was associated with stronger left parties. The same period, roughly since 1965, witnessed the most rapid expansion of social services and social security in the history of capitalism. None of this meant that the prospects for socialism were good; if anything, it was a reminder that the labour movement in the past had nearly always been a minority affair, isolated from large sections of the working class as well as governmental power.[6] What the British called the 'crisis of the post-war consensus', soon to become evidence of the corresponding crisis of social democracy, could be interpreted at the beginning of the 1980s as one of the reasons for the period of relative labour strength since the late 1960s. This is because the turn to the left, the growth in trade union membership and the increased social democratic participation in government of these years might be perceived as related to the end of the long post-war economic boom and the onset of capitalist economic crisis, visible since the early 1970s. Labour movements grew in organisational strength and in a number of countries (Britain, Sweden, France, Greece) adopted demands for more radical measures for the redistribution of wealth and a degree of democracy in industry.[7]

But, as the economic crisis stretched out over the rest of the 1980s these elements of apparent strength for the left were surpassed by indicators of growing weakness such as chronic mass unemployment, which began to undermine trade union power and promote divisions within the working class. In the longer term the economic crisis could be seen as evidence of 'a geological shift ... in the historical geography of capitalism', evidence of restructuring to the detriment of Western Europe and parts of North America and to the benefit of the Pacific Rim and Asia. Observers also noted that if the crisis was one of welfare capitalism, welfare appeared to be far more endangered than capitalism. The success of the attack on welfare in the 1980s, it could be argued, was ultimately connected to the vivid failure of actually existing socialism – symbolised by the inability of the communist regimes to feed themselves, as signified by their dependence on food imports from North America. Already by 1981 there was a sense that capitalist logic was the only form of economic reason available in practical politics.[8]

Evidence of capitalist crisis abounded, but so too did evidence that the left could not take advantage of it. While the 'international monetary and credit system [was] walking along the precipice of a major collapse', the left could only look on. The 'extreme case of Britain' was only 'a more dramatic version of the troubled state of the left elsewhere' and it showed already in 1982, according to Eric Hobsbawm, Britain's most illustrious Marxist historian, that the Labour Party was so 'disrupted, demoralised and defensive' that most of its members had written off the chance of effectively opposing Thatcher.[9] The Keynesian and communist alternatives – so powerful from the 1930s to the 1960s – now held little or no promise in Hobsbawm's view.

The Labour Government in Britain had already accepted this verdict in 1976 when, on discovering that it was not possible to spend its way out of a recession, to paraphrase the Prime Minister, James Callaghan, it implemented austerity measures and borrowed from the International Monetary Fund (IMF). The turn away from Keynesian priorities of full employment was also signalled in the USA in October 1979 when the chairman of the Federal Reserve Bank, Paul Volker, 'engineered a draconian shift in US monetary policy' that focused on the suppression of inflation, whatever the consequences for unemployment rates.[10] The welfare state was transformed in public rhetoric from a capitalist asset, supporting Keynesian macro-economic management, to an insatiable cost and liability, at first in Britain and the USA but later even in social democratic Sweden.[11]

Britain was ahead of the curve because, along with the USA, it had been among the first countries to be hit by the rapid decay of old industries, combined with rising unemployment and faster inflation of prices. There were already signs of other weaknesses too, as Hobsbawm pointed out in his Marx Memorial Lecture in London in 1978. The presumed 'forward march' of labour had arguably ceased in the UK since as far back as the late 1940s, when measured against important criteria.[12] The old blue-collar industrial working class had been shrinking as a proportion of the work-force in all the advanced capitalist economies during the post-war period. The class and occupational structure had changed radically, becoming more fragmented and more feminised, but not more trade unionised or more inclined to support Labour or a rival to its left. In some countries, the USA and Britain in particular, there was talk of 'de-industrialisation' before the 1970s came to an end. Changes to the class and occupational structure were possibly connected to evidence that class identity was of diminishing importance in voting behaviour.[13] Certainly the ties that bound the manual working class to the left parties were weakening even as that class diminished in size. The return of mass unemployment had not favoured and would not automatically favour the left.[14]

The Reagan approach

In the USA, the New Deal coalition forged by Roosevelt was in an advanced stage of decomposition and Ronald Reagan's success in the presidential election in November 1980 was secured with an agenda sufficiently similar to Thatcher's that this was noted by observers. 'Reaganomics' in practice cemented the alliance as trade unions were weakened or destroyed, real wages stagnated or fell for most workers and the wealthiest benefited from deregulation and tax cuts. But the Republican Party had been making great incursions into the white working-class vote for some time and Republican dominance of the White House mattered in Western Europe because of the importance of the USA in the global political economy. A new right-wing alliance had taken shape since the failed campaign of Barry Goldwater in 1964. Foregrounded in Republican rhetoric in the late 1970s was the need to restore American power in the world.

The domestic foundations of such power were to rest on the reduction of welfare dependency, cuts in direct taxes and the removal of other obstructions to free enterprise such as trade unions. Yet Reagan's victory drew on support across the class and ethnic map of the USA. Only black Americans and, to a lesser extent, Hispanics rejected him emphatically. Reagan's winning formula was based on his ability to attract interest groups with overlapping concerns comprising themes of anti-statism, nationalism and the concerns of the 'moral majority'. 'Big government' was blamed for stagflation, the stifling of enterprise and the encouragement of welfare dependency (and evils which the right associated with it, such as the decay of family values and the growth of crime). Reagan's success in making these equations and attributing responsibility to 'liberal' (left) ideology echoed Thatcher's a year earlier. It also revealed the parlous condition of the Democrats' mass organisations, his rivals' 'lack of programmatic and ideological vision' and their internal divisions.[15] Already the suggestion was that these problems of the American left were of a secular rather than episodic character, connected to the social and economic restructuring that heralded post-industrialism and the fragmentation of contemporary society.[16]

The Soviet invasion of Afghanistan in December 1979 assisted Reagan's campaign for the presidency and provided an additional platform for a Reagan–Thatcher alliance once he was elected. The *détente* of the early 1970s had been in decay since the middle of the decade, but after the invasion of Afghanistan the tone of East–West polemics, the emphasis on military matters (such as NATO's siting of Pershing and Cruise missiles in Western Europe, in response to Soviet upgrades of intermediate-range missiles) and the polarisation of opinion suggested a return to the Cold War.[17] This was the context in which the Campaign for Nuclear Disarmament (CND) was revitalised and European Nuclear Disarmament was launched in April 1980 to campaign for a nuclear-free Europe. Alarm was fuelled not merely by the revival of familiar Cold War rhetoric and a new generation of nuclear weapons but by talk of 'limited nuclear war' – the 'Schlesinger doctrine' – emanating from NATO and Washington DC. This helps to explain why West German peace activism took on the dimensions of a mass movement in the early 1980s, focusing its oppositional energies on the NATO decisions. West Germany was one of the anticipated 'theatres' in which limited nuclear war would take place and from which Pershing and Cruise missiles would seek to prevail against Soviet SS-20s; the West German left noticed the assumption and reacted with some anger. Socialists nevertheless could also recognise that the hopes placed in *détente* in the early 1970s had been dashed by Soviet decision making as well as by the imperatives of American domestic politics.[18] Expressions of dissent continued to be suppressed in the Communist bloc, contrary to the promise of *détente*, while Soviet investment in weapons, Moscow's military support for insurgencies overseas and the decision to invade Afghanistan confirmed the sceptics in their belief that the USSR understood only force or the threat of force.

It was a feature of the early Reagan years that the USA was prepared to use force or support force against its ideological opponents overseas, thus underlining the West European left's perceptions of US foreign policy as a support for reactionaries. Fears of military confrontation had already been stoked in the late 1970s by the Carter administration, in its support for the neutron bomb (presented by the media as lethal to people but kind to property) and its decision to deploy intermediate nuclear forces in Europe. In December 1979 the Thatcher government decided to buy Trident missiles from the USA, while NATO resolved to deploy Cruise and Pershing missiles in Europe. Soviet and Cuban interventions in Africa (Angola and Ethiopia) formed a sinister pattern for some observers, and when Soviet troops invaded Afghanistan in late December 1979 they concluded that one of the overall aims was Soviet domination of the Persian Gulf.

The sense of crisis was heightened by the hostage stand-off in revolutionary Iran which began when the American embassy in Teheran was occupied in November 1979 by followers of the Ayatollah Khomeini. Vietnam, Iran and Afghanistan were all of a piece, according to Reagan, as evidence of the USA's failure to lead the 'free world' by standing up to its enemies. The incoming administration thus increased US defence spending, while some of its members talked openly about prevailing in nuclear war, and the President announced, in March 1983, that the USA itself could be protected from missile attack by a protective shield.[19] Protests on the streets against the perceived bellicosity of the Reagan administration increased in Britain, West Germany, Belgium, Holland, Denmark, Sweden and Norway – the so-called 'Arch of Angst'.[20]

This is the context in which the British Labour Party was led by a founder-member of CND in 1980–83, Michael Foot (and another staunch supporter of CND, Foot's successor, Neil Kinnock). Labour remained committed as a party to unilateral nuclear disarmament and the removal of all US nuclear bases from Britain until 1989, by which time Gorbachev's policies had virtually ended the Cold War.[21] Labour was not alone in taking fright at American foreign policy – the governments of Denmark and Norway considered declaring a Nordic nuclear-free zone and the Reagan administration's support for low-intensity warfare against the Soviet Union in Afghanistan was publicly supported in Europe only by the Thatcher government. Reagan's support for the Contras against the Sandinista government in Nicaragua and US diplomatic and military aid interventions in the civil wars in Angola and Cambodia generated little public enthusiasm. The American invasion of Grenada – a member of the British Commonwealth – in the autumn of 1983 provoked criticism even from the Thatcher government, despite US support for the Conservatives' own war with Argentina over the Falklands in 1982.

The example of France

The progress of the first majority socialist government in France inevitably produced lessons for the left in Britain. It was proof, according to one prominent commentator, that 'far-reaching political changes were possible'.[22] One year into the experiment it was clear that France was polarised: the right had been mobilised against the government and the left was deeply divided, despite the participation of both major parties in the coalition. Only a 'façade of governmental solidarity' concealed the divergences that officially ended left unity in 1978.[23] A radical programme of economic and social reform had been implemented, although without popular mobilisation and on the basis of a legislative majority elected by only one third of the voters. The government contained Marxists, but also anti-Marxists like Michel Rocard, Minister of the Plan, and influential moderates such as Jacques Delors, Minister of the Economy. Together they had boosted domestic demand, increased aid to small and medium-sized firms, reduced unemployment and the length of the working day, lowered the retirement age and created a large programme of professional training for young workers. They had also gone ahead with extensive nationalisations of finance and manufacturing and higher rates of taxation on wealth, business and higher-income groups. Yet industrial unrest was on the increase and opponents of the reforms were far more active than supporters in organising their side of the argument. The decline of the Communist Party (PCF) since 1970 showed no signs of slowing down. The fortunes of the French left were in the hands of social democrats. After just twelve months of socialist government there was already evidence of an investment strike.[24] By March 1982 the government began to retreat and by December 1983 definite signs of fatigue in the left project were visible.

The right had seized the initiative in cantonal and municipal elections in 1982, making use of law and order and immigration issues to feed its vision of France on the brink of economic and moral disaster at the hands of the left. Worse was to come. The Front National entered a united right coalition for the second ballot of a by-election in the town of Dreux in September 1983 – a major breakthrough for this neo-fascist force which was already making inroads in the erstwhile red suburbs of Paris. A divided and shrunken left could only look on, such was the apathy on the streets. The dominant intellectual discourses, despite the socialist government, flirted with Reaganomics and equated socialism with totalitarianism, while sound economics and the open society were paired with the theories of Milton Friedman and Friedrich von Hayek. The French left had discovered the Gulag in the 1970s and the PCF further obliged its opponents after 1978 by abandoning the Eurocommunist rapprochement with liberal democracy, disapproving Polish Solidarity and turning back to an uncritical defence of the Soviet Union and it actions (such as the invasion of Afghanistan). Marxism in France was in clear retreat, while xenophobia and racism were becoming commonplace.[25] The victory of the socialists in 1981 proved only to be a temporary detour in this political trajectory.

In the course of 1983–84 the government's U-turn covered every area of policy. Reducing inflation became the most important economic objective, while major concessions were made to the opposition's demands for stronger immigration controls. British observers were clear, however, that the 'crisis' of the French left was not to be explained in terms of the politics of the last few years but, rather, with reference to the 'long-term process of social and ideological change' affecting the country.[26] The by now familiar ingredients of this process were said to include changes in the economic and class structure of France, involving the growth of the tertiary sector and the decline of both blue-collar manufacturing and the relative weight of agriculture. This fundamental restructuring was said to be 'reflected in the trade union and political spheres' – in the events of 1968, the recent electoral success of the Socialist Party, the initial rise of the CFDT (French Democratic Confederation of Labour) as a competitor to the Communist-led CGT (General Confederation of Labour) and the subsequent loss of membership in both trade union federations. The new social strata that supplied the personnel of the new social movements in 1968 and after were only temporarily aligned with the left, according to this argument. What were permanent among them were values of individualism and anti-statism – values which the New Right could champion effectively, all the more so in the context of the recent 'discovery' among French intellectuals that socialism led to totalitarianism.[27]

The U-turn of the Socialist government, it was argued, also demonstrated the power of the objective constraints on the relatively open French economy – notably a world economy hostile to socialist priorities. Internally, the government provoked the ire of farmers, doctors, lawyers, lorry-drivers, Catholics, the police and most of the mass media. The right sought to mobilise these different interests under the banner of neo-liberalism and a harder line on law and order and immigration – echoes of the 'free economy, strong state' formula that had proved efficacious in Britain for Margaret Thatcher.[28] A mass radical right had emerged and its appearance signalled more than the short-term problems of 1981–86, according to British commentators.[29] It was the 'direct result of the ideological earthquake' shaking French politics since the 1970s. Socialism had ceased to be a viable alternative. Governments, it was now fashionable to believe, could make only a small difference when confronted by the realities of power in contemporary society. This was said to be the meaning of the Socialists' U-turn.

The Communist Party's steep decline – by 1986 down to its lowest share of the vote for fifty years (at 9.8 per cent) – reflected a broader revulsion from Stalinism and was even more marked among the young (and students in particular). The rising forces promised markets, privatisation and deregulation combined with tougher constraints on trade unions, anti-social elements and immigrants. The French Socialists had entered office with old ideas worked out in the 1960s, innocent of modern business and its requirements yet assuming an environment of economic growth congenial for their reform programme. Instead they got inflation, a balance of payments deficit, an investment strike and a weakening franc. The Socialist government began by wanting to control the economy and ended with the roles reversed, the evidence of its failures contained in the electoral setbacks of 1982, 1983, 1984 and 1986.[30]

European co-operation

By the end of March 1986, the debit side of the left balance sheet included the defeat of the French Socialists and the formation of a right-wing government under Jacques Chirac. Reagan had been resoundingly re-elected in 1984 and Helmut Kohl was as comfortably ensconced in government in West Germany as Thatcher was in Britain. The socialist governments in Spain and Greece offered little consolation. The Spanish Socialists (PSOE) in office made a virtue of pragmatism and moderation, justifying their policies in terms of the country's necessary modernisation via integration into the European Economic Community (EEC) and NATO. They had no use for socialist economic policies and there was no sign of a mass movement in support of them.[31] PASOK was re-elected in Greece with 45.8 per cent of the vote in 1985. It continued to talk against NATO and the EEC but there was no sign of any action being taken against either, and this was true of the other prominent demands of its nominally radical programme. In practice it was dominated by its charismatic leader and was bereft of ideological and organisational roots in the Greek population.

It was widely accepted by socialists that the working class was shrinking in size in all West European economies and that a general convergence was taking place in their economic and social structures. Their national economies were increasingly woven together and all were affected by the decline of heavy industry, the growth of unemployment and curtailment of public spending. Old assumptions about the efficacy of the nation-state as the vehicle for social reform and economic management were subject to questioning. Though the term 'globalisation' was still confined to business literature and entered popular usage only ten years later, people on the left were already saying farewell to the nation-state.

Peter Glotz, secretary-general of the West German Social Democratic Party (SPD), told the *New Statesman* in 1985 that 'Social democracy and democratic socialism can *only* be achieved today as European concepts; in national terms these ideals become more illusory and hopeless every day ... an effective economic policy for democratic socialism is now scarcely possible within the empty vessel of the nation-state'.[32] Donald Sassoon thought that it was one of the New Right's ideological achievements that it was able to critique statism, deregulate the economy so that the citizens and their state were left at the mercy of international capital and yet promote itself as the defender of the nation.[33] This verbal conjuring trick was something that the populist and radical right was perhaps beginning to see through, as was obvious in France with the rise of the Front National and similar divisions in the right in other parts of Western Europe.

But Sassoon identified three trends on the left which responded to this problem differently, although they were perfectly capable of cohabiting within the same parties: 'Europeanist', 'centrist' and 'traditionalist'. The 'Europeanist' trend – strong in the SPD and PCI – recognised both the crisis of a particular structure of capitalism and a crisis of socialism and looked to the EEC for answers to both. The centrists – strong among Spanish and Italian socialists – had concluded that the crisis of socialism was irreversible and accepted most of the neo-liberal alternative and the idea that the best antidote to 'overloaded' government was to reduce the demands placed upon it. The future, according to the centrists, entailed reorganising Europe around an American model of political economy. Among those who denied this, Sassoon identified 'traditionalists', comprised of those who admitted that the left was in crisis but who blamed social democracy and called for new issues to be integrated into working-class politics operating within national parameters.[34]

Sassoon clearly favoured the Europeanist approach and he took this to entail recognition of the need for supranational power in order to control transnational economic processes. The supranational power had to have popular legitimacy, and already socialist Europeanists in the SPD, PCI and French Socialist Party were calling for political union of the EEC. On this basis they could imagine a European industrial policy, monetary union and a trade policy that could face the challenge of the USA and Japan. But it was not clear how political union could be achieved on the basis of popular consent. In fact, of course, European integration took a huge step forward with the signing of the Single European Act in February 1986, the first major revision to the Treaty of Rome since 1957. It envisaged the creation of a single market by 1992. But this step was determined by political elites working in close alliance with big business. Their intention was to strengthen capitalism. The drive for further integration successfully fused the priorities of British neo-liberals with those of continental enthusiasts for federalism, and those who believed that nation-states were increasingly defunct as agencies of domestic economic management.

British Labour's interest in all of this was stimulated only when Jacques Delors, President of the European Commission, set out his vision of social reform at the 1988 Trades Union Congress, apparently demonstrating that preparations for the single market included commitments to enhanced workers' rights. Unlike Thatcher, Delors realised that if most of the remaining work to remove barriers to trade involved non-tariff issues such as different national standards, there was an opportunity to raise standards for citizens and workers rather than allow market forces to promote 'a race to the bottom'. Workers' rights in Britain had been degraded by the Thatcher governments, many of whose supporters were already voicing fears about a 'creeping federalism' at Brussels that threatened to undo their work in the manner Delors favoured.

Labour's fleeting conversion to a pro-European stance took place in this context. For Labour, the prospect of placing Britain 'at the heart of Europe' promised, by the end of the 1980s, to raise standards in Britain across a range of industrial relations and social policy issues. But this proved to be a brief and unstable opportunism and from the mid-1990s, under Tony Blair's leadership, the rhetoric of getting closer to Europe had to be made compatible with preservation of what New Labour had come to believe was the comparative economic advantage of the UK bequeathed by the Thatcher reforms – a relatively low-paid and flexible work-force and a relatively deregulated business environment in which financial institutions were particularly dynamic and in tune with the realities of globalisation. This Blairite modification was always sensitive to the growth of popular 'Euroscepticism' in Britain, which increased as the process of European integration accelerated after the passage of the Maastricht Treaty.[35] As always, domestic and national foreign policy considerations informed the stance of parties, and these changed over time as they chased the votes that mattered – the ones cast in national elections.

Success and failure of neo-liberalism

The Lawson Boom in Britain in the second half of the 1980s may have reinforced the sense – at least for many – that Thatcher's reform programme, although painful, was beginning to work. The collapse of the communist regimes of Eastern Europe during 1989 provided evidence that a viable systemic alternative to capitalism did not exist. There was also evidence that capitalism was the truly radical force in the world. The consumer experienced this creative dynamism partly in the flow of new commodities – such as personal computers, video recording, gaming, compact discs, cellular phones and other gadgets – together with rising house prices and expanding areas of commodification, like health, sport, expanding retail chains and shopping centres. The 'business knows best' philosophy preached by the Thatcher Government was given expression in diverse ways such as the cult of business studies, business schools and the MBA; the uncritical admiration expressed for Japan and the Asian Tiger economies of Singapore, Hong Kong, South Korea and Taiwan; and the increasing reliance of mass media, like the BBC, on agencies with a vested interest in the economic practices they were asked to comment on, such as the firms that operated in the City of London. The deregulatory dynamic affecting finance spread quickly after the 'Big Bang' measures taken to liberalise the City by the Thatcher government in October 1986, and it would not be long before this sector was celebrated as a triumph of globalisation.

But many of the problems which brought Thatcher to power were still present, not only in Britain. The Lawson Boom was no sooner named than it had to be restrained by British membership of the European Exchange Rate Mechanism in October 1990, as inflation surged towards 10 per cent and the rate of unemployment began to grow again.[36] In reality, the 1980s continued the trend of the 1970s, signalling the end of the era of strong economic growth, low rates of inflation and full employment of the post-war boom years and the decay of the party systems and corporatist arrangements that had dominated the first twenty-five years after the Second World War.[37] The claim that the social democratic movement was especially suited to the macro-economic management tasks of welfare state capitalism had of course dissolved in the course of the same decades as policies prioritising the battle against inflation and promoting the revival of market dynamism came to the fore.

During the Reagan presidency, the World Bank and IMF became proselytisers for neo-liberalism across the globe, imposing 'structural adjustment programmes' which traded immediate debt relief for domestic reforms, forcing debtor countries to adopt the ruling neo-liberalism.[38] The same institutions, according to observers, were 'pivotal in squeezing Communism and collectivism out of the world economy in the 1980s'.[39] In the liberal democracies capital controls had been reduced from the 1970s onwards as offshore markets grew rapidly free from state regulation.[40] The USA, Britain, Canada, the Netherlands, Japan, Germany and Switzerland had all taken this path by 1979. The process deepened and spread in the 1980s. 'Most of the major markets were completely unfettered by capital controls by the early 1990s.'[41] The impetus was competitive and political as well as technological. Transnational capital flows rapidly increased in the 1980s both as foreign direct investment and as portfolio investment. National deposit banks began to operate internationally and became heavily involved in financial speculation. New financial instruments were invented to deal with volatility in exchange rates and interest rates. Futures markets expanded in value from about $220 million in 1975 to $440 billion in 1986.[42] But, by the end of the 1980s, it was far from clear that these measures could be accounted a success in stimulating economic growth. One authority concluded in 1990 that in respect of the 'eleven years of the Thatcher experiment' there was no ambiguity of verdict:

> All the signs point in the same direction: the experiment ended in almost unmitigated failure. By the end of the period, in 1990, Britain had the highest rate of inflation among advanced economies, though the curbing of inflation had been the Government's declared priority number one. It had, correspondingly, the highest interest rates; and it also had high and rising unemployment; large-scale bankruptcies of firms in all sectors of the economy, falling output and declining national income; and the largest deficit on the current balance of payment in history. Over the period as a whole, despite the [North Sea] oil, Britain had, unbelievably, a slower rate of growth than in comparable periods before.[43]

But this poor record served to underline the failure of the Labour Party to find a popular alternative policy, and this was an aspect of a bigger failure of socialists right across Europe. Instruments of economic policy associated with national macro-economic management such as monetary and fiscal aggregates could be undermined by global capital, as the French Socialists discovered in the early 1980s. Mitterand had entered government at a time of international deflationary pressures, chronic deficits on current account, currency speculation, financial disorder and capital flight.[44]

The end of the communist states in Eastern Europe also seemed to many to signal the defeat of the socialist project in another way. The spread of capitalism across the former Soviet empire proceeded apace with little sign that anything was to be retained from the old collectivism. The rapid pace of change was not confined to the communist bloc. The decline of old industries in the liberal democracies accelerated during the 1980s as economies became more open, international competition intensified, governments deregulated financial sectors, employers sought more flexible ways to manage, trade unions diminished in size and influence, unemployment increased and governments in most liberal democracies cut the top rates of income tax. Some socialists in Britain by the end of the 1980s theorised these and other changes as a transition from Fordism, amounting to an 'epochal shift' characterised by fundamental changes in the structures of industry, class and occupation.[45] In political terms they added up to a shift in the balance of power towards global capital, against states and national labour movements, promoting social fragmentation and an undermining of class solidarity.

Conclusion

From the perspective of 2014, the process underway in the 1980s, and begun at the end of the 1960s, has been called the 'dissolution of the regime of postwar capitalism'.[46] It showed a similar pattern across the advanced capitalist countries, but the USA was where the various trends originated – 'the ending of the Bretton Woods system and of inflation, the growth of budget deficits as a result of tax resistance and tax cuts, the rise of debt-financing of government activity, the wave of fiscal consolidations in the 1990s, finance market deregulation as part of a policy of privatising government functions and of course the financial and fiscal crisis of 2008'.[47] States did not become less important after waves of privatisation and deregulation but, as the British case vividly showed, were active instruments in the promotion of the new dispensation in restoring the power of markets. Governments sought to depoliticise all those areas that the state had encroached upon to make the Keynesian welfare state work. The politically regulated Keynesian welfare state was supposed to have been crisis free. It was tolerated, even celebrated, for as long as this seemed to be true. Once that illusion was exposed, as it was in the 1970s and 1980s, the main components of the post-war settlement were jettisoned – including the maintenance of full employment, public ownership, universal welfare and social policies, redistributive taxation, tripartite consultations, strong trade unions and collective bargaining. Democratic pressure on government expenditures was curtailed by such methods and although economic inequality grew rapidly, those opposed to it were able to offer only feeble resistance, the more so as social democratic parties failed to find a compelling alternative to the regnant neo-liberalism. Voter turnout fell in almost all liberal democracies in the 1980s, especially within the lower-income groups, suggesting rising levels of resignation and alienation from mainstream parties. The contradictions between capitalism and democracy observed in the 1930s were back in force and democracy was once again the loser.[48]

Notes

1 James O'Connor, *The Fiscal Crisis of the State* (New York: St. Martin's Press, 1973); Jürgen Habermas, *Legitimation Crisis* (London: Beacon Press, 1975); Anthony King (ed.), *Why Is Britain Becoming Harder to Govern?* (London: BBC, 1976); Claus Offe, *Contradictions of the Welfare State* (Cambridge, MA: MIT Press, 1984).
2 Paul Kennedy, *The Spanish Socialist Party and the Modernisation of Spain* (Manchester: Manchester University Press, 2013), pp. 23–4.
3 The states are Iceland, Ireland, Britain, France, Italy, West Germany, Switzerland, Austria, Luxemburg, Belgium, Norway, Sweden, Holland, Denmark and Finland.
4 'Europe's Socialists Are Losing Their Taste for Power', *Economist*, 7 August, 1982, pp. 39–40; 'Social Democracy Doesn't Thrive Abroad', *Economist*, 28 March, 1981, p. 26.
5 Kennedy, *The Spanish Socialist Party*, pp. 23–9.
6 Goran Therborn, 'Prospects for the European Left', *Marxism Today*, November 1981, p. 23.
7 Andrew Glyn (ed.), *Social Democracy in Neo-Liberal Times: The Left and Economic Policy Since 1980* (Oxford: Oxford University Press: 2001), pp. 6–7.
8 Therborn, 'Prospects', p. 23. The planned socialist alternative was subject to influential critiques from across the political spectrum in a succession of books published

around this time. I have in mind Friedrich A. Hayek, *The Constitution of Liberty* (Chicago: University of Chicago Press, 1978) and Alec Nove, *The Economics of Feasible Socialism* (London: George Allen and Unwin, 1983); André Gorz, *Farewell to the Working Class* (London: Pluto Press, 1982); Rudolf Bahro, *Socialism and Survival* (London: Heretic Books, 1982); André Gorz, *Ecology as Politics* (London: Pluto Press, 1987).

9 Eric Hobsbawm, 'The State of the Left in Western Europe', *Marxism Today*, October 1982, p. 9.
10 David Harvey, *A Brief History of Neoliberalism* (Oxford: Oxford University Press, 2005), p. 23.
11 Jenny Anderson, *Between Growth and Security: Swedish Social Democracy from a Strong Society to a Third Way* (Manchester: Manchester University Press, 2006), pp. 1–3.
12 Eric Hobsbawm, *The Forward March of Labour Halted?* (London: Verso, 1981), pp. 1–19.
13 Ivor Crewe, Bo Sarlvik et al., *Decade of Dealignment: The Conservative Victory of 1979 and Electoral Trends in the 1970s* (Cambridge: Cambridge University Press, 1983).
14 Hobsbawm, 'State of the Left', p. 14.
15 David Plotke, 'Reagan: Is It as Bad as It Sounds?', *Marxism Today*, February 1981, p. 8.
16 Plotke, 'Reagan: Is It as Bad as It Sounds?', p. 9.
17 See Fred Halliday, *The Making of the Second Cold War* (London: Verso, 1983).
18 Dan Smith, 'Goodbye to Détente?', *Marxism Today*, February 1981, pp. 22–4.
19 Geir Lundestad, *The United States and Western Europe since 1945* (London: Oxford University Press, 2003), pp. 211–12.
20 Lundestad, *The United States and Western Europe Since 1945*, p. 212.
21 John Callaghan, *The Labour Party and Foreign Policy: A History* (London: Routledge, 2007), pp. 282–3.
22 Eric Hobsbawm, 'The State of the Left', p. 8.
23 Keith Dixon and Daniel Perraud, 'The French Experiment', *Marxism Today*, May 1982, p. 15.
24 Dixon and Perraud, 'The French Experiment', p. 29.
25 Keith Dixon and Daniel Perraud, 'France's Resurgent Right', *Marxism Today*, December 1983, pp. 16–21.
26 Keith Dixon and Daniel Perraud, 'Le Fin: France Abandons Socialism', *Marxism Today*, January 1985, p. 24.
27 Dixon and Perraud, 'Le Fin', p. 25.
28 Andrew Gamble coined this phrase as a summary of Thatcherite policy in Andrew Gamble, *The Free Economy and Strong State* (London: Macmillan, 1988).
29 Keith Dixon and Daniel Perraud, 'The French Paradox: France after the Election', *Marxism Today*, May 1986, p. 17.
30 Denis McShane, *French Lessons for Labour* (London: Fabian Society Tract 512, 1986), pp. 22–4.
31 Kennedy, *The Spanish Socialists*, p. 54.
32 Peter Glotz, 'Europe – The Helpless and the Silent Continent', *New Statesman*, 20–27 December 1985, pp. 30–2.
33 Donald Sassoon, 'Europe's Left: A New Continental Blend', *Marxism Today*, May 1986, pp. 22–4.
34 Sassoon, 'Europe's Left', p. 24.
35 Paul Taggart, 'A Touchstone of Dissent: Euroscepticism in Contemporary Western European Party Systems', *European Journal of Political Research* 33 (1998), 363–88.
36 By John Smith in the House of Commons in 1990.
37 John Callaghan, *The Retreat of Social Democracy* (Manchester: Manchester University Press, 2000), pp. 26–53.

38 See Michel Chossudovsky, *The Globalisation of Poverty: Impacts of IMF and World Bank Reforms* (London: Zed Books, 1997).
39 Robert Skidelsky, *The World after Communism: A Polemic for Our Times* (London: Macmillan, 1995), pp. 169–70. Skidelsky is here citing Jeffrey Sachs, *Understanding Shock Therapy* (London: Social Market Foundation, 1994).
40 Beth Simmons, 'The Internationalisation of Capital', in Herbert Kitschelt et al. (eds), *Continuity and Change in Contemporary Capitalism* (London: Cambridge University Press, 1999), pp. 36–69, pp. 40–1.
41 Simmons, 'The Internationalisation of Capital', p. 41.
42 Simmons, 'The Internationalisation of Capital', p. 55.
43 Sidney Pollard, *The Development of the British Economy, 1914–1990* (London: Edward Arnold, 4th edn, 1992), p. 379.
44 Serge Halimi, 'Less Exceptionalism than Meets the Eye', in Anthony Dayley (ed.), *The Mitterand Era: Policy Alternatives and Political Mobilisation in France* (London: Macmillan, 1996), pp. 83–96.
45 Communist Party of Great Britain, *Manifesto for New Times* (London: Communist Party of Great Britain, 1989), pp. 6–7.
46 Wolfgang Streeck, *Buying Time: The Delayed Crisis of Democratic Capitalism* (London: Verso, 2014), p. ix.
47 Streeck, *Buying Time*, p. xii.
48 See, for example, Harold Laski, *Democracy in Crisis* (London: Allen and Unwin, 1933).

PART III
Currents of the wider left

7

Militant's laboratory: Liverpool City Council's struggle with the Thatcher Government

Neil Pye

The rise and fall of the Militant Tendency (also known as the Revolutionary Socialist League; RSL) in Liverpool, where its members took over the local party machinery and dominated the running of the City Council, proved to be a watershed for Labour and the left in the 1980s. Peter Taaffe and Tony Mulhearn, two leading figures of Militant, wrote in their book, *Liverpool: A City That Dared to Fight*, that Merseyside was used as a laboratory in which to test Militant's ideas and their opponents.[1] The experiment was conducted against a backdrop of central government cuts to local government spending. Two major struggles between the Militant-led, Labour-run Liverpool City Council and Margaret Thatcher's Conservative Government not only resulted in chaos and turmoil but also called into question the purpose and existence of the Labour Party, damaging its reputation and harming its fortunes in the 1987 general election.

The historiography of Militant's experiment in Trotskyite socialism can be divided into three strands. The first of these celebrates its achievements and has been written by the main protagonists of the hard-left organisation, which include Peter Taaffe, the editor of the *Militant* newspaper, and Derek Hatton and Tony Mulhearn, who were councillors directly involved in Liverpool City Council's struggle with the Thatcher Government. The successes that they identified were 'no redundancies', the creation of '2,000 jobs', the building of '4,000 council houses with front and back gardens, sports centres and even a park', along with the humbling of the Thatcher Government.[2] Although many houses were built and jobs were created, a key problem was the way in which those policies were delivered, bringing Militant into disrepute with both the Thatcher Government and the Labour Party.

In opposition to those celebratory views, the second strand comes from the staunch critics of Militant and what it stood for. During the mid-1980s, the journalist Michael Crick was attacked by the hard left for exposing Militant as 'a party within a party'.³ Furthermore, the Liverpool Labour Party politician Peter Kilfoyle has argued that Militant's sole intention was to 'eat away' at the party from the inside, 'taking away members and funding'. He added that 'they did it successfully'.⁴ A recent book by Labour's former director of organisation, Baroness Joyce Gould (nicknamed the 'Witchfinder General' by Militant after she purged its supporters from the party), and a re-issued publication of John Golding, document the intense struggle that the Labour Party faced in cleansing the far-left entryist organisation from its ranks.⁵

The third strand comprises sociological, economic and political interpretations which have sympathised with the Labour-run council on the grounds that Liverpool was dealt a bad hand by unfavourable conditions. One of the most comprehensive studies of the rate-capping rebellion was produced in 1985 by Professor Michael Parkinson, now executive director of the Heseltine Institute and then an academic in urban studies. Parkinson's study, in part, blamed Liberal administrations since 1974 for the city's plight. While Parkinson's analysis is quite strong and detailed, the book ends just as the fall-out of the rate-capping rebellion was about to start, especially within the Labour Party.⁶

There are also some studies which place the blame for Liverpool's problems in other quarters without really questioning the policies and motives of the Militant Tendency. Diane Frost and Peter North's *Militant Liverpool*, published to mark the thirtieth anniversary of the Labour group's taking control of the council, and based on oral testimonies, mainly argues that Merseyside's plight was caused by policies of the Thatcher Government which showed very little sympathy towards the city region's circumstances.⁷ Brian Marren also adopted this line of argument in a chapter about Militant in his book on working-class resistance, again largely based on oral testimonies. In a 'history from below', he charts the responses of Liverpool's working classes to redundancies, factory closures and government cuts and offers a critique of Thatcherism, neo-liberal policy and globalisation.⁸

Both Marren's study and Frost and North's book overlook the wealth of government documents, released under the thirty-year rule (now twenty years), that cast light on critical mistakes made by Militant and the Labour group in the running of Liverpool City Council. Both studies also appear to be one sided, as they largely ignore Conservative Party opinion and the difficulties which the Thatcher administration encountered in its policy towards Liverpool. Many of the problems which Merseyside faced during 1980s pre-dated Margaret Thatcher's election as Prime Minister in 1979. At the same time that Militant used Liverpool as a laboratory for its experiment in socialism, the Thatcher Government was using Britain to experiment with its own brand of monetarist economics. Thus a battle of ideas ensued over how jobs and prosperity could be created.⁹

The rise of Militant in Liverpool

Militant asserted that its socialist experiment raised the political consciousness of the working class in Liverpool. Yet, even before the hard-left organisation came to dominate Liverpool City Council from May 1983, there was a strong political awareness among its population. Militant tapped into this and successfully mobilised support as it tried to turn the Labour Party into an 'explicitly mass socialist party'.[10] According to the journalist Liam Fogarty, this mobilisation was able to occur because Liverpool in the early 1980s was 'a city on the verge of a nervous breakdown'.[11]

The main activity of the Merseyside economy revolved around its port, which by the 1980s was run down and had systemic problems. When Britain joined the European Economic Community (EEC) in 1973, trade moved away from Merseyside, to ports on the opposite side of the United Kingdom. Further, containerisation and the reluctance of Merseyside's labour force to embrace new technology meant that cargo was switched to ports such as Southampton.[12] What followed was a gradual exodus of port-related businesses from the region, resulting in unemployment.[13]

Linked to this was the gradual disappearance of Liverpool's manufacturing base throughout the 1970s. A process of deindustrialisation was in motion. Restrictions on public expenditure imposed by the Wilson and Callaghan governments led to 'disinvestment' and Liverpool came to be known as a 'service city', with an economy based on banking and insurance as well as its port.[14] Margaret Thatcher's Conservative Government, elected in May 1979, emphasised the free market and private enterprise. As a result of Thatcher's monetarist experiment between 1979 and 1984, over 50 per cent of Merseyside's manufacturing jobs were lost and Liverpool became known as the 'Bermuda Triangle of British Capitalism'.[15] One of the most devastating blows was the closure of the Tate and Lyle sugar refinery in March 1981.[16]

During the 1970s, the EEC recognised Merseyside as one of the worst areas for unemployment across the entire community. The region had a reputation for militancy and poor industrial relations among its workforce, and this dissuaded many firms from setting up businesses there. In an analysis of all stoppages and the ratio of workdays lost from 1968 to 1973, Merseyside was almost three and a half times as bad as other regions across the United Kingdom as a whole. It also had a very poor reputation for absenteeism and low production, as was highlighted by the inefficient operation of the British Leyland plant at Speke, where 50 per cent more manpower was needed to produce a given number of vehicles in comparison to an average plant.[17]

Alongside economic factors, Merseyside had deep-seated social problems, including some of the worst housing conditions in Europe. During the post-war era both Labour and Conservative governments invested in the construction of high-rise, high-density blocks of flats and system-built housing estates.[18]

The *Militant* newspaper described one of those estates at Cantril Farm, Knowsley as being 'planned by someone in the middle of a nervous breakdown'.[19] As the 1980s dawned, such was the paucity of Liverpool's housing stock, especially in the inner city, that major problems with overcrowding, slums and waiting lists surfaced.[20] This had contributed to an exodus of roughly 80,000 people from the city between 1973 and 1978.[21]

Another social problem that Militant targeted was education. A declining birth rate and low pupil numbers resulted in over-capacity in Merseyside's schools. At the same time, problems within the education system across Merseyside gave rise to episodes of strong community backlash, such as the 1982 Croxteth Comprehensive School lock-in.[22] There were also long-term structural issues, in so far as both schools and businesses were failing to address skills shortages in the local economy which went hand in hand with problems of both cyclical and youth unemployment. As firms such as Lucas and Spillers made workers redundant, youth apprenticeships became scarce. The lack of opportunities gave rise to criminal activity.[23]

Throughout the 1970s, Liverpool's inner city had one of the worst crime rates in Britain. A representative from the Confederation of British Industry (CBI) warned Prime Minister James Callaghan that the crisis affecting Merseyside would become 'a law and order problem'.[24] By the early 1980s that prophecy became a reality. Alongside mass unemployment, poor housing and social conditions, racial tensions caused social unrest.[25] The black community complained about a lack of racial justice in housing and under-representation among Liverpool City Council's work-force, as blacks occupied less than 1 per cent of posts in council services.[26] Grievances were raised about the heavy-handed approach of Merseyside police toward ethnic communities. As a result, tensions boiled over, culminating with the Toxteth Riots during the summer of 1981.[27]

In the wake of those disturbances, Margaret Thatcher's Government appeared to show very little sympathy towards Liverpool. Sir Geoffrey Howe, then Chancellor of the Exchequer, wanted the city to be left in a state of 'managed decline'.[28] However, Michael Heseltine, then Secretary of State for the Environment, was given a mandate by Margaret Thatcher to turn Liverpool's fortunes around. This led to the creation of joint public and private sector initiatives such as the Merseyside Task Force, the Albert Dock regeneration scheme, Wavertree Technology Park and the International Garden Festival, most of which created a lasting legacy in the city.[29] Previously, Heseltine had visited Liverpool and gauged from people's opinions that there was no leadership in the city, and nobody putting forward solutions to long-standing problems.[30]

This political void was filled by the Militant Tendency, which, from the mid-1960s onward, had built up a power base in the city. The emergence of Militant was largely due to the decline of sectarianism in Liverpool. An exodus of people from the city due to poor housing, unemployment and social conditions had weakened traditional allegiances to political bosses and the membership of local political parties.[31] During the early 1970s, the Scotland Road area of the city was still seen as 'a sectarian fault-line'. On one side of this line Labour-voting Catholics were situated in areas located towards the River Mersey, and on the other side people mainly of a Protestant and Unionist persuasion were generally based in the Anfield and Everton districts.[32] Further, rather than being a broad church, the Liverpool District Labour Party was highly selective about who could join its ranks. As people left the city and the influence of political bosses waned, apathy set in. With only a small number of people occupying the local party structures, a vacuum emerged which Militant's members willingly filled.[33]

The rise of Militant represented the Liverpool trait of struggle.[34] Historians such as John Belchem and Sam Davies have pointed to Liverpool's radical traditions and its 'exceptionalism' as an Irish city based on the British mainland, with a distinct cultural identity and labour relations. Belchem has argued that socialism arrived in Liverpool during the 1910s and peaked during the 1980s.[35]

Militant's origins date back to 1938 and a meeting of local Liverpudlian radicals Jimmy Deane and Tommy Birchall with Ted Grant, who, according to Peter Taaffe and Tony Mulhearn, was 'the theoretician and principal leader of Trotskyism in Britain'.[36] That same year the RSL was created, and for over two decades the RSL developed a Trotskyite power base in the city's Walton constituency. This was based on appealing to youth and impressionable young workers through its newspapers, *Rally* and *Socialist Fight*.[37]

In 1964 the *Militant* newspaper first appeared. The title *Militant* came about at an RSL conference held inside a pub at Kennington, South London. Initially, the twenty-five members present wanted to call the newspaper *Spark*, *Forward* or *Vanguard*, while Ted Grant wanted to continue with the name *Socialist Fight*, but that idea was dismissed. In the end, delegates settled on the name *The Militant*, which had been the title of the Trotskyite American Socialist Workers Party journal since 1928.[38]

Ideologically, Militant stood for democratic centralism (as opposed to democratic socialism), which was rejected by the Labour Party when its constitution was adopted in 1918, along with the notion of being a 'vanguard party'.[39] Militant also encouraged 'entryism', which was a tactic commonly associated with Leon Trotsky during the 1930s. After his involvement with Lenin during in the 1917 Russian Revolution, Trotsky urged people to abandon communist parties and join mass democratic parties.[40] Militant used Trotsky's writings as an ideological foundation as it attempted to radicalise, subvert and transform the Labour Party by developing a revolutionary consciousness within its ranks.[41]

In Liverpool, Militant's ascent was gradual. During the first decade, 1964–74, the far-left organisation canvassed the support of 'Trade Unions', the 'Labour Party', 'youth' and 'shop-stewards committees' on factory shop floors and in staff canteens.[42] In the main, Militant's growth on Merseyside was aided by two factors. First, a decision taken at the 1973 Labour Party annual conference to abandon the Proscribed List, which was a register that ensured extremist groups with radical hard-left leanings could not infiltrate and pursue their own agendas within the party. The naive abandonment of this list enabled Militant to exert influence at both constituency party and annual conference levels.[43] Second, when Labour lost control of Liverpool City Council in 1973 as the result of a dispute about rent increases following the introduction of the 1972 Housing Finance Act, Militant exploited major splits within the Liverpool District Labour Party (DLP).[44]

Following the 1978 local council elections, Eddie Roderick, who was 'neither right or left', launched a coup attempt to remove John Hamilton as leader of the Labour group. Although Hamilton was sacked and later reinstated, the failed coup divided the Labour group.[45] It was during this period that Militant hijacked the DLP. Derek Hatton, who later served as deputy leader of the Liverpool City Council, said that once Militant controlled the DLP, it 'controlled the machine'.[46] Orchestrated from its headquarters in London, the Militant-led Labour Party in Liverpool broke existing national party rules and standing orders, as political meetings were decided by aggregate voting and policies were formulated in small caucuses.[47]

Another key factor in Militant's ascendancy was the 1978–79 'Winter of Discontent' and the election of Margaret Thatcher as Conservative Prime Minister in May 1979. Thatcher's beliefs in the free market, privatisation and 'rolling back the state' were the absolute antithesis of everything that Militant stood for, which included public ownership, the living wage, a 35-hour working week and the defence of all public services from cuts and job losses.[48] From the moment that Thatcher was elected, a struggle was signalled. Immediately after the May 1979 local elections, which resulted in a hung council, Militant's members organised a coup inside the Labour group. Deputy leader Eddie Roderick and party chief whip Bill Snell were sacked and the group was split between 'moderates versus left-wingers'.[49] In December 1979, Militant, seen as 'young, unsmiling radicals ... but not infiltrators', attacked moderate Labour Party MPs, whom it labelled as 'Tories' who had 'masqueraded as socialists' and were 'content in finding careers within the party'.[50]

Both Derek Hatton and Tony Mulhearn, Labour Party members dating back to the 1960s and 1970s, joined Militant because successive governments, including Labour administrations, had done very little to stem the tide of industrial and social decline which affected the Merseyside region. They had become tired of the apathy and the lack of drive among local politicians to tackle high unemployment and poor housing.[51] By consistently homing in on those issues, Militant gained traction among the Liverpool electorate.

At the same time that Militant was manoeuvring to take control of Liverpool City Council, in December 1981 Labour Party leader Michael Foot moved against the hard-left organisation, which he later described as a 'pestilential nuisance'.[52] Through its National Executive Committee (NEC) the Labour leadership instructed general secretary Ron Hayward and national agent David Hughes to 'provide a report on the activities of the Militant Tendency'.[53] This investigation found that Militant possessed 'a hard core of supporters who had formed an organisation with its own programme and policy for distinctive and separate propaganda ... deemed outside the structure of the Labour Party and its Annual Conference'.[54] Following the publication of Hayward/Hughes report in August 1982, and legal battles, the Labour Party expelled five members of *Militant*'s editorial board in October 1983, including Peter Taaffe and Ted Grant.[55] The expulsions set the tone for future conflict between Labour and Militant.

The high tide of Liverpool Militant

In May 1983, the Militant-led Labour group under the leadership of the moderate John Hamilton took control of Liverpool City Council. The Liverpool journalist Ian Williams said that Militant 'never had a strategy for Liverpool, except a naive belief that an "all-out strike" would spread nationwide from Liverpool Town Hall and topple the Government'.[56] But this is not true. Militant did have a strategy, which had been tried before, at Poplar during the period 1919–24.

The parallels between Poplar during the 1920s and Liverpool throughout the early 1980s are striking. Poplar, situated in the East End of London, like Liverpool, had an economy based on docks and warehouses that depended on a casual labour force.[57] When the First World War ended Poplar, like Liverpool, experienced high unemployment and the council's outdoor relief structures were unable to cope with the demands placed on them by 'unwanted soldiers, engineers, munitions workers' and 'coal-miners'.[58] Elected in 1919, the Labour-run socialist council spent money on the unemployed, essential services and schemes to alleviate the poverty; already major social problems were caused by poor and overcrowded housing conditions. In doing so, the council ran up debts and was unable to pay the precepts owed to London County Council and the Metropolitan Asylums Board, as well as the Metropolitan Police Rate Warrant.[59] Just as Neil Kinnock warned Liverpool councillors to stay within the law during the 1980s, so were Poplar's councillors told by Herbert Morrison (the grandfather of Peter Mandelson; ironically, sixty years later Mandelson advised Neil Kinnock on how to tackle Militant) to stay within the law. Poplar's councillors ignored Morrison's advice and demanded an equalisation of rates across London. Following court proceedings, thirty councillors, 'guilty and proud of it', were imprisoned for breaking the law, amid much fanfare and publicity.[60]

Sixty years later, and determined to go one better, throughout 1984 the Militant-influenced Liverpool City Council used the Poplar slogan, 'Better to break the law than break the poor'. The council demanded £30 million in revenue to maintain services, on the basis that it had been under-funded for a number of years previously. Liam Fogarty said that decisions taken by previous authorities to hold down rents had delivered a knock-on effect which determined the grants provided by Whitehall.[61] Liverpool's council leaders warned the Thatcher administration that if extra funds were not provided for local services they would set an illegal budget.[62]

Liverpool City Council's clash with the Thatcher Government was planned for a number of years in advance. A trigger for the rebellion was the introduction of the 1982 Local Government Finance Act, which stipulated that councils had to fix the rates at or below a level set by the government.[63] In an interview given in 1981, Derek Hatton said:

> Pressure would be so great from Liverpool it would act as a beacon to many other local authorities to follow suit which would result in the bringing down of this Tory Government and the return of a Labour Government pledged to Socialist policies.[64]

On 12 June 1983, Hatton reiterated this call at a meeting of Young Socialists in Liverpool. He made a reference to the Clay Cross dispute, when councillors had refused to increase rents under the 1972 Housing Finance Act and had subsequently been surcharged by the District Auditor for defying the law. Hatton proclaimed that this new battle would be bigger.[65]

Throughout 1984, a wave of demonstrations, strikes and rallies gripped the city of Liverpool. With the miners' strike in full flow, the Thatcher Government feared that violence and disorder associated with the dispute would spread to the inner cities, especially Liverpool. As a precaution, Thatcher told her Cabinet that the Home Office Command and Control Unit, which was a 'clearing house for information', should play a part, and, as a 'last resort', the armed forces.[66]

The first major battle in the dispute between Liverpool City Council and the Thatcher Government took place on 29 March 1984, when the authority had to set a budget and a rate. The Town Hall was ringed by police and crowds of demonstrators who gathered for a mass rally, which jammed Castle Street.[67] Although the demonstration passed off peacefully, inside Liverpool Town Hall the ruling Labour group proposed an expenditure of £269 million for 1984/85, against the central government target of £216.1 million. In 1984/85, the City Council had to meet a deficit of £34 million that was carried over from 1983/84. It was estimated that a rate increase of 175 per cent would cover outgoings. The ruling Labour group proposed only 9 per cent.[68] As a consequence, no budget was set and deputy leader Derek Hatton said that the Labour Party would 'not flinch'.[69]

A stalemate ensued between Liverpool City Council and the Thatcher Government, despite numerous meetings and negotiations.[70] With both sides refusing to concede any ground, the *Liverpool Echo* launched a 'Save our City' campaign to persuade Environment Secretary Patrick Jenkin and the city's councillors to find 'a practical compromise' and end the budget crisis.[71] This dispute was later settled when, on 8 June 1984, Patrick Jenkin visited Liverpool and was led on a tour of 'urban blight'.[72] This began at the Tate and Lyle refinery and ended with a 'pause for photographs' in a butcher's shop at Edge Hill. Travelling on a Merseyside Transport bus, Jenkin saw the full scale of the city's appalling housing conditions. He was greeted by tenants carrying banners which proclaimed that 'if the Iron Lady lived here she would rust'.[73] *Militant* remarked that Jenkin's visit was 'like a criminal returning to the scene of the crime'.[74]

Shocked by what he had witnessed, Patrick Jenkin initiated a major climb-down by the Thatcher Government – which later cost him his ministerial post. In July 1984, Liverpool City Council secured an additional £20 million of funding from central government. Addressing a large crowd from the balcony of Liverpool Town Hall, Derek Hatton boasted that this was 'a major victory against the Tory government'.[75] *Militant* said that the Labour Party leadership's refusal to endorse Liverpool City Council's stance was an 'outright capitulation'.[76] A deal was struck which involved a rate rise of no more than 17.9 per cent and a raft of other financial measures.[77]

Following this victory, both Militant and Liverpool City Council's grip on the city unravelled, caused by a number of tactical errors. The biggest mistake was the appointment of Sampson (Sam) Bond as Principal Race Relations Adviser. As a Militant Tendency sympathiser, Bond was chosen ahead of better-qualified and more suitable candidates.[78] This episode precipitated a year-long race relations crisis. The council's leaders were accused of promoting 'jobs for boys', especially when Bond was allowed to continue in his role amid huge opposition, especially from the black community.[79] Derek Hatton's response was that Militant wanted people 'who understood the plan' and 'who were committed to it'.[80]

The running of Liverpool City Council by the Militant-led Labour group was sectarian and based upon coercion, as its belief in democratic centralism and a workerist approach to politics did not allow dissent.[81] The extent of this control came into the open during 1988 when, in his book *Inside Left*, Derek Hatton described John Hamilton as 'a nowhere man ... a Mr Magoo bumbling his way through life like a genial uncle'.[82] In response, Hamilton said that Hatton not only 'blustered and bullied' but was a 'cypher' for Militant and its leaders, who manipulated the council from their London headquarters.[83]

As well as within the Labour group, intimidation and violence was used against political opponents. This was often meted out by the infamous Static Security Force, labelled as 'Derek Hatton's Private Army', which guarded the Town Hall and council premises.[84] During the first budget rebellion threats were made against six councillors who refused to support the Labour group's stance against the Thatcher Government. Derek Hatton said that those councillors would be treated like political lepers if they failed to toe the line, and they were duly ostracised.[85] Similar threats were made against council employees who did not agree with ruling Labour group policies. One example was the ill-treatment of the 'Harthill six' gardeners, who refused to take part in a day of action organised by the General, Municipal, Boilermakers and Allied Trades Union (GMBATU).[86] This led to a year-long dispute that was settled at the High Court, after which Liverpool City Council deliberately demolished the glasshouses in Calderstones Park, citing health and safety reasons. This was seen as a cruel act of vandalism and the *Liverpool Echo* called the council 'legal wreckers'.[87]

Such incidents led to a rebellion against Militant. In February 1985, the Tendency was wiped out in the Vauxhall ward of the city when, at the Labour Party's annual ward meeting, all eighteen official positions from the chairman downwards passed into the hands of moderates, who beat off the Militants by fifty-eight votes to twelve. The ward secretary claimed that the Vauxhall party had 'lanced the boil of Militant', describing it as 'a virus poisoning the arteries of democratic socialism'.[88] This rebellion was linked to the Eldonian housing co-operative, whose residents had joined together to remove the Militant councillor Paul Luckock, who opposed their wish to keep the houses they had been allocated. Malcolm Kennedy, who at the time was secretary of the local Co-operative Party, became involved in the struggle to remove Militant and later succeeded Luckock as Vauxhall's first non-Militant councillor. The remnants of this group were later influential in Louise Ellman's election as the Liverpool Riverside MP in 1997.[89]

Amid this opposition, Liverpool City Council challenged the Thatcher Government for a second time, and this turned out to be an act of political suicide. Free of its year-long struggle with the coal miners, which had ended in March 1985, the Thatcher administration concentrated greater energy on the Liverpool dispute. Anticipating much tougher opposition from the Government, Derek Hatton said that councillors had to 'up the ante' and involve more councils in the protest.[90] On 28 November 1984, Liverpool City Council's leaders reiterated their commitment to defending jobs and services and began a campaign for the return of 'stolen' money in the form of Rate Support Grant for education and housing. Patrick Jenkin was accused of going back on an alleged promise of a £130 million capital allocation.[91] In a repeat of the first rebellion, this campaign led to a series of rallies and demonstrations across the city.

On 7 March 1985, Liverpool's councillors met at the Town Hall to set a budget and a rate. That day, most of the council's 30,000 workers struck and marched on Castle Street.[92] *Militant* reported that it was 'the biggest ever one-day strike by Liverpool local authority workers'.[93] At the meeting no rate or budget was set and John Hamilton's motion to defy the Thatcher

Government was passed by forty-eight votes to thirty-seven, with the opposition made up of combined Liberal and Conservative councillors.[94] In Whitehall this decision was greeted with huge concern. Margaret Thatcher's policy advisor, Oliver Letwin, urged the government to stick to its policy of 'no negotiations'.[95] Letwin urged Thatcher to send commissioners into Liverpool and give them the power to levy a poll tax which would 'bite on everybody'.[96]

In April 1985, the leaders of Liverpool City Council met the leaders of Sheffield City Council and six London boroughs. While they agreed to defer setting a rate, concerns were raised about the deployment of the District Auditor by central government.[97] Councillors were warned to fix a rate or face heavy fines, along with a ban from holding public office. Further, legal action was threatened to recover from elected members any cash losses suffered by these eight authorities through their failure to set a rate.[98] One by one, the rebel councils, including Sheffield and Greater London Council (GLC), set rates. By the end of May 1985, the rebellion had crumbled but Liverpool, along with Lambeth, led by 'Red' Ted Knight, refused to back down and was out on a limb.[99] On 27 June 1985, the District Auditor issued formal notices of surcharge to forty-nine Labour Councillors in Liverpool. The initial estimate of loss was £106,103, caused by the delay in setting a budget. As the amount exceeded £2,000, councillors faced automatic disqualification from holding public office for five years.[100] *Militant* said that the Tories had 'criminalised' councillors who opposed their social and economic policies.[101]

Managing Liverpool

Peter Taaffe and Tony Mulhearn have claimed that Liverpool City Council, under the domination of Militant, tried to ameliorate and improve the conditions of the working class in Liverpool.[102] Militant made a critical mistake in adopting moderate policies, alongside its overall campaign of challenging the authority of the Thatcher Government. This distracted the council and weakened its bargaining stance in trying to attract more funds to the city. Further, the public expectation and eventual failure to deliver those policies opened Militant and Liverpool City Council to severe criticism, once the after-effects of the council's conflict with the government took hold. Despite assertions made by Diane Frost and Peter North that Militant and Liverpool City Council were dealt a bad hand by social, economic and political circumstances, such was the council's belief in municipal solutions that the Archbishop of Liverpool, Derek Worlock, said that it was 'antagonistic' to any co-operation with the private sector.[103]

Liverpool City Council's flagship policy was housing. Supporters of Militant argue that more council houses were built in Liverpool during the years 1983–84 and 1984–85 than by all other local authorities in England put together. However, according to official figures submitted to the Department of Environment by Liverpool City Council, only 1,979 dwellings were built between June 1983 and June 1985, while the total for the rest of England was 41,189.[104] Launched in July 1983, Liverpool City Council's housing policy revolved around a five-year urban renewal strategy based on seventeen 'priority areas'. The programme was devised by the council's chief finance officer, Tony Byrne. Designated developers' sites, formerly allocated for sale, were acquired and reallocated for housing and development.[105]

On the one hand, this policy regenerated some housing estates and received support from sections of the city's population. Peter Hooton of the rock band The Farm said that at Cantril Farm 'all of a sudden, people had front and back gardens'.[106] However, there were flaws in the policy. Critics have argued that the homes built were too small and resembled 'dolls houses'.[107] There were criticisms about the allocation of the houses, as no proper procedures for vetting tenants were put in place. One of the newly built 'unemployed' housing estates later became known as 'smack valley' after being populated by drug dealers.[108]

As vast resources were pumped into the council's housing projects other key services, such as education, were affected. A frequent celebratory claim made by Militant was the council's creation of pre-school nursery education.[109] However, its response to more pressing educational needs, such as improving Liverpool's poor skills base, fell short. From September 1983, the council's education committee ambitiously tried to reorganise secondary schools and end all single sex-education, as well as to introduce rigid catchment areas. Parents' groups and opposition councillors criticised this policy for a lack of consultation.[110] Under the reorganisation, Croxteth Comprehensive School was allowed to remain open, while other schools were closed. Also, measures pushed through by the ruling Labour group were later watered down by the Secretary of State for Education, Keith Joseph.[111]

Alongside education, under the leadership of the Militant-led Liverpool City Council, the voluntary sector contracted. When the Labour group took control in May 1983, good neighbour schemes, which covered 80 per cent of the city, were removed from Age Concern and passed to the council's social services department. This was seen as a 'power grab' by the council in order to manipulate the activities of voluntary groups, as it wanted to assume control of twenty-three voluntary projects at a cost of £630,000. A representative from Age Concern said that 'it's like the council saying to us – you are not good enough to run them anymore'.[112] The council also attacked church charities and missions, including a mission run by Mother Theresa's nuns for homeless women, which was closed down and replaced by a council-run hostel.[113]

When Liverpool City Council chose not to set a budget during 1985, many critical and voluntary services were cash starved and unable to function.

In October that year, Social Services Minister Norman Fowler received reports from the Social Services Inspectorate about Liverpool City Council's 'apparent lack of preparedness' to keep essential services going for vulnerable groups. Voluntary bodies which received grants or were contracted to provide services for the council found themselves in 'a desperate position'. One such organisation, Catholic Social Services (Liverpool), which had existed since the 1850s and provided a wide range of services for children in need, as well as for mentally and physically handicapped people, faced bankruptcy, while 'a good many others' faced 'extinction'.[114]

The Labour group's decision to divert finances toward housing and to create public sector jobs, in an attempt to reverse the long-term cyclical unemployment and redundancies across Merseyside, was also flawed. Council leaders came up with a controversial £5 million scheme to create 1,000 full-time skilled and unskilled jobs in departments including cleaning, housing repairs and parks. Derek Hatton said that 'in this city, we have some of the dirtiest streets in the country. There is only one way to tackle the problem – employ people to clean them.'[115] However, there were two major problems with this strategy. First, although as a result Liverpool had some of the cleanest streets in the North-West, the cost of maintaining services was expensive in comparison to those run by other local authorities. In Liverpool the cost of street cleaning amounted to £2,547 per swept mile, while in Sefton it was £1,040, St Helens £828, the Wirral £853 and Sheffield £784.[116] Also, the cost of refuse collections in Liverpool was more than the metropolitan district average, amounting to more than £3 per head.[117] Second, the strategy of adding more employees to a 31,000-strong work-force resulted in over-manning and added further debt to the council's budget – all of which later had serious consequences.

Downfall

One of Militant's guiding principles was to tell working-class people the truth about its struggle with the ruling class.[118] As the second budget rebellion faltered and the implementation of moderate reforms fell apart, the leaders of the Labour-run Liverpool City Council refused to deviate from their default course of toppling the Thatcher Government. The council's refusal to set a budget meant that, following the Rate Support Grant Supplementary Report for 1985/86, issued on 4 July 1985, 'holdback' was implemented. This meant that Liverpool City Council would not receive any further grant payments for six months, until February/March 1986.[119] Once this was enacted, what followed were a number of deceptions by the Militant-led Labour group over the state of Liverpool City Council's finances.

First, the Conservative Government was misled, due to Militant's refusal to allow access to the council's financial records. Patrick Jenkin told Margaret Thatcher that district auditors could not gain access to the council's books, and central government accounting officers could not ascertain how much money was being spent. As information was being withheld, some government ministers panicked about the financial collapse of Liverpool City Council. Margaret Thatcher's advisors wanted Commissioners to take over the running of the council. Because this was not feasible, they sought an interested local party to challenge the council's rate in the courts, but nobody came forward.[120]

Amid this confusion, on 19 July 1985, the District Auditor issued a formal report to the council on its budget deficit and a range of options was set out which included 'financial collapse', 'major spending cuts' and 'quashing' the original rate.[121] While the report was being prepared, Knowsley Borough Council repaid Liverpool City Council £21 million worth of debt, owed on council houses transferred to Knowsley in 1974. This arrangement gave the council an immediate cash injection, which enabled it to deal with a major debt-refinancing requirement at the end of August 1985.[122] Despite receiving those funds, Liverpool City Council still demanded £25 million from central government to cover a shortfall between its planned revenue expenditure and the amount raised by its illegal rate.[123]

Following the parliamentary summer recess, Liverpool City Council lost face when, on 27 September 1985, it decided by forty-six votes to thirty-five to serve redundancy notices to all of its 31,000 employees.[124] According to Derek Hatton, letters were sent out to all council employees warning them that if the Thatcher Government did not do a deal over the budget, their jobs would be at risk.[125] Instead of uniting people, this high-risk strategy completely undermined the morale of the council's work-force.[126] The trade unions Union of Construction, Allied Trades and Technicians, National Union of Public Employees, National Union of Teachers and National and Local Government Officers' Association refused to support the council over the redundancy notices, which left Militant's main backer, the GMBATU, isolated.[127]

The fall-out from this episode angered the leadership of the Labour Party. At its 1985 annual conference at Bournemouth Neil Kinnock spectacularly said:

> You start with far-fetched resolutions. They are then pickled into a rigid dogma, a code, and you go through the years sticking to that, out-dated, misplaced, irrelevant to real needs, and you end in the grotesque chaos of a Labour council hiring taxis to scuttle round a city handing out redundancy notices to its own workers. I am telling you, no matter how entertaining, how fulfilling to short-term egos – you can't play politics with people's jobs and with people's services or with their homes.[128]

For a number of months, Neil Kinnock had tried to find the correct time to strike against Militant. Against the backdrop of the redundancy notices and the fear they had generated, his attack was timed to perfection. While moderates praised his speech as a 'masterpiece', the hard left vilified Kinnock as the biggest traitor since Ramsay MacDonald.[129] This speech was a watershed moment in Labour Party history and began a process that led to New Labour, culminating with the general election victory in 1997 under the leadership of Tony Blair.[130]

After Neil Kinnock's speech the tide turned against Militant and the hard left. Within the Liverpool Labour group itself, Roy Gladden made an unsuccessful attempt to remove Derek Hatton as deputy leader of Liverpool City Council, after Hatton had described the plotters as 'gutless cowards'.[131] This was followed by a huge demonstration by the group Liverpool Against The Militants, when thousands of people turned up at Liverpool Pier Head and listened to a range of speakers. One of those in attendance said that Militant had 'raped the city'.[132]

Under mounting pressure to end its struggle with the Thatcher Government, Liverpool City Council lost a High Court legal challenge by the NUT and National Association of Head Teachers over the unlawful sacking of the 31,000 council employees.[133] Following this, on 29 October 1985, the Stonefrost Report was published, in which the Labour Party's Association of Metropolitan Authorities (AMA) Policy Committee placed demands on Liverpool's councillors to end the dispute. Jack Cunningham, Labour's environment spokesperson, said that by the council's not producing a budget as agreed the saga had become a 'charade of dishonesty and downright lies'.[134]

In November 1985, Liverpool City Council finally set a legal budget. This included £23 million capitalisation coupled with a £60 million loan from Swiss banks. The deal meant that funds destined for the council's housing programme were re-routed towards paying the wages of council employees. Council leader John Hamilton said that the move was 'a retreat', for which the authority had 'lost on points in this round'.[135] Neil Kinnock called the council's decision to take out a loan 'an act of political perversity when a very small rate rise with insignificant effects on the people of Liverpool would have safeguarded jobs, services and the housing programme without going into hock'.[136] In response to Kinnock's criticism, Derek Hatton accused the Labour Party leadership of doing the 'dirty work' of the Tories.[137]

Following the swift end to the second budget crisis, Kinnock and the NEC investigated the practices and procedures of Liverpool City Council, the Liverpool DLP and Militant's influence over its affairs.[138] In November 1985 this resulted in the suspension of the DLP. As more evidence was gathered, during May 1986, the NEC expelled prominent Liverpool members of Militant, including Derek Hatton and Tony Mulhearn.[139] Finally, on 12 March 1987, the forty-seven councillors involved in the struggle with the Thatcher Government over the council's budget were disqualified from public office for five years and ordered to pay surcharges and costs totalling £330,000, after losing a long appeal in the House of Lords.[140]

Conclusion

Overall, this episode proved that local government could not take on central government and win. In terms of legacy, Militant's Trotskyite experiment not only caused harm to the reputation of Liverpool but also set back its development. Since the demise of the Militant Tendency and its domination of Liverpool City Council during the 1980s there has been a determination among council leaders and politicians not to repeat the same mistakes. In a speech delivered by the Mayor of Liverpool, Joe Anderson, at a Labour Party campaign event in 2012 before the city's mayoral elections, he described the Labour group in Liverpool during the 1980s as a 'basket case' and said that many lessons had been learned from that era. Those comments were made in relation to the current Labour group's handling of the conditions – considered worse than those experienced by its predecessor – resulting from austerity measures and cuts to local government finance brought about by the aftereffects of the 2007–8 global financial crisis.[141]

In the context of Labour and the left during the 1980s, Militant wanted to move the party to the left, but, in the end, its actions pushed it to the right. Militant's revolutionary policies and practices were clearly both unacceptable and incompatible with those of the Labour Party. Neil Kinnock's action against Militant, which resulted in the numerous expulsions of its members, helped to enable the Labour Party to become an electoral force once more. By the early 1990s the rapid descent of Militant into oblivion marked a watershed because it signalled a critical breaking point between Old Labour and the rise of New Labour.

As a postscript, in 2015, following the Labour Party's crushing general election defeat under the leadership of Ed Miliband and an ill-thought-through decision to introduce a £3 registered membership fee, the hard left rose to the surface, culminating in the shock election of Jeremy Corbyn as leader.[142] With that came the creation of Momentum, which has many similarities with Militant in terms of organisation and tactics. But whereas Militant was 'a party within a party', Momentum is 'a party outside a party' that attempted to take over the Labour Party, which became hugely divided following the outcome of the 2016 referendum on European Union membership and faced a far bigger existential crisis than in the 1980s.[143] The battles over Militant in Liverpool therefore continue to resonate in contemporary politics.

Notes

1. Peter Taaffe and Tony Mulhearn, *Liverpool: A City That Dared To Fight* (London: Fortress Books, 1988), p. 68.
2. Derek Hatton, *Inside Left: The Story So Far ...* (London: Bloomsbury, 1988); Peter Taaffe, *The Rise of Militant: Thirty Years of Militant* (London: Militant Publications, 1995), pp. 264–5.

3 Michael Crick, *Militant* (London: Faber & Faber, 1984); *The March of Militant* (London: Faber & Faber, 1986).
4 'Who, What, Why: What was Militant?', BBC News, 28 May 2015; see also Peter Kilfoyle, *Left Behind: Lessons from Labour's Heartland* (London: Politico's, 2000), pp. 39–57, 137.
5 Joyce Gould, *Witchfinder General: A Political Odyssey* (London: Biteback Publishing, 2016); John Golding, *Hammer of the Left: The Battle For the Soul of the Labour Party* (London: Biteback Publishing, 2016).
6 Michael Parkinson, *Liverpool on the Brink: One City's Struggle against Government's Cuts* (Cambridge, MA: Burlington Press, 1985).
7 Diane Frost and Peter North, *Militant Liverpool: A City on the Edge* (Liverpool: Liverpool University Press, 2013).
8 Brian Marren, *We Shall Not Be Moved: How Liverpool's Working Class Fought Redundancies, Closures and Cuts in the Age of Thatcher* (Manchester: Manchester University Press, 2016).
9 The National Archives (TNA), PREM 19/1363, Prime Minister Margaret Thatcher speech, 2 October 1984.
10 Frost and North, *Militant Liverpool*, pp. 124–5.
11 Liam Fogarty, 'The Mersey Militants', BBC Radio 4, 8 November 2014.
12 Kilfoyle, *Left Behind*, pp. 2–4; Frost and Lane, *Militant Liverpool*, pp. 7–11; Chris Couch, *City of Change and Challenge: Urban Planning and Regeneration in Liverpool* (Aldershot: Ashgate, 2003); Eric Heffer, 'Biased Rubbish', *Spectator*, 22 June 1985, p. 22; Derek Hatton interview with Fogarty, 'Mersey Militants'.
13 TNA, PREM 16/1750, Leslie Young, Chairman of the North-West Region, CBI, speaking at a meeting with Prime Minister James Callaghan and representatives of the city of Liverpool, 27 April 1978.
14 TNA, PREM 16/1750, Alfred Stocks, Chief Executive of Liverpool City Council, 27 April 1978.
15 Parkinson, *Liverpool on the Brink*, p. 12.
16 TNA, PREM 19/1590, Closure of Tate and Lyle sugar refinery, 1 March 1981.
17 TNA, PREM 16/1750, 'Industrial Relations', Prime Minister James Callaghan's meeting with Merseyside, background brief, 27 April 1978.
18 TNA, PREM 19/1614, 'Patrick Jenkin and Liverpool City Councillors and MPs', 13 April 1984.
19 *Militant*, 11 February 1983, p. 7.
20 TNA, PREM 19/1614, 'Patrick Jenkin and Liverpool City Councillors and MPs', 13 April 1984.
21 TNA, PREM 16/1750, Peter Shore, Secretary of State for the Environment, 27 April 1978.
22 Taaffe and Mulhearn, *Liverpool*, pp. 71–2.
23 TNA, PREM 16/1750, Councillor Eddie Roderick, 27 April 1978.
24 TNA, PREM 16/1750, Leslie Young, Chairman of the North-West Region CBI, 27 April 1978.
25 *Guardian*, 30 December 2011, p. 1.
26 People's History Museum Archives (PHM), L46, Merseyside Community Relations Council, 'Race and the Labour Party', 21 October 1985.
27 TNA, HO 266/119, Merseyside Police: The Toxteth disturbances, 1981; TNA, ET 16/6, Race relations: proposed research into employment in Liverpool, September 1983 to December 1989; Merseyside Record Office, The Report of the Chief Constable to the Merseyside Police Committee, 1981, pp. 9–12, 15–16.
28 *Independent*, 30 December 2011, p. 2.

29 See TNA, PREM 19/1363, Draft speeches and background notes to Margaret Thatcher's visit to Liverpool, 2 October 1984.
30 Lord Heseltine interview with Fogarty, 'Mersey Militants'.
31 Taaffe and Mulhearn, *Liverpool*, pp. 35–6.
32 Fogarty, 'Mersey Militants'.
33 See Kilfoyle, *Left Behind*, pp. 39–43, 49–52.
34 Felicity Dowling interview with Fogarty, 'Mersey Militants'.
35 See Sam Davies, *Liverpool Labour: Social and Political Influences on the Development of the Labour Party in Liverpool, 1900–1939* (Keele: Keele University Press, 1996); John Belchem, *Liverpool: City of Radicals* (Liverpool: Liverpool University Press, 2011).
36 Taaffe and Mulhearn, *Liverpool*, pp. 33–4.
37 Taaffe and Mulhearn, *Liverpool*, pp. 36–7.
38 Crick, *Militant*, pp. 46–7.
39 *Labour Weekly*, 10 September 1982, p. 7.
40 Crick, *Militant*, p. 22.
41 *British Perspectives and Tasks* (Cambridge: Cambridge Heath Press 1975), p. 14: Militant internal document – a copy can be found in PHM, LP/ESH/09/09.
42 *British Perspectives and Tasks*, p. 13.
43 Andrew Scott Crines, *Michael Foot and the Labour Leadership* (Newcastle: Cambridge Scholars Publishing, 2011), p. 10.
44 Kilfoyle, *Left Behind*, pp. 13, 15–16, 23–5; see Taaffe and Mulhearn, *Liverpool*, pp. 35–6.
45 *Liverpool Echo*, 6/7 May 1978, p. 1; 23 May 1978, p. 3.
46 Hatton, *Inside Left*, pp. 41, 60–1.
47 *Liverpool Echo*, 17 December 1979, p. 6; see PHM, LP/ESH/09–10, Labour Party NEC investigation into the practices of the Liverpool District Labour Party, 1985–86.
48 *Liverpool Echo*, 24 December 1979, p. 9.
49 *Liverpool Echo*, 24 December 1979, p. 9.
50 *Liverpool Echo*, 24 December 1979, p. 9.
51 Fogarty, 'Mersey Militants'.
52 *Labour Weekly*, 10 September 1982, p. 7.
53 *Labour Party Annual Conference Report*, 1982, Appendix A, p. 135.
54 *Labour Party Annual Conference Report*, 1982, Appendix A, p. 136; Ron Hayward, General Secretary and David Hughes, National Agent, 'Militant Tendency Report', 23 June 1983.
55 PHM, SEC/3/2/83, Alexander Irvine QC and Tony Blair, 'Joint Opinion', 23 February 1983; Document II, 'Militant Tendency', Labour Party Conference and National Executive Committee Decisions', November 1983.
56 Ian Williams, 'Now Militant Conducts a Witch-hunt of Its Own', *Tribune*, 26 October 1985, p. 10.
57 PHM, Edgar Lansbury, *'Poplarism', The Truth about the Poplar Scale of Relief and the Action of the Ministry of Health* (London: ILP Publications, 1924).
58 PHM, *The Poplar Story, 1921* (London: East London Communist Party, 1953), p. 5.
59 TNA, MEPO, 5/97, Police Rate Warrants: Poplar Borough Council's refusal to pay, 1921–2.
60 TNA, HO 45/11233, Disturbances: Imprisonment of Poplar Borough Councillors for contempt of Court, 1921–3; Poplar Board of Guardians, *Guilty and Proud of It! Poplar's Answer* (London: Victoria House Printing, 1922); PHM, LP/ESH/09–10, Labour Party NEC investigation into the practices of the Liverpool District Labour Party, 1985–86.

61 Fogarty, 'Mersey Militants'.
62 *Militant*, 3 February 1984, p. 13. The Local Government Finance Act of 1982 and the Rates Act of 1984 imposed limits on local authority spending. In May 1983 the Labour council inherited a debt from the previous Liberal-Conservative administration. When the council failed to obtain additional financial resources from central government, it threatened to set an illegal budget in order to get its own way.
63 'How Heseltine Will Rig His "Consult the People" Bid', *Tribune*, 13 November 1981, p. 9.
64 *Liverpool Echo*, 5 March 1984, p. 7.
65 *Liverpool Echo*, 13 June 1983, p. 1; see David Skinner and Julia Langdon, *The Story of Clay Cross* (London: Spokesman Books, 1974).
66 TNA, PREM 19/1614, Cabinet Office to Prime Minister Margaret Thatcher, 23 March 1984.
67 *Liverpool Echo*, 29 March 1984, pp. 1–3, 8.
68 TNA, PREM 19/1614, Prime Minister Margaret Thatcher, 'Confidential: Background Note', 19 April 1984.
69 *Liverpool Echo*, 29 March 1984, p. 3.
70 TNA, PREM 19/1614, 'Recorded minutes of meeting between Secretary of State for the Environment Patrick Jenkin and Liverpool City Councillors and MPs', 13 April 1984'.
71 *Liverpool Echo*, 6 May 1984, p. 1.
72 *Liverpool Echo*, 6 May 1984, p. 1; *Liverpool Echo*, 8 June 1984, p. 8.
73 *Liverpool Echo*, 8 June 1984, pp. 8–9.
74 *Militant*, 15 June 1984, p. 11.
75 *Liverpool Echo*, 11 July 1984, p. 3.
76 *Militant*, 13 July 1984, p. 2.
77 *Liverpool Echo*, 11 July 1984, p. 3.
78 See Frost and North, *Militant Liverpool*, pp. 147–54, pp. 155–8.
79 Frost and North, *Militant Liverpool*, pp. 158–63.
80 *Guardian*, 15 February 1988, p. 4.
81 Frost and North, *Militant Liverpool*, pp. 170–5.
82 Hatton, *Inside Left*, p. 68
83 *Guardian*, 16 February 1988, p. 2.
84 Hatton, *Inside Left*, pp. 116–19; Frost and North, *Militant Liverpool*, pp. 168–77.
85 *Militant*, 27 January 1984, p. 2; *Liverpool Echo*, 23 February 1984, p. 1.
86 *Liverpool Echo*, 3 August 1984, p. 2.
87 *Liverpool Echo*, 3 August 1984, p. 2, *Liverpool Echo*, 18 October 1984, p. 9.
88 *Liverpool Echo*, 20 February 1985, p. 2.
89 Interview with Councillor Malcolm Kennedy, Deputy Lord Mayor of Liverpool City Council, 16 September 2016.
90 Derek Hatton interview with Fogarty, 'Mersey Militants'.
91 TNA, PREM 19/1615, Secretary of State for the Environment Patrick Jenkin to Prime Minister Margaret Thatcher, 29 November 1984.
92 *Liverpool Echo*, 8 March 1985, pp. 2, 8–9.
93 *Militant*, 15 March 1985, p. 5.
94 *Liverpool Echo*, 8 March 1985, p. 8.
95 TNA, PREM 19/1616, 'Rate Capping: MISC 109', 25 March 1985.
96 TNA, PREM 19/1616, 'Rate Capping: MISC 109', 25 March 1985.
97 *Liverpool Echo*, 26 April 1985, p. 23.
98 *Liverpool Echo*, 22 May 1985, p. 1, 3.

99 PHM, Merseyside Labour Co-ordinating Committee, 'The Political Crisis in Liverpool: Evidence to the Labour Party National Executive Committee', December 1985.
100 TNA, PREM 19/1561, 'Liverpool: Situation Report', 8 July 1985.
101 *Militant*, 5 July 1985, p. 2.
102 Taaffe and Mulhearn, *Liverpool*, p. 69.
103 TNA, PREM 19/1615, 'Meeting with the Archbishop and Bishop of Liverpool', 16 November 1984.
104 Jack Straw, 'How Liverpool Undermined the Real Anti-Tory Struggle', *Tribune*, 29 November 1985, p. 1; Kilfoyle, *Left Behind*, p. 116.
105 Merseyside Record Office, Proceedings of Liverpool City Council, 1983/84, 27 July 1983, pp. 171–2.
106 Fogarty, 'Mersey Militants'.
107 Kilfoyle, *Left Behind*, p. 91.
108 Kilfoyle, *Left Behind*, p. 91.
109 Taaffe and Mulhearn, *Liverpool*, pp. 175–6.
110 Merseyside Record Office, Proceedings of Liverpool City Council, 1983/4, 12 October 1983, pp. 270–1.
111 See TNA, PREM 19/1615.
112 *Liverpool Echo*, 18 September 1984, p. 4.
113 TNA, PREM 19/1615, 'Meeting with the Archbishop and Bishop of Liverpool', 16 November 1984.
114 TNA, PREM 19/1562, 'Liverpool: Provision of Social Services', 11 October 1985.
115 *Liverpool Echo*, 6 June 1983, p. 1.
116 TNA, PREM 19/1614, 'Patrick Jenkin Meeting with Sir Trevor Jones', 12 April 1984.
117 TNA, PREM 19/1614, 'Patrick Jenkin and Liverpool City Councillors and MPs', 13 April 1984.
118 Taaffe and Mulhearn, *Liverpool*, p. 69.
119 See Fogarty, 'Mersey Militants'; TNA, PREM 19/1561, MISC 109, 'Liverpool City Council Situation Report', 29 July 1985.
120 TNA, PREM 19/1561, MISC 109, 'Liverpool City Council Situation Report', 29 July 1985.
121 TNA, PREM 19/1561, MISC 109, 'Liverpool City Council Situation Report', 29 July 1985.
122 TNA, PREM 19/1561, MISC 109, 'Liverpool City Council Situation Report', 29 July 1985.
123 TNA, PREM 19/1562, Secretary of State for the Environment Kenneth Baker to Prime Minister Margaret Thatcher, 13 September 1985.
124 TNA, PREM 19/1562, MISC 109, Liverpool Situation Report, 27 September 1985 (TNA).
125 Derek Hatton interview with Fogarty, 'Mersey Militants'.
126 PHM, Merseyside Labour Co-ordinating Committee, 'The Political Crisis in Liverpool', December 1985.
127 *Liverpool Echo*, 27 September 1985, pp. 1–2.
128 *Labour Party Annual Conference Report*, 1985, p. 128.
129 *The Times*, 2 October 1985, p. 1.
130 Kilfoyle, *Left Behind*, pp. 141–6; Lord Kinnock interview with Fogarty, 'Mersey Militants'.
131 Councillor Roy Gladden interview with Fogarty, 'Mersey Militants'; *Liverpool Echo*, 5 October 1985, p. 8.

132 *Liverpool Echo*, 7 October 1985, p. 5.
133 *Liverpool Echo*, 17 October 1985, p. 14.
134 PHM, Note of a meeting of the AMA Policy Committee Labour Group, 21 November 1985.
135 *Liverpool Echo*, 23 November 1985, p. 1.
136 *Liverpool Echo*, 23 November 1985, p. 1.
137 PHM, NEC/27/11/1985, Liverpool District Labour Party meeting report, 22 November 1985.
138 David Basnett, General Secretary of the GMBATU to Larry Whitty, General Secretary, Labour Party, 26 November 1985.
139 See PHM LP/ESH/09/09 and LP/ESH/09/10, Labour Party NEC investigation into the procedures and practices of the Liverpool District Labour Party.
140 Hatton, *Inside Left*, p. 163.
141 Joe Anderson speaking at the Labour Party's North West Local Government Day, 25 February 2012.
142 Ray Collins, *Building a One Nation Labour Party: The Collins Review into Labour Party Reform* (London: Labour Party, 2014).
143 Interview with Baroness Gould, former Director of Organisation of the Labour Party, 29 September 2016.

8

'Fill a bag and feed a family': the miners' strike and its supporters

Maroula Joannou

> I cannot interfere ... it breaks my heart to see what is happening in our country today. A terrible strike is being carried on by the best men in the world. They beat the Kaiser's army and they beat Hitler's army. They never gave in. (Harold Macmillan, First Earl of Stockton, debut in the House of Lords, 13 November 1984)[1]

The miners' strike of 1984–85 was the most protracted and bitterly contested strike in the history of late twentieth-century Britain: its importance as a watershed in industrial relations that was likely to determine the distribution of power between labour and capital for the foreseeable future was generally recognised at the time by supporters and opponents alike. Striking miners were the *corps d'élite* of the trade unions in 1984 and had famously humiliated Edward Heath's administration at the Saltley Gate coke depot in 1972, forcing him to introduce the three-day working week before his electoral defeat in 1974. But it was not only the left who believed the miners to be invincible in 1984–85. In contrast to Prime Minister Margaret Thatcher, many Conservative politicians privately believed the same. The Deputy Secretary to the Cabinet remembered the reaction of pure disbelief ('The woman's mad. You can't win miners' strikes. All you can do is buy them off') when Thatcher announced on taking office in 1979: 'The last Conservative government was destroyed by the miners' strike. We'll have another and we'll win.'[2]

The strike, called in response to the National Coal Board's projected closure of Cortonwood and another twenty pits at a cost of 20,000 jobs, ran throughout the long, cold winter of 1984–85. Neither the 1972 strike, which started in January and ended in February, nor the 1974 strike, which started in February and ended in March, had been long lived. The National Union of Mineworkers (NUM) did not issue strike pay but it did make a small picketing allowance. The miners were ineligible for social security benefits and their dependants were ineligible for 'urgent needs payments' under the National Security Act of 1980, although £15 was deducted from benefits to cover 'notional strike pay'.[3] Incomes had been depleted by the previous year's overtime ban and poverty became endemic once household savings ran out. Thus many striking miners and their families found themselves perilously near to destitution.

What emerged was a historic mobilisation of the mining areas in their own defence, coupled with a humanitarian relief effort to the beleaguered coalfields organised through a network of miners' support committees working with the mining communities to raise the millions of pounds that would prevent the miners' being starved into submission. As Paul Mackney put it, this perhaps 'involved more people at a greater pitch of activity over a lengthier period than any other campaign in the history of the labour movement'.[4] In March 1985 the miners accepted defeat, processing back to the pitheads behind their bands and banners with all the pride and dignity that the instigators of the 'orderly return-to-work', the South Wales Federation of Miners, had intended the world to see. However, sacked and victimised miners were not reinstated and the National Coal Board (NCB) was able to implement its programme of pit closures virtually unhindered.

As Mike Sanders suggests, the 'danger threatening the 1984–5 miners' strike is not that of being forgotten, of being consigned to historical oblivion, but rather of being only available to the memory in ways which separate its historical significance from its current relevance'.[5] How, then, can the historian return to the dispute in order to provide resources of hope for those with no memory of a lost industrial past? This chapter avoids the Thatcher/Scargill polarities in which the strike is usually discussed, and analyses the remarkable support for the miners, mobilised by the organised labour movement but encompassing countless groups and individuals far beyond its usual orbit, as an enduring legacy of the strike that demonstrates the traditions of that movement at their very best.[6] I argue that the miners' refusal to separate their own well-being from that of their dependants, coupled with the aggregation of the miners and their families by the miners' support groups, differentiated the strike from previous disputes, and that this accounted, in part, for its longevity as well as the reversal in how the miners were perceived by the public and how they perceived themselves. If, as Beatrix Campbell put it, the 'socialist movement in Britain had been swept off its feet by the magic of masculinity, muscle and machinery', that 'magic' clearly no longer prevailed when machinery was idle and the miners were absent from the workplace that had traditionally conferred their masculinity, economic status and collective sense of self-worth.[7] Single men and active pickets apart – the latter often in the minority – striking miners found themselves at home and reduced to unwelcome passivity and dependency. Voluntarily designating themselves as family men, while ironically lacking the wherewithal to feed and clothe their children, strikers became reliant on their own fundraising efforts and on the supporters who stood between themselves, penury and capitulation.

The informal coalition that identified with the moral and political arguments for investment in coal was exceedingly broad. It included women, traditionally excluded from the labour aristocracy, the young, the poor, student and inner-city radicals, peace activists, the unemployed (for whom trade unionism had hitherto had little meaning), anti-racists, gays, lesbians and ethnic minorities. In consequence *new* forms of solidarity, *new* forms of self-help and *new* forms of sustenance emerged. Although the trade unions remained at the centre of the dispute, Thatcher rhetorically dubbed all NUM supporters as 'the enemy within' – a comparison with the military dictatorship of General Galtieri in Argentina in the Falklands War, the 'enemy without', which was at first resented but subsequently adopted as a badge of pride.

The strike was initially defensive. Called by the miners to safeguard their own jobs, pits and communities, it quickly acquired a symbolic importance inseparable from its industrial objective. 'Victory for the miners' became a clarion call for many who identified the NUM as the chief obstacle to the systematic deregulation of the labour market, opposed the Falklands War and the ideological project of the early Thatcher years and discovered in the praxis of the strike an alternative vision of mutuality, effective trade unionism and co-operative ideals.

The dispute generated the passions that it did precisely because it was not perceived as narrowly economistic. Unlike the strikes of 1972 and 1974, this one was not about pay. On the contrary, its rhetoric invoked the right to work (resonant in the slogan 'coal not dole'), reiterated the importance of close-knit communities and demanded consultations about proposed job losses, an ethical non-nuclear energy policy and that the welfare of human beings rather than profitability should feature prominently in calculations about economic planning, restructuring and change. What can loosely be termed the 'moral case for coal' appeared of concern not only to the miners but to all with a stake in a sustainable future. As the critic Raymond Williams put it, the 'miners' strike is being represented as the last kick of an old order. Properly understood, it is one of the first steps towards a new order.'[8]

By insisting on the importance of their own gender and sexuality while fighting alongside the miners, Women Against Pit Closures and Lesbians and Gays Support the Miners presented a substantive challenge to the chauvinistic old labourist attitudes of the coalfields. Working-class women's activism, to which I will return below, was not new. Rather, it drew strongly upon equal rights traditions that were established in the mining areas between the wars and on traditions of women's protest during strikes going back to 1926, while inflecting those traditions in radical, innovative ways.[9] It was women who emerged as the public spokespersons for their communities, articulating the case for coal as a common resource held in trust for future generations, and women who developed the links with the peace movement based upon a shared approach to a coal-based energy policy and opposition to the development of nuclear weapons and nuclear power.

From the start, the NUM was beset with problems brought about by its lacerating internal divisions. In Nottinghamshire, miners who responded to the national strike call were heavily outnumbered by others who voted against it in a series of locally organised pithead strike ballots which were made possible by the federal nature of the union. Each of the county's thirty-one pits continued to work, ensuring that 'the nation's lights, even at mid-winter, would not even flicker'.[10] Ironically, it was the NUM's weakness rather than its strength which brought it into a new relationship with the marginalised and the dispossessed or, rather, which forced it to renew its old historic relationship with those who, in Hywel Francis's words, were 'penned in by police and poverty'.[11] As Hilary Wainwright and Doreen Massey noted: 'Movingly, impressive support has come from those who are themselves experiencing industrial dereliction. Liverpool 8 [Toxteth] was one of the first paces to spawn a support group.'[12] 'On Merseyside there are fourteen support groups which between them have sent off £1 million so far (a million pounds – from a city itself in desperate poverty).'[13] Inez Macormack co-ordinated the NUPE (National Union of Public Employees) 'Fill a Bag and Feed a Family' campaign, which was supported by Belfast's lowest-paid workers: school cooks, council employees and cleaners. 'However much it plastered over the all-too-real cracks, one of the leading narratives of much strike literature was that of a united Wales standing against an external foe.'[14] Indeed, so broadly based was the Welsh Congress in Support of the Mining Communities, established in Cardiff in October, that it was able to adopt the slogan 'The NUM Fights for Wales'.[15]

The strike marked the high point of a brief, if now largely forgotten, period of popular protest between 1979 and 1984 which was characterised by student radicalism, new wave music, alternative bookshops and massive peace demonstrations organised by the re-energised Campaign for Nuclear Disarmament after the publication of E. P. Thompson's influential broadside *Protest and Survive* (1980). The feature film *Pride*, directed by Matthew Warchus in 2014, unerringly evokes the mood of the young at the time. What began as a conventional labour dispute quickly became attached to a politics of struggle in the inner cities, linked to the discontents of urban poverty and laced with the concerns of environmentalists and feminists. Black and ethnic minority groups and gays and lesbians rallied to the miners, recognising affinities between the latter's mistreatment and their own. Long-standing tensions between the police, the urban poor and the black community had fuelled the riots in Brixton and the Liverpool 8 district in 1981, and distrust of the police also became common within the mining communities: 'Harassment by some police of men and women taking coal from wherever they could find it became a dominating feature of daily life.'[16] In Nottinghamshire extra forces were drafted in to turn away 'presumed pickets', and quiet villages became habituated to inordinate numbers of police, house-to-house searches, road blocks and unprecedented restrictions on freedom of movement. The National Council for Civil Liberties reported that 'many police officers from other forces who for the first time have had to work alongside colleagues from urban forces have not been at all happy with what they have seen'.[17] The police deployed had been 'systematically retrained in riot control, and readily mobile Police Support Units set up in every force [sic], following a review of police training in 1981 initiated in response to the urban riots of that year'.[18]

Money poured in from the troubled Broadwater Farm Estate in Tottenham. In Haringey leaflets and badges were printed in Turkish and Greek. Support for the miners, pastoral and practical, was received from Quakers, churches and other faiths. In Liverpool, riven with unemployment, sectarian division and social unrest, the Anglican bishop, David Sheppard, an outspoken critic of Thatcher, worked alongside the Catholic archbishop, Derek Worlock, in ministering to Lancashire miners and their dependants. The Asian community in Southall adopted the Betteshanger pit in Kent.[19] In Glasgow collections were organised by the Indian Workers' Association and in Birmingham worshippers at Sikh temples donated food.

Industrial chaplains working with the NUM in Selby, Durham and Nottingham warned of the damage as pits were left unattended and spoke of the suffering they had witnessed at first hand. A Church of England briefing paper reported strategic interventions from the archbishop of Canterbury and the bishops of Sheffield and Birmingham and the exchanges in *The Times* of 2 October 1984 between Peter Walker, Secretary of State for Energy, and the bishop of Durham: 'Unfortunately, the Government to which you belong does not seem to care for the steadily increasing number of people who are unemployed, and are otherwise marginalised in society, and does not *seem* to care that it does not care.'[20]

The strength of feeling for the miners was prompted by the extent to which Thatcher had *already* restructured the economy, producing massive job losses and a drastic reduction in the size of Britain's industrial base. Two million manufacturing jobs had been lost between 1979 and 1981 in what William Keegan termed 'the worst recession since the war, with manufacturing output dropping by nearly 20 per cent and unemployment more than doubling from 1.3 million to nearly 3.5 million in 1983'.[21] To make explicit comparisons with the 1930s, the organisers of the People's March for Jobs in 1981 had followed the route of the Jarrow March of 1936.

By 1984 Thatcher had become closely identified with the controversial monetarist policies implemented to control inflation, improve Britain's global competitiveness and reverse Britain's long-term economic decline. Moreover, she was often held personally responsible for the human misery that ensued from the Conservative Government's policy of allowing 'uncompetitive' and 'uneconomic' industries to go to the wall. It was largely the dramatic success of the expedition to reclaim the Falkland Islands from Argentinian military occupation in April 1982 that transformed the prime minister's personal fortunes and resulted in an electoral landslide for the Conservative Party in June 1983.[22]

A key legacy of the disastrous 'winter of discontent' of 1978–79 was the public equation of the right to strike with trade union irresponsibility and the misuse of power. The spectacle of uncollected rubbish festering, ambulances ignoring emergency calls and grave diggers refusing to bury the dead moved industrial relations to the forefront of the Conservative agenda. As Robert Saunders put it, the '"Winter of Discontent" not only damaged the Labour Party and created a mood of revulsion against the unions; it also helped to resolve the incoherence within the Conservative's own union policy.'[23] Hence, the miners' strike took place in the context of three pieces of employment legislation (1980, 1982 and 1984) although 'Only the South Wales National Union of Mineworkers which was sued at different times by two haulage firms and whose assets were sequestrated in August 1984 as a result, can be said to have been seriously affected by what were supposedly the Thatcher government's major anti-strike devices.'[24] As Thatcher wrote in her memoirs, 'had we fought an October general election the manifesto would have included no significant measures on union reform'.[25]

Confidential papers released by The National Archives in 2013 and 2014 reveal unprecedented stockpiling of coal over the winter of 1983/84 and just how high the curtailment of union power ranked in Thatcher's strategic thinking. The minutes of a secret meeting in September 1983 set out the full extent of the projected pit closure programme. Ian MacGregor, whose appointment as Chairman of the National Coal Board in March 1983 had been personally approved by Thatcher, planned to shut seventy-five 'uneconomic' pits over three years (1983–85) and to cut 64,000 jobs. Two out of three Welsh miners would be made redundant, 35 per cent of mines in Scotland, 48 per cent in the North East of England, 50 per cent in South Yorkshire, 46 per cent in the South Midlands and the entire Kent coalfield were to close.[26] In January 1983 Nigel Lawson advised that 'If Scargill succeeds in bringing about such a strike, we must do everything in our power to defeat him, including ensuring that the strike results in widespread closures.'[27] Ferdinand Mount noted that 'We must neglect no opportunity to erode trade union membership wherever this corresponds to the wishes of the workforce.'[28] It was hoped by the end of the century to see 'a trade union movement whose exclusive relationship with the Labour Party is reduced out of all recognition'.[29]

The strike was sustained through an extensive network of miners' support groups stretching from Aberdeen to Belfast and from Ipswich to the Isle of

Wight. They were responsible for collecting money, groceries, clothing, toys, toiletries, shoes and other essentials. 'Twinning' arrangements were common: Norwich with Ollerton, Harlow, Huntingdon and Stevenage with Welbeck, St Albans with Newstead. Supporters overcame vocal objections to 'bucket' collections in shopping precincts and town centres, especially in Conservative-controlled areas, and maximised public sympathy by the strategy of aggregating the miners and their dependants: children were widely perceived as innocent parties in the dispute and women as (relatively) untarnished by unpopular picket-line violence. Leaflets promoting the Gwent Food Fund, for example, emphasised that all food was distributed to strikers *and their families*. The Labour Research Department estimates that the numbers in groups varied from 'six to 110, with most in the ten to fifty range and the average being thirty'.[30] Moreover, 'weekly collections ranged from £25 (Waveney Town, Suffolk) to £1,000 (Isle of Wight and Kirby) but the average amount collected was almost £240 a week'.[31] The support committees were, in the main, run by members of the Labour Party, the Communist Party and non-aligned trade unionists; many were set up by constituency Labour parties or local trades councils. A wide spectrum of Trotskyist, anarchist and other left groups either put aside their sectarian differences to work inside these committees or operated separately. In the provinces supporters of the Campaign for Nuclear Disarmament, which had some 90,000 national members and a further 250,000 in local branches, were often active.[32]

The strongest groups were large, efficient and formidably well organised. The Oxford Miners' Support Group 'raised £111,000 in cash and food and received regular donations from ninety-two trade union organisations in Oxfordshire and forty-five Labour Party organizations'.[33] Others were informal and extempore in nature. There is no national register of miners' support groups. Many did not keep systematic records, leaving few, if any, traces of their existence behind. As Alison New of the Cambridge Miners' Support Group put it: 'We were too busy creating the historical record to document it.'[34] What is true in Cambridge is true of hundreds of similar groups in England, Scotland and Wales.

Lifelong personal friendships developed out of solidarity and sustenance. As Norma Dolby from Derbyshire wrote in her strike diary: 'whenever we were in trouble, or needed anything they were there. Never will those ties be broken; we will be friends for life.'[35] Miners' families in Nottinghamshire villages enjoyed free holidays in supporters' homes: 'everybody got close to one family in Cambridge and so that is where they always stayed whenever we went there'.[36] In St Albans 600 toys were carefully labelled so that every child in Newstead and Annesley received an age-appropriate present at Christmas. Dundee 'adopted' more than seventy East Fife coalfield babies born during the strike.[37] Raphael Samuel suggests that support of this kind 'owed more to the humanitarian spirit of Good Works than, in any classical trade union sense, solidarity'.[38] David Edgar wrote that fundraising 'was closer to the impetus of Live Aid [July 1985] than the proletarian solidarity that won the miners their emblematic victory at Birmingham's Saltley Gate in 1972'.[39]

Traditional proletarian solidarity was demonstrated by the rail unions (National Union of Railwaymen, Transport Salaried Staffs' Association, and ASLEF (Associated Society of Locomotive Steam Enginemen and Firemen)), which blocked attempts to move coal from Nottinghamshire by rail, by lorry drivers (Transport and General Workers' Union) and seafarers (National Union of Seamen) handling coal at the ports. Fleet Street print workers stopped a front page in *The Sun* appearing with the headline 'Mine Führer' and a photograph of Arthur Scargill supposedly giving a Nazi salute.[40] Equivocal attitudes at the highest echelons of the Trades Union Congress (TUC) contrasted markedly with the enthusiasm demonstrated by the rank and file. Virtually every TUC-affiliated union had members fundraising voluntarily. The prodigious activities of the Birmingham Trades Council were chronicled in *Birmingham and the Miners' Strike* (1986). The GMBATU (General, Municipal, Boilermakers and Allied Trades Union) gave £1 million centrally.[41] NALGO (National and Local Government Officers Association) donated a national total of £66,342. Many trade union branches set up their own support groups, with women trade unionists often working directly with women's action groups in the coalfields.[42] In August a '26-truck convoy arrived in Yorkshire from London conveying £100,000 worth of food', organised by SOGAT (Society of Graphical and Allied Trades).[43] Of the twenty-four trades councils in a Labour Research Department survey, the 'average council collected £230 per week'.[44] The miners' families' Christmas appeal with full-page press advertisements signed by Howard Brenton, Judi Dench, Margaret Drabble, David Edgar, Harold Pinter, Salman Rushdie and Fay Weldon raised a quarter of a million pounds, as well as 130,000 toys from the French trade unions.[45]

Well-wishers frequently bypassed the official NUM Miners' Solidarity Fund, sending their money directly to pits or women's groups. Twinning arrangements were often haphazard: workers in Sheffield City Council Employment Department 'stuck a pin in a map and it landed on Thurcroft'.[46] There was no parity of income between pits. Those with backing from big trade unions and constituency Labour parties or prosperous hinterlands fared better. Barnsley, Sheffield and Doncaster 'provided free meals, food and clothing vouchers, and lodgings allowances for single miners as well as deferring or waiving rents and rates'.[47] Blaenau Gwent Council gave food vouchers to every miner and Torfaen Council waived miners' rents.[48]

Two contentious issues accounted for the equivocation of the TUC and the Labour Party nationally. The most divisive was the decision of the NUM not to hold a national ballot requiring a majority of 55 per cent (later changed to 50) under union rule 43. Instead, a national executive committee resolution of 19 April called upon all areas to join those already involved in area strikes based on rule 41.[49] Since an estimated 80 per cent of NUM members were on strike in April, critics argued that a strategic opportunity had been lost to win over Nottinghamshire and demonstrate the legitimacy of the strike to the rest of the trade union movement.[50] Scargill's tactics and conduct of the strike were also controversial. The refrain, 'Arthur Scargill, we'll support you ever more', sung to the tune of 'Cwm Rhondda', echoed across the picket lines in the militant coalfields of Yorkshire and Kent, where Scargill was lionised as the defender of working-class interests. But his reluctance to work more closely with the TUC put him at odds with General Secretary Norman Willis and union officials intent on brokering a settlement with MacGregor. For this and other reasons the TUC General Council proved largely ineffective in mobilising support.

Television images of violent confrontations with the police did nothing to help Labour's electoral prospects. Moreover, Scargill's strategy of 'picketing out' the working collieries created difficulties with senior figures in the Labour Party, including Neil Kinnock and Stan Orme, shadow secretary for energy, who were arguing strongly for the alternative energy policy outlined in *The Case for Coal* (1984). Kinnock, the son and grandson of a miner, representing a mining constituency, Islwyn, had replaced Michael Foot in 1983 in a closely fought leadership contest in which he had rounded on Scargill, accusing him of 'destroying the coal-industry single-handed' and of being the 'labour movement's nearest equivalent to a First World War general'.[51] Kinnock's personal support for the strike was never in question, although he did not visit a picket line until 3 January, following a promise to his constituents.[52] He was close to the leaders of the South Wales Federation and his brother-in-law was in charge of the pickets at Wylfa power station.[53] Kinnock made 'seventy speeches in favour of coal as the opinion polls displayed a continuing and – for a long time worsening – effect of the strike on Labour's standing', but came to believe it essential to distance himself from the strikers if the Labour Party was to win the next election.[54]

Many Labour-controlled authorities, councillors, constituency Labour parties, MPs, and party officials worked tirelessly for the miners until the end: Joyce Gould, the Women's Officer, 'was constantly syphoning funds to us and trying to make the contacts and encouraging women's councils and women's sections to make contact with us'.[55] The disappointment of Labour Party supporters who had formed the backbone of the miners' support groups and 'adopted' striking collieries was palpable. As Huw Beynon put it, the 'failure of the Labour Party to initiate action in support of their cause, to point vigorously to questions of unemployment and energy policy; to raise clearly important issues about civil rights and the workings of the police force and the legal system, was not simply treacherous, it was incomprehensible'.[56]

Also backing the strikers was the Communist Party, dwindling in size and internally divided between its Eurocommunist leadership, who looked to the theoretical journal *Marxism Today*, and the 'hardline' readers of the *Morning Star*, which had passed out of party control. Seriously weakened by its internal problems, the party was still able to exert a disproportionate influence in the NUM, largely due to the positioning of its key activists. These included Jean Miller in Barnsley, Kath Mackay and Vicky Seddon in Sheffield, Hywel Francis and George Rees in Wales, Ida Hackett in Nottinghamshire, Mark Ashton in the gay community and Ella Egan, daughter of Scottish president Abe Moffat, who co-ordinated the National Union of Mineworkers' *Scottish* Area (NUMSA) women's groups. Egan and Lorraine Bowler from Yorkshire were both on the committee of Women Against Pit Closures (WAPC).

Broad leftism, represented by Mick McGahey as vice president of the NUM, was the dominant political force within the NUM in South Wales and Scotland, the areas known to be most critical of the national conduct of the strike. McGahey, although persistently rumoured to have serious reservations, remained publicly loyal to Scargill throughout. A Scottish miners' leader, George Bolton, vice president of the NUMSA, was the chairman of the Communist Party. Historically, there had always been a strong communist presence in the NUM – the Scottish presidents, Abe and Alex Moffat, Laurence Daly (Peter Heathfield's predecessor), Arthur Horner and Will Paynter had played important roles in earlier struggles. The funeral of Paynter, a former president of the South Wales Miners' Federation, took place during the strike. The party was still important in regions of the NUM where it had officials at pit or area level, and in coalfields where rank-and-file members were veterans of the industrial disputes of the 1970s. Malcolm Pitt, leader of the NUM in Kent in 1972, was jailed briefly during the 1984 strike.

In 1984 the Communist Party was intent on building a 'broad democratic alliance' to reflect the importance of the 'new social forces' in British society in accordance with the position in its manifesto, the *British Road to Socialism* (1977). The manifesto marked a radical departure in asserting that the struggle for socialism needed to extend beyond the working class and involve 'not only an association of class forces but of other important forces in society which emerge out of areas of oppression not always directly connected with the relations of production'.[57] Those with whom communists sought to engage included the women's movement, campaigners for black and minority ethnic rights, the peace movement, gays and lesbians and progressive elements within Scottish and Welsh nationalism. This theoretical position, with its rejection of 'workerism' and understanding of the importance of identity politics, made it possible for many key academics, activists and intellectuals, such as Beatrix Campbell, to support the miners while foregrounding aspects of their own identities (feminism, Welsh identity, gay activism).

As Peter Ackers suggests, the leadership of the Communist Party were 'much more critical of the official conduct of the strike than their measured written statements would suggest'.[58] This was because 'solidarity with the miners was an extremely emotive and morally loaded issue of loyalty on the left' and

> Eurocommunists with official positions in the party and trade unions could ill-afford to launch frontal assaults on the leadership of the NUM or policies like striking without a national ballot. This would have led to immediate internal defeat by labor [sic] movement loyalists at Party Congress or *Morning Star* meetings. The struggle to stay 'on-side' was constant.[59]

The eleven gay and lesbian support groups formed during the strike reflected the policies of the organised left in London and local authorities such as Manchester, Liverpool, Southampton and, notably, Sheffield under David Blunkett. Members of Bristol South Labour Party, which supported Welsh miners, had belonged to the Bristol Campaign for Homosexual Equality and the Labour Campaign for Lesbian and Gay Rights.[60] The London boroughs of Brent, Hackney, Greenwich, Islington and Lambeth were particularly active in the promotion of gay rights. Between 1981 and May 1984 'grants totalling at least £292,548 were approved for gay groups' in London and the £751,000 committed to the London Lesbian and Gay Community Centre in Islington brought the total to £1,043,548.[61] In 1983 the Greater London Council, chaired by Ken Livingstone, set up a Gay Working Party which advised on grant applications and maintained contact with over 100 such groups.[62] Livingstone also chaired the Mineworkers' Defence Committee during the strike.

Diarmaid Kelliher has analysed one group that put socialist politics on the agenda of the London gay community and sexual politics on the agenda of the trade unions. Lesbians and Gays Support the Miners, whose activities were memorialized in *Pride*, was set up by Mike Jackson and Mark Ashton (a former chairman of the Young Communist League). The £20,000 raised is estimated to have paid about a quarter of the bills in Dulais, helping to break down homophobic attitudes in rural Wales: 'Rather than their sexuality it was the metropolitan lifestyle of the young activists that posed the biggest problem.'[63] Their solidarity was transformative largely because they refused to allow their own sexuality to be subsumed. In consequence, the NUM was invited to lead the London Gay Pride March in 1985 and supported the first resolutions in favour of gay rights passed at the TUC and Labour Party conferences that year.

WAPC was launched in May 1984 at a rally in Barnsley attended by 10,000 women and a national delegate conference in Chesterfield in November. Because their key objectives, preventing colliery closures and job losses, were endorsed nationally by the NUM they were accepted, albeit with some resistance, in coalfields where patriarchal attitudes had been naturalised in the workplace and the home for generations. However, they differed from working-class women who had defended their own jobs in the Grunwick (1978) and Dagenham machinists' (1967) disputes: the jobs underground which they fought to save were tightly regulated by unions which had excluded women from membership and in which women had been prohibited from working under the Mines and Collieries Act of 1842. Women were thus engaged in a struggle on two fronts: to stop pit closures and to enable women to participate fully in the coal dispute and to have their own distinctive voices and perspectives heard.

To this end, WAPC accentuated their credentials as loyal miners' wives and family members, thus legitimising women's involvement, winning themselves plaudits from the labour movement and access to the male-dominated political spaces hitherto occupied exclusively by the NUM. 'Miners' wives' is, of course, an inaccurate (albeit common) misnomer for activists who attempted to make contact with *all* the women in the coalfields whose lives were affected by the strike and who 'believed that the dispute was as much our dispute as the men's because we had as much suffering as the men who worked down the pit'.[64] Many miners' wives did not take part in the strike or were actively opposed to it, while some women working in colliery canteens were on strike in their own right. Even the 'seventy five rule' stipulating that three-quarters of WAPC members should be from mining families still left one in four women with no familial connection to a miner.

Without consciously using a feminist vocabulary, WAPC recognised that sexist and patronising attitudes constituted a deterrent to women's political involvement and insisted on their right to engage separately in the strike. They used their influence with the NUM and status as 'authentic' representatives of the mining districts to make women's perspectives heard on issues such as peace, jobs, health and education, and other subjects on which the union had no policy, developing relationships with protestors at the Greenham Common peace camp. Reciprocal visits led to the formation of Greenham Women for a Miners' Victory and to regular collections at the camp gates. 'Mines not missiles' became a popular slogan on badges and T-shirts and 'Mines not Missiles' groups were set up.

While the women's action and support groups should not be romanticised, the very existence of hundreds of groups organised by women for which documentary evidence exists was clearly of major political significance – whatever comparators may be used – as were the role that these groups played in mitigating day-to-day hardship and their impact on the lives and consciousness of the women who ran them.[65] Women's groups fed and clothed entire communities, acquiring expertise on all strike-related matters, from Department of Health and Social Security claims to mortgage repayments and international solidarity, as well as providing many sought-after public speakers. For example, Lynne Cheetham, a miner's wife from Point of Ayr, 'very nervous and apprehensive', addressed the European Parliament in Strasbourg, won instant acclaim and toured mining towns and car factories in France, raising thousands of pounds.[66] The strike brought together 'accidental' or 'circumstantial activists' whose commitment was a product of their life circumstances and 'long term activists' whose political outlook had been formed over an extended time-span. The distinction was a loose one. Many miners' wives made the transition from 'circumstantial' to long-term activist: Sian James, MP for Swansea East, is the best known. Neither were 'long term activists' invariably feminist or middle class ('parachuted into the coalfields and, once the action was over headed back to their middle-class London homes to write their Ph.Ds').[67]

WAPC, which held committee meetings in the NUM headquarters in Sheffield, was never a monolith and the group was subject to internal fissures, divisions and tensions. The prominence of Anne Scargill and Betty Heathfield as ex officio members led to criticisms that the organisation was being orchestrated at a national level by the NUM president and general secretary.[68] However, WAPC enjoyed remarkable success in drawing many women into political activity for the first time. What women brought to the strike was the disregard for hierarchy that was the hallmark of the women's movement in the 1980s, coupled with a spontaneity that challenged the procedures and assumptions of the trade unions. 'Without a formal structural base, without such things as standing orders, rules and constitutions, the women of the coalfields launched a massive political education campaign, publicising through the country and abroad what was happening in the coalfields and its implications for other workers.'[69]

WAPC tactics, such as overnight occupations of empty properties or the use of the suffragette colours on banners, were reminiscent of Edwardian first-wave feminism, while their 'women only' groups placed WAPC on a continuum with other feminist organisations of the 1980s. However, working-class women often saw feminism as a procrustean bed in which they did not wish to be placed, simultaneously attempting to disassociate themselves from the negative connotations attached to the word in many working-class communities while acting in recognisably feminist ways. Attitudes have mellowed considerably over time. Interviewed for the British Library's 'Sisterhood and After' oral history recordings of the Women's Liberation Movement, the WAPC's treasurer, Betty Cook, hoped that 'future generations will gain inspiration from not only Women Against Pit Closures but the women's movement as a whole because we are now part and parcel of the women's movement'.[70]

Women's activism had a historical precedent in the Lock-Out of 1926, when Labour MP Ellen Wilkinson (1891–1947) led a massive humanitarian effort organised by the Women's Committee of the Labour Party and collected £313,000, clothes, food, milk, shoes and medicines. As Arthur Cook wrote in appreciation: 'the Women's Committee worked night and day to collect funds, to arrange for our choirs and bands, and to dispatch money, clothes and boots … The Labour Women cared for Humanity, when the Government led by Baldwin tried to starve our people.'[71] In her biography, *A Woman's*

Work is Never Done, Elizabeth Andrews, Labour Party Women's Organiser for Wales, recollects miners' wives, Mrs Beatrice Green of Abertillery, Mrs Johnna James of Tonypandy and Mrs Herman of Pentree, making effective fundraising speeches in London during the Lock-Out.[72] Andrews recalls the Labour Advisory Councils and the Relief Committee of the Standing Joint Committee of Industrial Women's Organizations, under whose guidance 'we set up in Wales in a very short time a wonderful network of organisations to look after expectant and nursing mothers, children, and sick people'.[73]

Wilkinson spent many weeks living and working with women in the Yorkshire coalfields during the Lock-Out, helping to initiate a tradition of mutual respect and understanding, which was revived by middle-class women 'outsiders' active in the pit villages during in the 1984–85 strike. For example, women from the Cambridge Miners' Support Group regularly helped with the cooking in the Blidworth communal kitchen: 'It was great for us to have them, they really helped to take some of the burden off us and it made us realise how hard we worked to see how tired it made them.'[74] Relationships between women from differing social and educational backgrounds were initially complicated by pre-existing imbalances of power and class differences, as well as some suspicion of motives: 'Sometimes I got annoyed as it felt like every organisation that wanted attention was jumping on our bandwagon,' wrote a striking canteen worker and NUM member, Catherine Paton Black.[75]

What middle-class women like Alison New and Lucy Munby from Cambridge still recollect, however, is the warmth of their reception in the mining villages after hazardous weekly journeys to deliver much-needed money and foodstuffs to places like Rainworth that they could not previously have identified on the map.[76] Small children were an 'ice breaker', as were the ubiquitous Saturday night social evenings at which supporters were welcomed. 'The capacity of Newstead folk to create enjoyable community events, even in hard times, was impressive,' recalls Vivien Bailey of the St Albans support group.[77]

'Equal rights feminism' was strongly embedded in the Staffordshire mining areas, where the reputation of the legendary Fanny Deakin (1883–1968), a working-class maternity rights and childcare campaigner from the mining village of Silverdale, lived on. Deakin had been a communist county councillor and an Alderman in Newcastle-under-Lyme for many years. Jim Phillips suggests that women's activism in the Scottish coalfields may 'have owed something to Communist Party Tradition, especially in Fife, Communist women expected a greater involvement in public life, and Communist Party men – more or less – accepted the desirability of this'.[78] Indeed, women's local knowledge and expertise was crucial to the strike's maintenance. Notts Women Against Pit Closures, which co-ordinated all the Nottinghamshire women's groups, was chaired by Ida Hackett, a veteran communist who had been prominent in the equal pay campaign during the Second World War:

> Mrs Hackett liked to tell a story about the time she and fellow union members got involved in a dispute over pay. In the hosiery union, female workers received a higher rate of pay than men and the men weren't happy about the situation. When two national union officials visited Mansfield to persuade the women to accept lower rates, rather than equal pay for men and women, the angry women chased them out of the meeting and up the hill.[79]

In Nottinghamshire, where families were torn apart on 'pro' and 'anti' lines, the visibility of women in the action groups counteracted media attention on miners' wives supporting their husbands' 'right to work'. Women joined picket lines, strengthened one another's morale and combated individual feelings of isolation. Women's groups were set up for some thirty Nottinghamshire pits, their nomenclature (such as the Ashfield Women's Support Group or the Langold Women's Action Group) emphasising the importance attached to action and support, respectively.

Working relationships between men and women could sometimes be acrimonious. In Normanton 'The men wouldn't let us join forces with them, we couldn't speak at Union meetings, we hit a brick wall.'[80] Elsewhere, there were disagreements between NUM officials attempting to exercise local control and women demanding decision-making powers. One hundred and six women's groups were organised centrally from Cardiff, covering twenty-seven pits.[81] However, as Geoffrey Goodman notes, there was a 'long tradition and reputation for male chauvinism in Wales in general, and perhaps South Wales in particular', and the 'women's activities were not universally welcomed by the men'.[82] Although women in Gwent set up their food centre and distributed 6,000 parcels every week it was men who met weekly to make decisions: 'At no point during the strike were women allowed to attend one of those meetings.'[83]

Extreme poverty and hardship inevitably put a strain on intimate relationships and necessitated questioning and readjustment of domestic roles. While some marriages were cemented by a sense of common purpose, others fell apart.[84] One NUM area official found 'one in six of those who came to see me experiencing very distressing marital problems ... the trauma of the strike was directly related to the break-up of the marriage'.[85] A Methodist minister in Barnsley equated women's altered self-perceptions and new understandings of their potential 'with the New Testament experience of "transfiguration"'.[86] Many working-class women gained confidence to study for higher qualifications, for example at Northern College, or to apply for jobs which would previously have seemed unattainable. However, shifts in consciousness are intractably difficult for the historian to map. The feelings of emancipation, agency and self-esteem which women activists reported were frequently qualified by unhappy personal recollections of the dispute as a time of great personal anxiety, insecurity and distress. The desire to return to normality was strong.

The 'tradition of women's protests in British mining communities has always been largely community based, deriving its authority as well as its form from commonly understood values'.[87] However, the notion of community is itself problematic. As a consequence of earlier pit closures, new housing developments and changing patterns of migration, the terms 'mining community' and 'mining village' were far from synonymous. Yet, as Jean Spence and Carol Stephenson point out, the 'frequent references to "mining village" … in the discourse of the strike suggested the continuing vibrancy of historically discrete, spatially isolated and bounded places in the imagination of the Left'.[88] Nevertheless, the longevity of the strike demonstrated the value that the miners attached to their trade union and the loyalties learned in both workplace and home, as well as the contempt that was ubiquitously felt for the 'scab' labour in Nottinghamshire and the working minority elsewhere. Solidarity was transmitted through the family, with women acting as the bearers of communal consensus. 'In my family and Dave's we have between us seven miners who all work down the pit, not one of them returned to work during the strike of which I am very proud,' testified Janine Head, a Normanton activist.[89]

The miners' epic struggle in defence of their industry and their communities secured them a place in the annals of English radical protest alongside the Jarrow marchers and the demonstrators at Peterloo. However, what few had envisaged at the time was the magnitude of Thatcher's victory or the eradication of the coal industry in places like the Welsh valleys where mining had been a way of life for generations. In 1984, Britain had 180 working deep-cast coal mines and 181,400 miners.[90] In 2013 the NUM's figures revealed 1,283 mineworkers left in the industry.[91] With the closure of Kellingley pit in Yorkshire in December 2015, the history of deep-cast mining in Britain came to an end.

And the price of the miners' defeat? Kinnock estimates that 'by all reasonable reckoning' breaking the strike had 'cost 47 billion pounds in today's money'.[92] It is impossible to calculate exactly how much was collected by the organised labour movement and their supporters, although the mobilisation of money, solidarity and resources was arguably on a scale that had not been witnessed since the Aid for Spain Movement in the 1930s. One estimate is £60 million.[93] The value of groceries, toys, clothing, toiletries, infant necessities and holidays can never be known.[94]

Notes

1 House of Lords Debates, 13 November 1984, 457 col. 240.
2 Charles Moore, *Margaret Thatcher: The Authorised Biography* vol. 1 *Not for Turning* (Harmondsworth: Penguin, 2013), p. 537.
3 Lesley Sutcliffe and Brian Hill, *Let Them Eat Coal: The Political Use of Social Security During the Miners' Strike* (London: Canary Press, 1985), p. 3.

4 Paul Mackney, *Birmingham and the Miners' Strike: A Story of Solidarity* (Birmingham: Trades Council, 1987), p. 1.
5 Mike Sanders, '"Alive to Production, Misery, Slavery – Dead to Enjoyment and Happiness"', in Simon Popple and Ian W. Macdonald (eds), *Digging the Seam: Popular Cultures of the 1984/5 Miners' Strike* (Cambridge: Cambridge Scholars Publishing, 2012), pp. 10–22, at p. 11.
6 See, for example, Seamus Milne's pro-Scargill, *The Enemy Within: The Secret War Against the Miners* (London: Verso, 1994) and Ian K. MacGregor with Rodney Tyler's pro-Thatcher, *The Enemies Within: The Story of the Miners' Strike, 1984–5* (London: Collins, 1986).
7 Beatrix Campbell, *Wigan Pier Revisited: Poverty and Politics in the Eighties* (London: Virago, 1984), p. 97.
8 Raymond Williams, 'Mining the Meaning: Key Words in the Miners' Strike', in Richard Gable (ed.), *Resources of Hope: Culture, Democracy, Socialism* (London: Verso, 1989), p. 125.
9 See Jaclyn J. Gier-Viskovatoff and Abigail Porter, 'Women of the British Coalfields on Strike in 1926 and 1984: Documenting Lives Using Oral History and Photography', *Frontiers: A Journal of Women Studies* 19 (1998), 199–230.
10 W. John Morgan and Ken Coates, *The Nottinghamshire Coalfield and the British Miners' Strike 1984–85* (Nottingham: University of Nottingham Department of Adult Education, c.1990), p. 27; Peter Wilsher, Donald Macintyre and Michael Jones, *Strike: Thatcher, Scargill and the Miners* (London: Hodder and Stoughton, 1985), p. 107.
11 Hywel Francis, *History on our Side: Wales and the 1984–5 Miners' Strike* (Ferryside, Wales: Iconau, 2009), p. 45.
12 Doreen Massey and Hilary Wainwright, 'Beyond the Coalfields: The Work of the Miners' Support Groups', in Huw Beynon (ed.), *Digging Deeper for the Miners: Issues in the Miners' Strike* (London: Verso, 1986), pp. 149–68, at p. 152.
13 Massey and Wainwright, 'Beyond the Coalfields', p. 154.
14 Daryl Leeworthy, 'The Secret Life of Us: 1984, the Miners' Strike and the Place of Biography in Writing History "From Below"', *European Review of History* 19 (2012), 825–46, at 830.
15 Francis, *History on our Side*, p. 61.
16 Francis, *History on our Side*, p. 45.
17 John Alderson, Larry Gostin, Sarah McCabe, Ian Martin, Christopher Mason and Peter Wallington, *The First Report of the Independent Inquiry Civil Liberties and the Miners' Dispute* (London: National Council for Civil Liberties, 1984), p. 17.
18 Sarah McCabe and Peter Wallington with John Alderson, Larry Gostin and Christopher Mason, *The Police, Public Order and Civil Liberties: Legacies of the Miners' Strike* (London: Routledge, 1998), p. 23.
19 Labour Research Department, *The Miners' Case* (London: LRD, 1984), p. 14.
20 *The Church and the Miners: Strike: a Briefing Paper* (London: General Synod Board for Social Responsibility Industrial and Economic Affairs, 1984), pp. 5–6.
21 Roger Middleton, *Government versus the Market: The Growth of the Public Sector, Economic Management and British Economic Performance, c.1890–1979* (Cheltenham: Edward Elgar, 1996), p. 630; William Keegan, *Mrs Thatcher's Economic Experiment* (Harmondsworth: Penguin, 1984), p. 10.
22 Francis Beckett and David Hencke, *Marching to the Fault Line: The 1984 Miners' Strike and the Death of Industrial Britain* (London: Constable, 2009), p. 36.
23 Robert Saunders, '"Crisis: What Crisis?": Thatcherism and the Seventies', in Ben Jackson and Robert Saunders (eds), *Making Thatcher's Britain* (Cambridge: Cambridge University Press, 2012), p. 39.

24 Eric J. Evans, *Thatcher and Thatcherism* (London: Routledge, 2013 [1997]), p. 38; Richard de Friend and Gerry R. Rubin, 'Civil Law and the 1984–85 Coal Dispute', *Journal of Law and Society* 12 (1985), 321–32, at 322.
25 Margaret Thatcher, *The Path to Power* (London: HarperCollins, 1995), p. 414.
26 See confidential minute, 15 September 1983, www.margaretthatcher.org, document 133121 (accessed 10 October 2014).
27 *Guardian*, 1 August 2013, p. 16.
28 *Guardian*, 1 August 2013, p. 16.
29 *Guardian*, 1 August 2013, p. 16.
30 Labour Research Department, *Solidarity with the Miners*, p. 17.
31 Labour Research Department, *Solidarity with the Miners*, p. 18.
32 James Hinton, 'Campaign for Nuclear Disarmament', in Roger S. Powers (ed.), *Protest, Power and Change* (London: Taylor and Francis, 1997), p. 63.
33 Alan Thornett (ed.), Preface, *The Miners' Strike in Oxford* (Oxford: Oxford and District Trades Union Council, 1985), p. 7.
34 Alison New, conversation with Mary Joannou, 1 October 2014.
35 Norma Dolby, *Norma Dolby's Diary: An Account of the Great Miners' Strike* (London: Verso, 1987), p. 17.
36 Lynn Beaton, *Shifting Horizons* (London: Canary Press, 1985), p. 211.
37 Jim Phillips, *Collieries, Communities and the Miners' Strike in Scotland, 1984–85* (Manchester: Manchester University Press, 2012), p. 117.
38 Raphael Samuel, preface to Raphael Samuel, Barbara Bloomfield and Guy Boanas (eds), *The Enemy Within: Pit Villages and the Miners' Strike of 1984–5* (London: Routledge and Kegan Paul, 1986), p. x.
39 David Edgar, 'The Miners' Strike: Coal not Dole', *Guardian*, Review, 5 April, 2004, p. 19.
40 Granville Williams, 'Trade Union Solidarity and the Miners' Strike', in Granville Williams (ed.), *Shafted: The Media, the Miners' Strike and the Aftermath* (London: Campaign for Press and Broadcasting Freedom, 2009), pp. 36–46, at p. 39.
41 Jonathan Winterton and Ruth Winterton, *Coal, Crisis and Conflict: The 1984–5 Miners' Strike in Yorkshire* (Manchester: Manchester University Press, 1989), p. 120.
42 Granville Williams, 'The Media and the Miners', in in Granville Williams (ed.), *Shafted*, p. 31.
43 Martin Harvey, Martin Jenkinson and Mark Metcalf, *The Miners' Strike* (Barnsley: Pen and Sword History, 2014), p. 120.
44 Labour Research Department, *Solidarity with the Miners* (London: LRD, 1985), p. 11.
45 John Rose, 'But Once a Year', *New Statesman*, 28 December, 1984, p. 15.
46 Peter Gibbon and David Steyne, *Thurcroft: A Village and the Miners' Strike, an Oral History* (Nottingham: Spokesman, 1986), p. 59.
47 Winterton and Winterton, *Coal, Crisis and Conflict*, p. 133.
48 Brian Curtis, *The South Wales Miners 1964–1985* (Cardiff: University of Wales Press, 2013), p. 211.
49 De Friend and Rubin, 'Civil Law and the 1984–85 Coal Dispute', p. 323.
50 De Friend and Rubin, 'Civil Law and the 1984–85 Coal Dispute', p. 323.
51 Cited in Robert Harris, *The Making of Neil Kinnock* (London: Faber & Faber, 1984), p. 164.
52 Winterton and Winterton, *Coal, Crisis and Conflict*, p. 113.
53 Martin Adeney and John Lloyd, *The Miners' Strike 1984–5: Loss without Limit* (London: Routledge and Kegan Paul, 1988), p. 293.
54 John Lloyd, *Understanding the Miners' Strike* (London: Fabian Society, 1985), p. 16.

55 Jean McCrindle, interviewed by Sheila Rowbotham, 'More than Just a Memory: Some Political Implications of Women's Involvement in the Miners' Strike, 1984–5', *Feminist Review* 23 (*Socialist Feminism: Out of the Blue*) (1986), 109–24, at 119.
56 Huw Beynon (ed.), Introduction, *Digging Deeper for the Miners* (London: Verso, 1985), p. 22.
57 The CPGB, *The British Road to Socialism* (London: CPGB, 1977), p. 16.
58 Peter Ackers, 'Gramsci at the Miners' Strike: Remembering the 1984–85 Eurocommunist Alternative Industrial Relations Strategy', *Labor History* 55 (2014), 151–72, at 156.
59 Ackers, 'Gramsci at the Miners' Strike', p. 156.
60 Daryl Leeworthy, '"Don't Worry about Him, He's a Scargill Man": The Strike and After', https://historyonthedole.wordpress.com, 12 March 2015 (accessed 20 March 2015).
61 Rachel Tingle, *Gay Lessons: How Public Funds are Used to Promote Homosexuality among Children and Young People* (London: Pickwick Books, 1986), p. 8; GLC Agenda, 22 May 1984, quoted Tingle, *Gay Lessons*.
62 Tingle, *Gay Lessons*.
63 Diarmaid Kelliher, 'Solidarity and Sexuality: Lesbians and Gays Support the Miners 1984–5', *History Workshop Journal*, 77 (2014), 240–62, at 242; Lucy Robinson, *Gay Men and the Left in Post-War Britain* (Manchester: Manchester University Press, 2007), p. 166.
64 Jean Miller, 'Barnsley', in Vicky Seddon (ed.), *The Cutting Edge: Women and the Pit Strike* (London: Lawrence and Wishart, 1986), pp. 227–40, at p. 228.
65 LSE Women's Library, Papers of Jean McCrindle, including records of Women Against Pit Closures, 7J MC.
66 Tony Heath, 'The Miner's Wife Who Found Her Voice and Spread the Word', *Guardian*, 2 June, 1984, p. 14.
67 Triona Holden, *Queen Coal: Women of the Miners' Strike* (Stroud: Sutton, 2005), p. 139.
68 Keith Laybourn, *Marxism in Britain: Dissent, Decline and Re-emergence 1945–c.2000* (London: Routledge, 2006), pp. 127–8.
69 Joan Witham, *Hearts and Minds: The Story of the Women of Nottinghamshire in the Miners' Strike 1984–5* (London: Canary Press, 1986), p. 25.
70 Betty Cook interview, *Sisterhood and After: an Oral History of the Women's Liberation Movement*, The British Library, www.bl.uk/learning/histcitizen/sisterhood/clips/activism/campaigns-and-protests/143237.html (accessed 24 March 2014).
71 A. J. Cook, quoted in Marion Phillips, *Women and the Miners' Lock-Out: The Story of the Women's Committee for the Relief of the Miners' Wives and Children* (London: Labour Publishing, 1927), p. 25.
72 Elizabeth Andrews, *A Woman's Work is Never Done* (Ystrad, Rhondda: Cymru Democratic Publishing Society, 1956), p. 25.
73 Andrews, *A Woman's Work is Never Done*, p. 24.
74 Lynn Beaton, *Shifting Horizons* (London: Canary Press, 1985), p. 211.
75 Catherine Paton Black, *At the Coalface: My Life as a Miner's Wife* (London: Headline, 2012), p. 303.
76 Conversations between Alison New, Lucy Munby, Vivien Bailey and Mary Joannou, all of whom were active in Nottinghamshire during the strike, 17 November 2014.
77 Vivien Bailey, *Thirty Years On: The 1984/5 Miners' Strike and the St Albans Nottinghamshire–NUM Miners' Support Group* (St Albans: privately produced pamphlet, 2014), no pagination.
78 Phillips, *Collieries, Communities and the Miners' Strike in Scotland, 1984–85*, p. 135.

79 *Nottingham Post*, 9 May 2012, www.nottinghampost.com/Obituary-Ida-Hackett/story (accessed 1 February 2015).
80 Janine Head, Mavis Watson and Teresa Webb, *Striking Figures: The Story of Normanton and Altofts Miners Support Group 1984–5* (Halifax: Artivan and Striking Figures, 1986), p. 23.
81 Jean Stead, *Never the Same Again: Women and the Miner's Strike 1984–5* (London: Women's Press, 1987), p. 17.
82 Geoffrey Goodman, *The Miners' Strike* (London: Pluto Press, 1985), p. 90.
83 Alex Gray, 'Women's Place in the Welsh Congress', in Seddon (ed.), *The Cutting Edge*, pp. 205–10, at p. 207.
84 Chrys Salt and Jim Layzell (eds), *Here We Go! Women's Memories of the 1984/85 Miners' Strike* (London: Political Committee, Co-operative Retail Services, c.1985), p. 4.
85 Janet Peters, 'A Day in the Life of a Pit Prop', *Guardian*, 2 June, 1984, p. 14.
86 Brian Jenner, *Christian Reflections on the Miners' Struggle* (Sheffield: New City, 1986), p. 64.
87 Gier-Viskovatoff and Porter, 'Women of the British Coalfields on Strike in 1926 and 1984', p. 202.
88 Jean Spence and Carol Stephenson, '"Side by Side with Our Men?": Women's Activism, Community, and Gender in the 1984–1985 British Miners' Strike', *International Labor and Working-Class History* 75 (2009), 68–84, at 74.
89 Janine Head, quoted in *Striking Figures*, p. 27.
90 *National Coal Board, Reports and Accounts 1985/6* (London: National Coal Board, 1986), p. 19.
91 Annual returns for 2013 as submitted to the Certification Office, published 24 November, 2014, www.NUM.org.uk (accessed 12 March 2015).
92 Neil Kinnock interview, www.historyandpolicy.org/…/the-miners-strike-30-years-on-conference (accessed 1 June 2015).
93 Alex Callinicos and Mike Simons, *The Great Miners' Strike of 1984–5 and its Lessons* (London: SWP, 1985), p. 127.
94 A multimedia archive and website on the work the Cambridge Miners Support Group including interviews with key activists has been compiled by the Labour History Research Unit at Anglia Ruskin University and can be accessed online at www.cambridgeminersstrike.com/.

9

'Race Today cannot fail': black radicalism in the long 1980s

Robin Bunce

No discussion of the British left in the 1980s would be complete without an account of the Race Today Collective. Simply put, the collective was the most influential group of black radicals in the UK, 'the centre, in England, of black liberation'.[1] From its foundation in the mid-1970s to its dissolution in 1991, the collective coalesced around the magazine *Race Today*. It was the embodiment of C. L. R. James's vision of a small organisation. Consequently, members saw their role in the following ways. First, they were a repository of strategic expertise who would help with the complexities of organising grass-roots campaigns. Second, they aimed to use the magazine to record the struggle of the 'black' British working class.[2] Finally, having established the collective, they were determined to influence mainstream debate and British institutions from a position of strength.

The Race Today Collective went through three main stages. First, from its foundation in the mid-1970s to the early 1980s, it was primarily concerned with helping to organise grass-roots campaigns. Second, from the mid-1980s, there was a change in emphasis and the collective threw its considerable weight behind the encouragement of black art and literature. Finally, having broken into the mainstream media, it dissolved in April 1991.

The origins of the collective

Farrukh Dhondy, one of the first people to write for *Race Today* under Darcus Howe's editorship, argues that the collective grew out of the most progressive politics of the British Black Panther movement.[3] The Panthers had been founded as a nationalist and Leninist organisation by Nigerian playwright Obi B. Egbuna in 1968.[4] Following Egbuna's trial for conspiracy to murder police officers, Althea Jones-Lecointe, a doctoral candidate in biochemistry at the University of London and recent migrant from Trinidad, became the leading figure in the Panthers.[5] According to Neil Kenlock, the Panthers' official photographer, 'Althea never called herself the leader, but she led us'.[6]

Under Jones-Lecointe the Panthers became transformed from a small group of 'Hyde-Park revolutionaries', intent on catching the headlines, to a low-profile but genuinely effective grass-roots organisation boasting 3,000 members, including its Youth League.[7] Jones-Lecointe also took the Panthers in a new ideological direction. She developed a library for the Panthers, introducing them to the work of Marx, Lenin and C. L. R. James and to E. P. Thompson's *The Making of the English Working Class*.[8] In this period the Panthers played a leading role in the trial of the Mangrove Nine, a court case which ended in December 1971 and which enabled black radicals, including Jones-Lecointe and Howe, to force the first judicial acknowledgement that there was 'evidence of racial hatred' in the Metropolitan Police.[9]

However, by 1973 the Panthers had split. A group of radicals including Howe and Dhondy walked away, believing that the group was moving in a reactionary direction.[10] Soon after, Howe was appointed editor of *Race Today*, a radical monthly magazine published by the Institute of Race Relations (IRR). Initially, Howe worked with Ambalavaner Sivanandan, the leading figure in the IRR. However, there was a fundamental disagreement between the two. Leila Hassan, Information Officer in the IRR's library and later editor of *Race Today*, argues that, for Sivanandan, 'it had to be about white racism, racism that had formed us and deformed us, that was our fight'.[11] Howe, by contrast, believed that black people were playing the leading role not only in the struggle against racism in Britain but also in the struggles of the British working class.

Against this background, a break with the IRR was inevitable. After eight months of working with Sivanandan at the IRR's offices in Kings Cross, Howe, Hassan and the *Race Today* team set up on their own. They decided to move their base of operations to Brixton and to root the magazine in the centre of London's biggest working-class black community. With the aid of Olive Morris, a former Panther who had turned squatting into a science, the magazine relocated, squatting at 74 Shakespeare Road.[12]

The collective, which took shape in 1974, was an eclectic mix. It included Farrukh Dhondy and Mala Sen, intellectuals and former members of the Panthers' Central Core; Leila Hassan and Jean Ambrose, who were part of the Black Unity and Freedom Party; Patricia Dick, a one-time member of the IRR; Barbara Beese, one of the Mangrove Nine and a former employee of Release; and Linton Kwesi Johnson, a member of the Panther Youth League, who became *Race Today*'s resident poet. By the mid-1970s the radicals who formed part of the collective had become an essential part of Brixton's black working-class community.

In 1980 the members of the collective broke through a wall connecting their house on Shakespeare Road with a house on Railton Road, in order to establish a second squat. The house on Railton Road later became the offices of *Race Today*. During the 1980s, the basement of 165 Railton Road was used for 'Basement Sessions' (discussed below); the ground floor was where *Race Today*'s production team was based, the first floor comprised editorial offices, and the top floor housed James.

The collective's influence was felt far outside London. Through contacts with Ali Hussein, Gus John and Max Farrar, and through developing a reputation as the authentic voice of the black community, it became the centre of the fight for black rights in Britain.

Ideological and strategic orientation

The collective was often regarded as something of an enigma. Recalling Darcus Howe and the collective in the mid-1980s, Linda Bellos, leader of Lambeth Council from 1986 to 1988, comments, 'I could see what he was against, I couldn't see what he was for.'[13] Hassan argues that misunderstandings of the collective abounded. The local black community, she recalls, initially mistook them for social workers. White radicals were also perplexed as the collective did not fit easily into any of the mainstream leftist schemas. What the white left found confusing was that while the collective rejected Black Nationalism and separatism, it also refused to embrace the slogan 'Black and White Unite and Fight'.[14]

While the collective's ideological and strategic orientation might have perplexed the mainstream left, the collective knew what it was about. Howe set out his vision for *Race Today* in his first four editorials, published between January and April 1974. First, Howe stressed black self-organisation. His first editorial, 'From victim to protagonist', signalled a rejection of 'liberal' assumptions that black people were 'helpless victims' who needed to be rescued by progressive whites or educated members of the black middle class. The editorial focused on the 'self-activity' of the 'Caribbean and Asian peoples'. Howe wrote:

> Our task is to record and recognise the struggles of the emerging forces as manifestations of the revolutionary potential of the black population. We recognise too the release of intellectual energy from within the black community, which always comes to the fore when the masses of the oppressed by their actions create a new social reality. *Race Today* opens its pages to the tendency which seeks to give theoretical clarification to independent grass roots self-activity with a view to its further development.[15]

Second, Howe argued that black people had a unique historical role to play in the context of late twentieth-century Britain. The February editorial addressed the energy crisis, the dominant issue in British politics at the time.

In the context of the miners' strike, Howe argued that anti-government feeling existed in black and Asian communities to a much greater extent than it did within the white working class. The roots of this disparity, he argued, were historical: the British working class had been socialised by capitalism for more than 400 years, whereas the mores of the new arrivals were at greater variance with prevailing capitalist values.

Howe's third editorial was on a similar theme. Discussing the relative positions of the white and black working class, 'Bringing it all back home' argued that there was 'an increasing tendency within the white working class to take on the British State'.[16] Howe attributed this to a historical change. Traditionally, British capitalism had exported its most repressive side to the colonies, while at home the white male working class had been bought off by paternalism, and latterly by social democracy. However, the policing of recent migrants had brought the horrors of the colonial system to the streets of Brixton, Handsworth and Notting Hill. Moreover, British capitalism refused to extend the niceties of social democracy to black workers or working-class women. As a result, some in the white working class were beginning to see through liberal assumptions about the essential fairness of British society. Consequently, there was a new possibility that black and white workers could draw strength from each other. What was needed, Howe concluded, was an acceleration of black 'self-organisation, indicating that we too are prepared to take on the British state'.[17]

For Johnson, the politics of the organisation was crucial to his decision to join:

> It was not just the politics of race, it was also the politics of class. The analysis from which we were working was that we were part of a working class struggle. So from an ideological point of view, the fact that it was a class orientated organisation, as opposed to one simply dealing with race meant that I was more likely to join than not.[18]

The emphasis on self-activity necessitated a rejection of the vanguard party, the Leninist notion of a small group of professional revolutionaries who initiated a revolution on behalf of the wider working class. Rather, the collective conceived of itself as a 'small organisation' in the Jamesian sense. The Jamesian influence was self-conscious. 'We were driven by the small organisation as opposed to the vanguard party,' Howe recalled.[19] Specifically, Howe was inspired by the analysis of the small organisation built around a journal that James had outlined in *Facing Reality*, a text that Howe had first read with James in the late 1960s:

> For thirty years the small organisation knew what it meant by success: success was growing membership and influence ... But the organisation of today will go the way of its forerunners if it does not understand that its future does not depend

on the constant recruiting and training and disciplining of professional or semi-professional revolutionaries in the Leninist manner. Its task is to recognize and record. It can do this only by plunging into the great mass of the people and meeting the new society that is there.[20]

Race Today was also inspired by James's conception of a radical journal:

The journal contemplated here ... exists so that workers and other ordinary people will tell each other and people like themselves what they are thinking, what they are doing, and what they want to do. In the course of so doing, the intellectuals and advanced workers, both inside and outside the organisation, will have their opportunity to learn. There is no other way.[21]

This Jamesian approach was evident in Howe's fourth editorial. The centrepiece of the April issue of *Race Today* was a series of interviews with Asian workers. Evoking the spirit of Marx's *A Worker's Enquiry*, Howe's editorial argued that the interviews were significant because they revealed 'the day-to-day struggles of the Asians on their introduction ... to factory life, their customs, their values, their ideas, hopes, aspirations and fears as well as their drive toward self-organisation'.[22]

The strategy of the Race Today Collective was also informed by a shift that was taking place in migrant communities in the 1970s and early 1980s. The members of the collective, like migrant communities more generally, made an important transition from seeing themselves as migrants or children of migrants to identifying themselves as British, in the sense that they had made Britain their home. For Howe, this new orientation was summed up in the phrase which emerged from campaigns for Asian rights in the East End: 'Come what may we are here to stay'. With this in mind, the collective's overarching objective was to play a part in the fight to secure the full rights of citizenship for migrants and to ensure that migrants played a full role in British society. This meant working with migrants to gain the attention and support of trades unions and, after the intervention of James, backing initiatives for black people to join the police.

The collective believed that through joining unions and working within existing institutions black people could advance their own struggle and play the leading role in radicalising institutions which had ossified during the period of social democracy, and which had tended to represent the interests of white men, rather than the working class as a whole. The collective's approach to journalism was also distinctive. Rather than writing about ideology, it deliberately focused on the experience of minority communities and women. This was not, however, a rejection of intellectual concerns. Rather, it was rooted in an intellectual position: the recognition of the truth of James's view that disenfranchised groups should articulate their own experience, formulate their demands and determine their own strategies.

During the 1970s this strategy led to success. The strike by Asian workers at Imperial Typewriters in Leicester, beginning in July 1974, won Asian workers better pay and conditions and, perhaps more importantly, forced the Transport and General Workers' Union to work whole-heartedly for the interests of its Asian members. In another campaign of the mid-1970s the collective threw its organisational expertise behind the Bengali Housing Action Group (BHAG), organising the largest squat in Europe.[23] The squatters' campaign won Bengali residents in Tower Hamlets decent, affordable housing which was safe from National Front violence. Moreover, the campaign forced the Tory-led Greater London Council to recognise the right of Bengalis living in Tower Hamlets to live in majority Bengali areas, which guaranteed the community safety from racist attacks.

Informed by five years of backing campaigns and publishing its paper, the collective formally set out the kernel of its ideological position in 1978:

> Race Today is an organisation which has had as its guiding principle, that its content and practice be guided by the activity of the black working class – what it is saying and doing. That the working class will always be in the leadership of any struggle or movement.[24]

The Black People's Day of Action

By 1980 the collective was a repository of considerable organisational experience. What is more, it had also been accepted by the black working class of Brixton as a group who genuinely understood their struggle and as people who could help them to effect change.

The early 1980s was a turning point in British politics. The post-war consensus, which had been under strain for some time, finally gave way to political polarisation. Anti-immigrant sentiment played an important role in the rise of Thatcherism. The Tories overtook Callaghan's government in the polls soon after Thatcher's highly publicised claim that 'people are really rather afraid that this country might be swamped with a different culture', declaring that she would not allow 'false accusations of racial prejudice' to stop her from tackling the 'problem' of immigration.[25] True to Thatcher's word, a White Paper was produced within a year of her election and a new British Nationality Act reached the statute book in 1981, further restricting the right of Commonwealth citizens to settle in the United Kingdom.

It was in this context that the New Cross fire, quickly dubbed the 'New Cross Massacre', occurred. In the early hours of Sunday, 18 January 1981, a terrible fire started at a birthday party held at 439 New Cross Road in Deptford, South London. Thirteen people aged between fourteen and twenty-two lost their lives and many more were injured. All were black.

In the immediate aftermath of the Massacre a new movement emerged. A week after the New Cross fire, 2,000 people arrived for a public meeting from as far afield as Bradford, Manchester and Leeds. The meeting established the Black People's Assembly, or General Assembly as it was known, a body open to everyone who supported the general aims of the campaign. The collective quickly became involved in the spontaneous movement which determined to force the political establishment to acknowledge the horrors of the Massacre, to conduct a full and fair inquiry into the causes of the blaze and to bring the perpetrators to justice. Howe was elected by an impromptu grass-roots assembly to give the emerging movement shape. The assembly met every week. It heard from the survivors of the fire, discussed the troubled history of the black community in Deptford and addressed the question, as Howe put it, of 'what has to be done?'

In concrete terms, the assembly made recommendations to the New Cross Massacre Action Committee (NCMAC), a body open to migrants from Asia, Africa and the Caribbean, which would decide how to implement its proposals. In the short term, the NCMAC established a Fact Finding Committee, which would take statements, gather evidence and oversee the police investigation. Additionally, the NCMAC called a press conference in response to the misleading reports which were beginning to appear in the press. In the longer term, the General Assembly and the NCMAC called for a Black People's Day of Action. Howe conceived this to be 'A general strike of blacks', an idea that had been circulating among black radicals since the late 1960s. Therefore, he argued that it should be held on a working day and during the school week, a deliberate break with the left's convention of calling national demonstrations on Saturdays. Howe later explained the reasoning behind the date of the Black People's Day of Action:

> I said 'Well if they are going to kill so many kids in a fire, we have to show them we got some power in this place, and the only way to do that is to call a general strike of blacks'.[26]

The General Assembly and NCMAC voted for Howe, along with the Race Today Collective, to organise the Day of Action, acknowledging that their experience of grass-roots organisation and their connections across the UK meant that they were best placed to organise a national campaign. Howe and the collective also played an important strategic role in shaping the march. The question of white participation emerged early in the planning process. Some argued that white people should be able to participate in the march on equal terms with black and Asian people. Others argued that the march should exclude white people. Howe's solution symbolised his conception of the role of white people in the movement. He argued that white people should be able to join the march, but should march at the rear. This symbolised the leading role of black people directing their own movement, while recognising that white people could legitimately play a supporting role.

The route of the march was also symbolic. Starting in New Cross, heading over Blackfriars Bridge, through the City and Fleet Street, past Scotland Yard and the Houses of Parliament before finishing in Hyde Park, the route took protestors from the site of the fire, past the symbolic centres of press, government and police power, in protest at the indifference, incompetence and institutional racism in the nation's institutions.

Finally, the collective played a leading role in the organisation of the march. The members of the collective, who acted as chief stewards, organised stewarding, instructing all stewards on the necessity to encourage discipline and restraint in the face of police provocation. Howe determined to start the march half an hour before it was advertised, in order to keep the police on the back foot. The police were also caught off guard by the scale of the march and the sophistication of the organisation. Howe said that they 'underestimated us … They thought we were a load of little, stupid, black people. They had never seen that size of demonstration by black people before. So the police didn't know culturally what to do.'[27] Over 20,000 marched, and thousands of protestors gathered to hear speeches by Howe and others. Against tremendous opposition, the marchers had triumphed. The collective had been responsible for organising the largest demonstration of black people in British history.

Insurrection

The march had an immediate effect on black communities in London and on London's police. Research funded by the Metropolitan Police into police behaviour at the time reveals how the Massacre and its aftermath 'had the effect of focusing racialist attitudes within the Met'.[28] At the same time, black people, Howe recalls, had a new self-confidence in the wake of the Day of Action.

In the immediate aftermath of the Black People's Day of Action the police initiated Operation Swamp 81, an operation which turned the police presence in Brixton into something akin to a colonial army of occupation. Interviews with police officers at the time indicate that many officers believed that black activists had come out on top in the Day of Action, but that the police hoped to even the score in what one chief inspector referred to as 'the return match'.[29] For Howe, Swamp 81 was nothing but 'an attempt to reassert police authority'.[30] By the end of the first week of Swamp 81, local organisations were overwhelmed by complaints from young black people about their treatment by the police. Hassan recalls that during Swamp 81 life in Brixton resembled reports that she had read of South African apartheid.

Meetings took place between community leaders, including members of the collective, and the police in order to try to persuade the authorities to end the operation. However, these led to nothing. The upshot was a spontaneous insurrection, which the press dubbed 'the Brixton Riots'. The *Daily Telegraph* and *Daily Mail* published reports soon after the riots referring to Howe and the collective as 'agitators', alleging that they had stirred up the conflict and demanding that they should be the subject of police investigation. The collective's role in the riots was also considered at Cabinet level. In a now declassified briefing prepared for the Cabinet in July 1981, after the riots had spread to at least twenty other cities, the contribution of 'extremists' in sparking the initial Brixton uprising was considered by the government. However, authorities would ultimately conclude that 'it seemed unlikely that in any major case the extremists have actually instigated the violence or been able to plan it'.[31] Indeed, while the collective was based one minute's walk away from the 'front line' on Railton Road, it members were effectively penned in by squads of police who used Shakespeare Road as a base. Consequently, the police themselves knew that the collective had played no part in initiating the uprising. Hassan recalls:

> Unless you were in it, you have no idea of what it was like. It was a feeling of euphoria, of freedom, of people really believing once and for all the oppression we had put up with for years, we were finally taking a stand against it … The black youth, they high-jacked a bus, there was a racist pub called the George they burnt it down, it was an absolutely targeted insurrection … there were military tactics, the way they would contact each other from the side roads … the way they came at the police in an armed way, when they were injured the way they were looked after in some of these houses where we had mini hospitals. For the days that it raged it was absolutely unbelievable to live in, but it's that feeling it gave us, that we are so fed up with the way you're messing with black people in this country that we are taking a stand. And for us, it was really freedom.[32]

Nonetheless, the collective did play a role in the events surrounding the insurrection. First, it was able to monitor events. Anticipating an uprising, all of the members of the collective, with the exception of Johnson, who was attending a conference in Amsterdam, met throughout the weekend at their Shakespeare Road headquarters in order to be ready should an uprising take place. Second, the collective was instrumental in establishing the Brixton Defence Committee (BDC), which campaigned for an amnesty for all those arrested during the confrontation. As the radical barrister and fellow BDC member Rudi Narayan made clear in his cross-examination of witnesses during the Scarman Inquiry, such a demand came not as a plea for clemency. Rather, it reflected the conviction that a revolt was inevitable, given such widespread police abuse, and that the uprising was a legitimate act of self-defence against an illegal police operation involving the unlawful stopping and searching of thousands of innocent people.[33]

Finally, members of the collective utilised their close ties within the community to assemble the leaders of the uprising, debrief them and interview them in extensive detail on the causes and course of the insurrection. The interviews confirmed what the collective had observed from the vantage point of the *Race Today* offices: the uprising had been organised with military precision, using the network of parallel streets and intersecting roads, to organise black and white resistance to the police.[34]

Looking back thirty years later, Howe viewed the People's Day of Action and the 1981 insurrection as a turning point:

> The Day of Action was the first organised mass intervention with a semblance of the March on Washington and the huge mobilisations in the Caribbean that I had been involved in. The thinking in Race Today was we could replicate it and we did. It represented an end to the easy going way and resignation to our lot, to the belief that things were bad but that we couldn't do anything about it. When the insurrection occurred it fundamentally broke with the past which had consisted of complaining quietly about our lot and whispering in the ear of white power. People acted in a massive spontaneous way and said 'if you continue to treat us as you have been doing we will burn down every city'.[35]

Relationship with C. L. R. James

As far as Dhondy was concerned, 'CLR was the ideological guide for Race Today'.[36] Speaking in 1992, Howe described the relationship between the collective and James in the following terms:

> he lived with us, the small organisation, for the last ten years of his life. He actually physically lived with us. He lived upstairs above the offices. By and large, people use the word 'consultant' these days – I don't think it means anything, but we had this relationship with him, he was a grand old man, suitably respected, who intervened and worked with us over ten years.[37]

In 1982 James moved into a flat above the *Race Today* offices and the collective began looking after him. The collective supported him in numerous ways. In 1981, in collaboration with the publishers Allison and Busby, they organised his Eightieth Birthday Lectures. On a more prosaic level, Hassan remembers shopping and cooking for him, and Dhondy polished his shoes. Others would fetch wine, brandy and flowers when James was entertaining, and on these occasions Howe recalled, 'if anybody called, you were entitled to say "C. L. R. James is dead" rather than interrupt him!'[38]

Harry Goulbourne, who had known Howe since the early 1970s, recalls spending a number of evenings at the *Race Today* offices, talking with Howe and James. 'It was wonderful spending evenings there, just sitting around and chatting. It was a part of a great Trinidadian tradition – liming.'[39] Goulbourne recalls Howe's relationship with James as one of 'nephew and protector. Darcus provided CLR with care, he made sure that visitors didn't exhaust the old man, and one got the impression that he felt very privileged to be in that position, to take care of him in the last leg of his life.'[40]

James's influence was evident in the collective's attitude to Western culture. Rather than rejecting it, as the nationalists had done, 'the Collective picked up from C. L. R. James that the western intellectual tradition has to be respected and built upon – that is absolutely the basis of *Race Today*, there is no way that that can be gainsaid'.[41]

The collective's strategy had always been to penetrate mainstream institutions, seeking 'integration on our terms'.[42] The events of 1981 propelled *Race Today* journalists into the mainstream media like never before. Following the New Cross Massacre, Howe appeared on *Skin*, directed by Trevor Phillips for the London Weekend Television (LWT) Minorities Unit. Rather than offering a political programme, Howe used the interview to reflect on what was going on in the community. His brief interview set contemporary events the context of black struggle since the mid-1960s and stressed the scale and potency of the self-organisation that had followed the fire.[43] Howe took a similar tack during his appearance on an episode of *The London Programme* dealing with the Scarman Report in November 1981.[44] A final example, an ITN News debate chaired by Peter Sissons, featuring Howe, Gerald Kaufman, Michael Mates and Leslie Curtis, the Chairman of the Police Federation, saw Howe setting out a forensic case against the police. Howe's critique of police racism appealed to the most progressive aspects of British political culture. Indeed, Howe situated the fight against stop and search in 'the British democratic tradition'.[45]

One of the most significant opportunities that Howe took hold of in the wake of the insurrection was the commission to write a lead article in *The Times* in response to the Scarman Report. His feature article, the first he had written for the mainstream British press, was published on 26 November 1981. Drawing on the material acquired from the leaders of the Brixton revolt to help inform his perspective, Howe rejected the plaudits that Scarman had received from the liberal press. While Scarman had resisted right-wing demands to recommend the granting of even greater police powers, he had failed to 'grasp the nettle' by addressing the systemic abuses which had led to the revolt. Next to Scarman's continued support for 'stop and search' and his failure to recommend safeguards against physical abuse and forced confessions of detainees, or greater scrutiny of the police evidence used by magistrates to convict black people, his call for a more independent police complaints system was 'mere tinkering'. Ignoring a wealth of personal testimony of widespread police racism towards black people, Scarman preferred police accounts which explained such racism in terms of a few inexperienced junior officers. He considered the image of a hostile police force held by black people, young and old alike, to be 'a myth'.[46]

These forays into the mainstream led to bigger things. In 1984 Howe did a screen test for LWT's *Black on Black*. Inspired by James, Howe viewed culture as a progressive force. Radicals had long seen the potential of the media as a propaganda weapon, but for James, the media's progressive role was rooted in the sociological dynamics of modern society. *American Civilization* argued: '[t]he modern popular film, the modern newspaper ... the comic strip, the evolution of jazz, a popular periodical like *Life*, these mirror from year to year the deep social responses and evolution of the American people ...'.[47] The bureaucratisation of modern life, James contended, stripped people of their freedom and threatened their individuality. As life became increasingly restricted, people sought liberty in the field of entertainment, demanding 'aesthetic compensation in the contemplation of free individuals who go out into the world and settle their problems by free activity and individualistic methods'.[48] In this sense, the modern media tended to reflect the desire for liberty and self-organisation. *Black on Black* was a false start, the screen test did not go well.[49] Howe would soon get a break, with much more scope for creativity, in the form of the Channel 4 television show *The Bandung File*.

The collective's interest in culture extended beyond Howe's career in television. As the 1980s progressed, *Race Today* became increasingly oriented towards black cultural movements. Under the direction of Akua Rugg, *Race Today*'s in-house literary critic, the magazine gained sections such as 'Poet's Corner' and 'Creation for Liberation', a regular section which covered music, theatre, films and books. The cultural orientation of the magazine was given further prominence from 1980 with the publication of an annual *Race Today Review*. The first *Review* contained 'a short story and poems' as well as reviews of 'novels, the work of poets, musicians, playwrights and film makers'.[50] Howe conceived of the *Review* as a small taste of the 'creative activities which flow from the terrain on which we do political battle', work that was 'forged in the heat of confrontation between the new society in the making and its suffocating and increasingly murderous opposite'.[51]

The second *Race Today Review* contained James's essay 'I am a poet', which championed the work of Ntozake Shange. Drawing inspiration from the 1981 Polish Spring, James argued that artistic expression in the modern world would reflect either the desire for freedom embodied in Solidarity or imperatives of the 'regimes that are described by Solzhenitsyn in his book, *The Gulag Archipelago*'.[52]

Howe returned to the topic of culture and politics in his 1981 'Introduction' to the *Race Today Review*. The essay addressed the conditions necessary to a flourishing cultural scene. Howe argued that artistic expression must be 'nurtured':

> artistic creativity is fed and stimulated in an ambience which generates work of the highest quality. It requires vibrant, social institutions in which the works are concentrated and made available to those who strive to create it.[53]

However, Britain in 1981 was characterised by cultural bankruptcy and therefore black artists should look to 'durable institutions' within the black community such as 'New Beacon Books, Bogle-L'Ouverture Publications and Race Today Publications', which 'continue to foster the ambience' in which artistry could flourish.[54] Akua Rugg's 'Introduction' to the 1984 *Race Today Review* indicates that Howe's notion of cultural 'nurture' was central to her own editorial view of literature. 'Artists', she argued, 'need to be nurtured by a receptive and critical audience' in order for their work to mature. Therefore, the 'publishing houses, bookshops, art galleries, theatres and public festivals' that had emerged as part of the 'struggles waged consistently over the years by blacks' were crucial to the black cultural scene.[55]

Creation for Liberation was one of a number of cultural institutions that thrived during the 1980s to nurture black artists. Established in 1975, the small group of artists and organisers set out the organisation's origins and purpose thus:

> Creation for Liberation was born out of the struggles the black community is engaged in for freedom. There is a cultural dimension to these struggles reflected in many areas of the arts, be it music, literature, the fine arts, the performing arts, film or sport. The cultural expression not only draws from the rich and powerful Asian, African and Caribbean heritage but also from the British and European tradition.[56]

To this end, the organisation set up cultural events, organised discussions and published leaflets and books recording and promoting black talent.

Creation for Liberation was responsible for a series of annual Open Exhibitions, starting in 1982, which showcased the work of black visual artists. The Greater London Arts Council and Lambeth Borough Council provided some assistance, but the greater part of the support came from the community itself, who gave their time and skills as curators, electricians, carpenters, painters and decorators to build the show from scratch.

Chila Burnam, who was involved in the 1987 Open Exhibition, described the Open Exhibition as 'dead important because it's the only exhibition by black artists, for black artists'.[57] Aubrey Williams, the elder statesman of the black British art world, argued that the importance of the exhibition lay in the fact that it gave young black artists the freedom to 'do their own thing. We're having a do in our own back yard, we're producing our own thing, for our own people ... it gives an avenue for pure unfettered black expression.'[58]

In addition to the visual arts, Creation for Liberation did much to promote the work of black poets, including Maya Angelou, Michael Smith, Grace Nichols, Lorna Goodison and Marc Matthews.[59] Indeed, the group was responsible for Ntozake Shange and Jean 'Binta' Breeze's 1988 national tour.[60] By 1990, with ticket receipts and various forms of sponsorship, Creation for Liberation was generating annual revenues in excess of £39,000.[61]

Basement sessions and outreach

In addition to publishing *Race Today* and supporting the flourishing of black culture, the collective was also engaged in self-education and reached out to other groups that were engaged in struggle with the British state. Self-education was facilitated through 'Basement Sessions'. These events were designed, in Howe's words, 'not to build anything, but to discuss the issues of the day'. Sometimes they were reading groups. Indeed, an early set of sessions was devoted to James's *Nkrumah and the Ghana Revolution* (1977). On other occasions, the basement sessions built bridges with other communities involved in their own acts of resistance. In 1984, to take one example, at Hassan's instigation, the collective paid for the wives of striking coal miners to come to London and tell their stories.[62]

Race Today also kept a constant eye on the politics of Northern Ireland. The magazine reported the Republican struggle as part of its wider coverage of anti-colonial movements. For this reason, it came to the attention of leaders of Sinn Fein and members of the IRA. As a result, Bobby Sands submitted a short story, 'Black Beard in Profile', which Howe published as part of the 1981 *Race Today Review*. 'It had very little literary merit', Howe recalls, but the submission came in the midst of Sands' hunger strike. Moved by compassion for the starving prisoner, Howe published the piece. It was one piece among many, but its publication clearly meant something for the Republican movement, for when Ken Livingstone invited Gerry Adams to London in July 1983, Adams requested a meeting with Howe. Howe recalls that the *Race Today* offices were circled by a police helicopter for the duration of Adams's visit. The two men spoke at length. Adams's physical presence made a deep impact on Howe. 'He did not smile once. To appropriate a Dickensian phrase, he was "so cold and hard". Icy even. He spoke literally without a blink. His stare was razor sharp.' Howe's abiding impression was of a man who had been forced to inhabit a 'dark grim dungeon'.[63]

Conclusion

As Howe and Dhondy gained greater access to the mainstream, *Race Today* changed. In the first few years, *Race Today* worked closely with media production company Bandung Productions, printing transcripts of segments of the show and publishing pamphlets based on the show's content. However, from the mid-1980s Howe's attention was increasingly focused on his television work. In 1985 Howe stepped down as editor and Hassan took over the running of the magazine. Hassan remembers this as a difficult time. 'When Darcus left *Race Today* we were very upset. We used to joke "are you selling out and becoming a TV personality?".'[64] The final issue was published in 1988. Howe was keen, at least between 1988 and 1990, to keep an organisation going. In a letter to the members of the collective written in 1989 he argued that the organisation should continue as a basis for future interventions in British national life.⁶⁵

The eventual agreement was to dissolve the collective and found a new organisation. The collective formally dissolved itself on 7 April 1991. The formal dissolution, proposed by Patricia Dick and seconded by Michael Cadette, passed all the collective's assets to a new association, The C. L. R. James Institute (Preparatory). From Johnson's point of view, Howe had lost interest in *Race Today*:

> Darcus decided that he wanted to be in the media, and I got the impression that he figured that we had more-or-less won the battle that we had been fighting. I wasn't around for any decision making, I just stopped attending meetings, I didn't think the leadership's heart was in the organisation any more. Also the death of C. L. R. James created a pall over everything. Some members were affected by it. I certainly was.⁶⁶

For Howe, *Race Today* had done its job. 'We had exhausted the moment.'⁶⁷

From its foundation in 1975 to its dissolution in 1991, the Race Today Collective was, as Hassan argues, the centre of black liberation in England. It was the realisation of James's vision of a small organisation, a repository of organisational expertise and journalistic excellence which kept black rights on the agenda, and which broke into mainstream consciences through the grass-roots campaigns it helped to organise.

In terms of their ongoing influence, it should be recognised that the members of the collective played a role in shaping the political consensus that emerged in the 1980s. It is usually assumed that this decade witnessed the emergence of a Thatcherite consensus which championed privatisation, deregulation and free enterprise, but that is only part of the story. While the right dominated the economic argument, the left, by and large, won the social argument. From the mid-1990s until around 2015 mainstream British politics was characterised by economic and social liberalism. Notably, although groups such as the Race Today Collective, which had campaigned for the recognition minority rights, were written off in the 1980s as 'looney left', by the mid-1990s the message of equality and diversity had been accepted, rhetorically at least, by front-bench politicians of both main parties. In this sense the collective is part of a broader story of self-directing groups, representing minority communities, which, during the 1970s and 1980s, shifted the political consensus radically to the left, an influence that was felt in the content of equality legislation, culminating in the 2010 Equality Act, introduced by the governments of Tony Blair and Gordon Brown.

Stepping back from broad claims about its influence, Hassan sums up the collective thus:

> Our history is really the history of Brixton, we were here for the '81 riots, the Uprising, the road out here had all the police from Herefordshire, Southampton and Bristol, literally lying in this road as the troops that were brought in as reserves to fight the black community who were giving them hell further up. So we would open the door of the offices and step over policemen … Here we had people coming from all over the Caribbean, Steve Biko from Soweto, Jerry Adams came down here … he came and talked to us about the Irish liberation struggle. I hope one day we do have the opportunity to tell the story of this building and what it did for the freedom of black people in this country.[68]

Notes

1. Leila Hassan, interview by Robin Bunce and Paul Field. Unpublished interview. Norbury, London, UK, 21 October 2011.
2. The Collective understood the term 'black' as universal; that is to say, comprehending people from Africa, the Caribbean, the Indian subcontinent and Asia. This chapter follows the Collective's use of the term. In that sense, black has a similar meaning to terms such as people of colour or BAME in contemporary usage.
3. Farrukh Dhondy, interviewed by Robin Bunce and Paul Field. Unpublished interview. Royal Festival Hall, London, UK, 20 September 2010.
4. Robin Bunce and Paul Field, 'Obi B. Egbuna, C. L. R. James and the Birth of Black Power in Britain', *Twentieth Century History* 22 (2010), 391–414.
5. W. Chris Johnson, 'Guerrilla Ganja Gun: Policing Black Revolutionaries from Notting Hill to Laventille', in Stephan F. Miescher, Michele Mitchell and Naoko Shibusawa (eds), *Gender, Imperialism and Global Exchanges* (Chichester: Blackwell Publishing, 2015), pp. 280–306.
6. Neil Kenlock, interview by Robin Bunce. Unpublished interview. Emirates Stadium, London, UK, 1 August 2016.
7. Darcus Howe, interviewed by Robin Bunce and Paul Field. Unpublished interview. British Library, London, UK, 20 August 2010.
8. Linton Kwesi Johnson, interviewed by Robin Bunce. Unpublished telephone interview, 14 November 2011; Farrukh Dhondy, interviewed by Robin Bunce and Paul Field. Unpublished interview. British Film Institute, London, UK, 15 September 2011.
9. Bunce and Field, 'Obi B. Egbuna, C. L. R. James and the Birth of Black Power in Britain', p. 414.
10. Robin Bunce and Paul Field, *Darcus Howe: A Political Biography* (London: Bloomsbury, 2014), pp. 137–40.
11. Leila Hassan, interview by Robin Bunce and Paul Field. Unpublished interview. Norbury, London, UK, 21 October 2011.
12. Darcus Howe, interviewed by Robin Bunce and Paul Field. Unpublished interview. Norbury, London, UK, 6 October 2011.
13. Linda Bellos, interviewed by Robin Bunce. Unpublished telephone interview, 31 December 2012.

14 The Collective rejected the slogan on the basis that, in practice, it was used to co-opt black people into white-dominated organisations, and to back campaigns over which they had no influence.
15 Darcus Howe, 'From Victim to Protagonist', *Race Today* 1974, p. 67.
16 Darcus Howe, 'Bringing It Back Home', *Race Today*, 1974, p. 126.
17 Howe, 'Bringing It Back Home', p. 126.
18 Linton Kwesi Johnson, interviewed by Robin Bunce. Unpublished telephone interview, 14 November 2011.
19 Darcus Howe, interviewed by Robin Bunce and Paul Field. Unpublished interview. Norbury, London, UK, 6 October 2011.
20 C. L. R., James, Grace C. Lee and Pierre Chaulieu, *Facing Reality* (Detroit: Bewick Editions, 1974), pp. 128–31.
21 James, Lee and Chaulieu, *Facing Reality*, p. 126.
22 Darcus Howe, 'Editorial', *Race Today*, 1974, p. 95.
23 The BHAG campaign had grown out of the Anti-Racist Committee of Asians in East London (ARC-EL) campaign which organised small community defence squads. The latter had quickly stamped out the skinhead and National Front 'Paki bashing', which took place in the early 1970s in East London.
24 University of Columbia Rare Books and Manuscript Library, Darcus Howe Papers, Race Today Constitution, 1978, Box VIII Folder 1.
25 Margaret Thatcher, interview with Gordon Burn, *World in Action*, Granada TV, 27 January 1978.
26 Mike Phillips and Trevor Phillips, *Windrush: The Irresistible Rise of Multi-Racial Britain* (London: HarperCollins, 1999), p. 328.
27 Darcus Howe, interviewed by Robin Bunce and Paul Field. Unpublished interview. Norbury, London, UK, 15 July 2011.
28 David J. Smith, and Jeremy Gray, *Police and People in London IV: The Police in Action* (London: Policy Studies Institute, 1983), p. 116.
29 Smith and Gray, *Police and People in London IV*, p. 116.
30 Darcus Howe, interviewed by Robin Bunce and Paul Field. Unpublished interview. Norbury, London, UK, 21 July 2011.
31 The National Archives (TNA), PREM 19/484, 57, Cabinet Papers, July 1981.
32 Leila Hassan, 'Our History Is the History of Brixton'. Filmed 1 November 2015, YouTube video, posted 1 November 2015, https://www.youtube.com/watch?v=H7YxeuqUHDs.
33 Rudy Narayan, *Barrister for the Defence: Trial by Jury and How to Survive It* (London: Hansib Publications, 1985), p. 143.
34 Darcus Howe, interviewed by Robin Bunce and Paul Field. Unpublished interview. Brixton, London, UK, 1 November 2015.
35 Darcus Howe, interviewed by Robin Bunce and Paul Field. Unpublished interview. Norbury, London, UK, 21 July 2011.
36 Farrukh Dhondy, interviewed by Robin Bunce and Paul Field. Unpublished interview. British Film Institute, London, UK, 15 September 2011.
37 Darcus Howe, 'C.L.R. James Lecture', Institute of Contemporary Art, July 1992.
38 Darcus Howe, interview with Humphrey Carpenter. *Great Lives*, BBC Radio 4, 1 November 2002.
39 Harry Goulbourne, interviewed by Robin Bunce. Unpublished telephone interview, 8 February 2012.
40 Goulbourne, interviewed by Robin Bunce.
41 Farrukh Dhondy, interviewed by Robin Bunce and Paul Field. Unpublished interview. British Film Institute, London, UK, 15 September 2011.

42 Leila Hassan, interview with Krishnendu Majumdar. *What's Killing Darcus Howe*, Channel 4, 24 November 2009.
43 Darcus Howe, television interview. *Skin*, London Weekend Television, 7 June 1981.
44 Darcus Howe, television interview. *The London Programme*, London Weekend Television, 20 November 1981.
45 Darcus Howe, interview with Peter Sissons. *ITN News*, Independent Television, 17 November 1983.
46 Darcus Howe, 'My Fears after This Failure', *The Times*, 26 November 1981, p. 106.
47 C. L. R. James, *The American Civilization* (Oxford: Blackwell, 1993), p. 119.
48 James, *The American Civilization*, p. 127.
49 Darcus Howe, interview by Robin Bunce and Paul Field. Unpublished interview. Norbury, London, UK, 16 March 2011.
50 Darcus Howe, 'Introduction', *Race Today Review*, 1980, p. 51.
51 Howe, 'Introduction', p. 51.
52 Darcus Howe, 'Introduction', *Race Today Review*, 1981, p. 2.
53 Howe, 'My Fears after This Failure'.
54 Howe, 'My Fears after This Failure'.
55 Akua Rugg, 'Introduction', *Race Today Review*, 1984, p. 3.
56 Akua Rugg, 'Creation for Liberation', *Race Today Review*, 1988, p. 3.
57 Chila Burnam, interview with Darcus Howe, *Bandung File*, Channel 4, 24 October 1987.
58 Aubrey Williams, interview with Darcus Howe, *Bandung File*, Channel 4, 24 October 1987.
59 Darcus Howe (ed.), *Race Today Review*, 1988, p. 12.
60 Howe (ed.), *Race Today Review*, 1988, p. 12.
61 University of Columbia Rare Books and Manuscript Library, Darcus Howe Papers, Creation for Liberation Accounts, 1990, Box VIII Folder 3.
62 Leila Hassan, interview by Robin Bunce and Paul Field. Unpublished interview. Norbury, London, UK, 21 October 2011.
63 Darcus Howe, 'Devil's Advocate', *Evening Standard*, 9 September 1994, p. 26.
64 Leila Hassan, interview by Robin Bunce and Paul Field. Unpublished interview. Norbury, London, UK, 21 October 2011
65 University of Columbia Rare Books and Manuscript Library, Darcus Howe Papers, Letter to the Collective, 1989, Box VIII Folder 4.
66 Linton Kwesi Johnson, interviewed by Robin Bunce. Unpublished telephone interview, 14 November 2011.
67 Darcus Howe, interviewed by Robin Bunce and Paul Field. Unpublished interview. Norbury, London, UK, 6 October 2011.
68 Hassan, 'Our History Is the History of Brixton'.

Index

Abse, Leo 71, 75, 78
Adams, Gerry 205, 207
affluent socialism 123, 124, 128
AIDS/HIV 2, 77
Ali, Tariq 74
Allaun, Frank 48
Alternative Economic Strategy 11, 30, 31, 49, 53, 95, 132
Ambrose, Jean 193
Anderson, Joe 166
Apartheid (South Africa) and anti-apartheid 13, 14, 199
Arbatov, Georgy 119
Archer, Peter 73
Attlee, Clement xii, 8, 10, 14, 50, 60, 93

Band Aid 2
Bank of England 93, 106
Banks, Tony 76
Beese, Barbara 193
Belchem John 155
Bellos, Linda 78, 194
Benn, Tony (Anthony Wedgwood Benn) x, xiv, 2, 4, 5, 10, 11, 36, 44, 46, 59, 75, 125
Berlin Wall 1, 113, 116, 127, 129
Bermondsey by-election (1983) x, 73–5
Bernstein, Eduard 127
Bevin, Ernest 13

Birchall, Tommy 155
Black Liberation 192, 206
Blair, Tony 7, 17, 18, 25, 26, 29, 30, 32, 35, 37, 38, 40, 41, 75, 84, 91, 95, 100, 101, 106, 143, 165, 206
Blue Labour 84–5
Blunkett, David 32, 37, 182
Bond, Sampson (Sam) 159
Bowker, Mike 118, 120
Bragg, Billy 4
Brandt, Willy 119, 127
Brezhnev, Leonid 118, 121, 126
Bright, Graham 80, 83
British Black Panther movement 192, 193
Brooke, Stephen 72, 79, 80
Brown, Archie 115, 127
Brown, George 71
Brown, Gordon 26, 32, 33, 34, 35, 37, 206
Buckley, William F. 47
Bush, President George H. W. 12
Byrne, Tony 162

Cairns, David 84
Callaghan, James (Jim) 5, 10, 13, 44–62, 136, 153, 154, 197
Campaign for Nuclear Disarmament (CND) 4, 5, 15, 118, 137, 138, 175, 178

Campbell, Beatrix 2
Cameron, David 15
Carter, President Jimmy 47, 138
Castle, Barbara 9, 71
Chamberlain, Neville 50
Chapple, Frank 47
Charter 15, 88
Chartism 3
Chernenko, Konstantin 118–21
Chernyaev, Anatoly 122
Clarke, Charles 118, 122
Clarke, John 85
class, social (class structure and class politics) x, 3, 8–11, 15–18, 30, 71, 77, 80, 82, 84, 85, 104, 120–2, 124, 135, 136, 137, 140, 141, 142, 145, 152, 153, 161, 163, 174, 180, 181, 182, 184, 185, 186, 192, 193, 194, 195, 196, 197
Cold War 3, 13, 19, 113, 118, 119, 133, 137, 138
Communist Party of Great Britain 2, 116, 178, 180, 181, 185
Communist Party of the Soviet Union (CPSU) 113–20, 122, 123, 127, 128
consensus politics, post-war x, xii, 3, 69, 85, 135, 197
Conservative Party x, xi, 1, 3, 5, 7, 8, 9, 15, 16, 18, 35, 37, 50, 55, 56, 57, 58, 59, 61, 69, 70, 72, 73, 76–84, 123, 134, 139, 172, 177, 178, 151, 152, 153, 156, 158, 159, 161, 163
consumerism 6, 9, 121, 124, 126
Cook, Betty 184
Cook, Robin 32, 120
'convergence' 103, 114, 115, 116, 120, 122, 123, 128
Corbyn, Jeremy xii, 3, 18, 19, 32, 40, 41, 75, 92, 95, 166
Craigie, Jill 73
Crewe, Ivor 73
Crick, Michael 152
Cronin, James 36
Crosland, Tony (Anthony) 7, 9, 30, 71–3, 84
Cunningham, Jack 79, 165
Curran, James 74
Currie, Edwina 84

Davies, Sam 155
Deane, Jimmy 155
Delors, Jacques 12, 139, 143
democratic socialism 7, 116, 117, 123–5, 127, 128, 142, 155, 160
Deng Xiaoping 13, 115
Desai, Meghnad 101
designer socialism 6
development state 7, 30, 32, 33
Diamond, Patrick 85
disarmament *see* nuclear weapons
Disraeli, Benjamin 50
Dobson, Frank 71, 85
Dhondy, Farrukh 19–23, 201, 205
Drucker, Henry M. 28, 39
Dubček, Alexander 121
Duncan, Peter 114

Eastern Europe 13, 98, 116, 122, 129, 143, 145
Eatwell, John 34, 101, 102, 105
economic liberalism 6, 15, 19, 69, 70, 121, 140, 142, 143–4, 146, 206
Edwards, Nicholas 103
Ellman, Louise 160
Elton, Ben 17
Empire, British 16
European Economic Community (EEC)/Common Market 5, 11, 12, 18, 32, 34, 53, 57, 60, 83, 141–2, 153, 166
European Investment Bank 94, 98
Evans, Moss 52

Fabian Society 12, 29, 37
Falklands War 10, 15, 55, 139, 174
feminism xi, xiv, 2, 4, 11, 14, 73, 81, 85, 181, 184–5
Field, Frank 46
Flynn, Paul 99
Fogarty, Liam 153, 158
Foot, Michael 2, 4, 5, 10, 16, 36, 44, 45, 50, 58, 73, 75, 91, 96–8, 106, 118, 138, 156
Fowler, Norman 163
France 132, 133, 134, 135, 139, 140, 142
Franklin, Stanley 54
Frost, Diane 152, 161

Index

Gaitskell, Hugh 9, 10, 49, 50, 56
Galbraith, John Kenneth 16
gay rights 14, 69–80
General Strike (1926) xi, 6
Gerasimov, Gennady 121
Gilmour, Alan 81
Gladden, Roy 165
Gladstone, William E. 48
glasnost' (openness) 126
globalisation 7, 11, 113, 115, 120, 123, 128, 129, 142, 143–4, 152
Golding, John 152
Gorbachev, Mikhail 2, 13, 113–29, 138
Gould, Bryan 7, 31–4, 36, 99, 102, 105
Gould, Joyce 152, 180
Gould, Philip 26, 27, 29, 35, 37, 56, 57, 60
Grant, Bernie 59, 79
Grant, Ted 155, 157
Greater London Council (GLC) x, xi, xiv, 2, 14, 71, 76–8, 81–2, 161, 182, 197
Greece 132, 134, 135, 141
Green Party 2, 18
Greenaway, Harry 82
Greenham Common peace camp 4, 13, 14, 183

Hall, Stuart 4, 15, 28
Hamilton, John 156, 157, 159
Hardie, James Keir 17
Hare, David 2, 17, 60
Harris, José 123
Hassan, Leila 193, 194, 199–200, 201, 205, 206–7
Hattersley, Roy 7, 31, 36, 37, 47, 53, 57, 72, 74, 75, 98, 104, 105
Hatton, Derek 2, 151, 156, 158–60, 163, 164–5
Hayward, Ron 48, 157
Healey, Denis 5, 36, 45–7, 52, 54, 56–7, 60, 75, 118–20
Heffer, Eric 49, 52, 56–7, 117
Heseltine, Michael 154
Hewitt, Patricia 49, 61, 78, 118
Hilton, Denis 39
Hobsbawm, Eric 3, 26, 136
Hodge, Margaret 78
Holland, Stuart 95

homosexuality *see* gay rights
Hooton, Peter 162
Howe, Darcus 192–4, 196–206
Howe, Geoffrey 154
Howell, Denis 82
Hudson, Hugh 55
Hughes, David 157
Hughes, Simon 73
Humane Democratic Socialism 123, 127, 128
Hyman, Peter 38

immigration 16, 73, 84, 139, 140, 197
International Monetary Fund (IMF) 5, 96, 136, 144
internationalism 3, 98, 115
Irish Republican Army (IRA) 75, 205
Italy 96, 98, 121, 122, 133, 134, 135

James, C. L. R. 192–8, 201–6
James, Sian 184
Jacques, Martin 28
Jeger, Lena 71
Jenkin, Patrick 159–60, 163
Jenkins, Clive 46, 47
Jenkins, Peter 48
Jenkins, Roy 4, 10, 46, 71–3, 83
Johnson, Linton Kwesi 193, 195, 200, 206
Jones, Oliver 124
Jones, Tudor 123, 126
Joseph, Keith 96, 162

Kaldor, Nicholas 101
Kaufman, Gerald 1, 47, 202
Kendall, Liz 40
Kennedy, Malcolm 160
Kenny, Michael 85
Keynes, John Maynard 1, 6, 19, 30, 31, 33–5, 115, 132–3, 136, 146
Kilfoyle, Peter 152
King, Anthony 73
Kinnock, Neil 3–6, 10, 13, 14, 16, 18, 30, 31, 44, 46, 50, 55, 58, 73, 75, 83, 84, 90–1, 95, 98–106, 113–29, 138, 157, 164–6, 180, 187
Knight, Jill 79
Knight, Ted 161
Kohl, Helmut 134, 141

Labour Campaign for Lesbian and Gay Rights 72, 73, 182
Labour Co-Ordinating Committee 37
Labour councils 78, 79, 151–66
Labour governments 1, 8, 9, 10, 30, 34, 47, 69, 72, 83, 84, 117, 136, 153
Labour and international affairs 12–14, 113–131, 132–148
labour movement (including trade unions) 1, 4, 6, 8, 9, 10–12, 15, 16, 27, 29, 35, 44, 45, 53, 82, 120, 122, 155, 164, 172, 174, 175, 177–80, 182, 184, 186–7, 197
Labour Party xii, xiii, xiv, 1–22, 25–43, 44–68, 69–89, 90–109, 113–31, 132–6, 138, 140, 143, 145, 151, 152, 153, 155, 156, 157, 158, 159, 160, 162, 163, 164–5, 166, 177, 178, 179, 180, 182, 184–5
  black and women's sections 11
  conference 4, 29, 48
  leadership 5, 9, 44–62, 74, 75, 79, 126, 157, 159, 164–5
    see also individual party leaders
  parliamentary Labour Party 5, 44, 48, 70, 81
Labour voters 9, 54, 77, 78, 85, 121
Labour Weekly 49
labourism 29, 37
Lansbury, George xii, 74
Lawrence, Ivan 76
Lawson, Nigel 57, 96, 143–4, 177
Lesbians and Gays Support the Miners x, 182
Letwin, Oliver 161
Leys, Colin 123
Liberal Party (after 1988 the Liberal Democratic Party) 1, 6, 9, 15, 46, 73, 74, 75, 79, 84, 152, 161
liberalism 4, 14, 69–85, 206
  see also economic liberalism
Limehouse Declaration, the 90
Livingstone, Ken xi, 2, 14, 17, 19, 53, 58, 71, 77, 81, 104, 182, 205
Liu, James 39
Liverpool City Council 151–66
'loony left' 1, 4, 14, 49, 70, 77, 79
Luckock, Paul 160

MacDonald, James Ramsay 165
Mackley, Simon 84
Macmillan Gap, the 92, 94, 96–7, 101, 102, 105
Major, John 1, 18, 55
Mahoney, James 29
Mandela, Nelson 13–14
Mandelson, Peter 26, 35, 37, 40, 51, 53, 55, 101, 157
Mao Zedong (Tse Tung) 13
Marquand, David 69
Marren, Brian 152
Marxism 11, 12, 17, 37, 69, 114, 116, 133, 140
Marxism Today 3, 7, 15, 122
Marwick, Arthur 77
Maxwell, Robert 16
McGahey, Mick 181
Mellish, Robert 73
Miliband, Ed 166
Militant and Militant Tendency 4, 5, 16, 31, 32, 38, 49, 50, 57, 74, 75, 90, 99, 116, 151–66
miners' strike x, 5, 10, 31, 38, 50, 56, 75, 158, 172–7, 179, 187
Minkin, Lewis 27, 36
Mitchell, Austen 47, 72, 120
Mitterand, President François 115, 134, 145
Momentum 166
Morgan, Kenneth O. 73
Morning Star 122, 181, 182
Morrell, Frances 78
Morrison, Herbert 80, 157
Mortimer, Jim 58
Mulhearn, Tony 151, 155, 156, 161, 165
Murdoch, Rupert 1, 6, 16

Naden, Gwendoline 78
National Coal Board (NCB) 172, 173, 177
National Enterprise Board 91, 94, 95
National Investment Bank, the (NIB) 91, 92, 94, 96–106
nationalisation xii, 8, 9, 11, 27, 29, 36, 37, 38, 50, 72, 77, 90, 97, 99, 100, 117, 123, 126, 139
NATO 13, 118, 119, 137, 138, 141
neo-liberalism *see* economic liberalism

New Labour 7, 8, 11, 15, 18, 19, 25–41, 53, 84, 92, 106, 123, 143, 165, 166
New Right 12, 69, 96, 113, 120, 122, 140, 142
New Statesman 6, 15, 16, 142
News on Sunday 1, 16
North, Peter 152, 161
Northern Ireland 14, 15, 72, 205
nuclear power 2, 174
nuclear weapons (and disarmament) x, xiv, 2, 5, 6, 13, 14, 52, 58, 90, 118, 120, 122, 126, 127, 137, 138, 139, 175, 178
National Union of Mineworkers (NUM) 172–6, 180–7
New Cross Fire 197–9, 202

O'Grady, John 73
'Old Labour' 7, 8, 18, 25–41, 166
Orme, Stan 180
Owen, David 47, 48, 71

Pan-Hellenic Socialist Movement (PASOK) 132, 134, 141
Parkinson, Michael 152
Parris, Matthew 82
Parshin, Lev 118
Pelling, Henry 120
perestroika (restructuring) 113–14, 115, 119, 121, 123, 127, 128, 129
Petley, Julian 82
Phillips, Trevor 202
Pimlott, Ben 114
Policy Review (Labour Party 1987–88) 3, 6, 13, 30–5, 37, 53, 103–4, 123–5, 127
Poll Tax (community charge) x, 4, 161
Ponomarev, Boris 119
Powell, Enoch 11
Pravda, Alex 114
Prescott, John 32, 106
Purton, Peter 73

Race Today and Race Today Collective 192–206
racism 4, 140, 193, 199, 202
Radice, Giles 90, 104, 106
Randall, Nick 37
Reagan, President Ronald 12, 13, 59, 113, 118, 120, 134, 136–41, 144

Red Wedge 2
republicanism 15
Richardson, Jo 75
Robertson, Geoffrey 82
Robertson, George 118, 120
Roderick, Eddie 156
Rodgers, Bill 52
Roper, John 52

Salter, Afred 74
Sandle, Mark 127
Sayle, Alexei 17
Scargill, Arthur 2, 35, 50, 56, 173, 177, 179–81, 184
Scottish politics 15, 181
Sen, Mala 193
Section 28 (Local Government Act 1988) x, 14, 69, 79–80, 84
sexuality 3, 14, 69–80
Shearman, Peter 118, 120
Shore, Peter 46, 47, 48, 49
Short, Clare 14, 81
Sinowatz, Alfred 118
Smith, Chris 2, 76
Smith, Clarissa 81
Smith, John 33–7, 57, 62, 102, 104
Snell, Bill 156
social democracy 6, 7, 9, 12, 13, 19, 37, 55, 90, 92, 113, 114, 115, 118, 121, 127, 128, 129, 132–3, 135, 142, 195, 196
Social Democratic Party (SDP) 1–6, 10, 16, 52, 72–3, 75, 78, 83, 85, 116, 134
socialism as political doctrine xi, 2, 4, 7–13, 15, 37, 55, 57, 71, 72, 76, 113–17, 121–5, 127–9, 135, 140–2, 151–2, 155, 160, 181
see also designer socialism
Socialist Party of Spain (PSOE) 134, 141
Socialist Workers Party 18, 116, 155
Soviet Union (USSR) 2, 3, 10, 12, 13, 113–23, 125–9, 137–40, 145
Soviet socialism 13, 114–16, 122, 125, 127–9
Spain 132–4, 141
Spitting Image 2, 55, 75
Stanbrook, Ivor 83
Steel, David 46–7
Strategic Defence Initiative ('Star Wars') 13, 118, 120

Stokes, Donald 91, 106
Straw, Jack 76
Sun, the 1, 14, 16, 18, 54, 77, 81, 179
Suslov, Mikhail 119
Sweden 98, 105, 115, 133, 135, 138
Swift, Jonathan 54

Taaffe, Peter 151, 155, 157, 161
Tatchell, Peter x–xii, 73, 74, 75
Taylor, Matthew 27
Tebbit, Norman 76, 83
Thatcher, Margaret and her governments (1979–90) xii, 6, 10–11, 13, 15–16, 18, 51, 57, 69, 77–8, 82–3, 90–1, 94–6, 98, 102, 114–15, 120, 128, 134, 136–41, 143–5, 151–4, 156, 158–61, 163–5, 172–4, 176–7, 187, 197
Thatcherism as political doctrine x, xi, xiii, 1–5, 7, 9–12, 15, 28, 70, 113, 120–3, 125, 128, 152, 197, 206
Thornton, Glenys 78
Tillett, Ben 17
Todd, Ron 124
Toynbee, Polly 78, 81–2
trade unions *see* labour movement
Tribune 16, 47, 52, 56
Tuffin, Alan 57
Turner, Alwyn 74, 82

Ullman, Tracey 55
unemployment xiv, 1, 5, 12, 15, 27, 35, 50, 90, 94, 105, 133, 135–6, 139, 141, 144–5, 153–7, 163, 176

United Kingdom Independence Party (UKIP) 12, 84

valence politics 91, 99–100, 106
Veber, Aleksandr 114
'video nasties' 70–1, 80–3
Vinen, Richard 79

Wainwright, Hilary 53, 175
Walker, Alexander 80–1
Wardell, Gareth 82
Weeks, Jeffrey 69
Weir, Stuart 15
Wellbeloved, James 75
West Germany 133, 135, 137, 138, 141–2, 144
Westlake, Martin 122
Whitehead, Alfred North 83
Whitehouse, Mary 69–70, 80
Williams, Charles 98, 106
Williams, Ian 157
Williams, Len 48
Wilson, Harold 9–10, 52, 59, 60, 71, 72, 85, 94, 102, 120, 153
Wistrich, Enid 81
Wogan, Terry 51
women's politics *see* feminism
Women Against Pit Closures (WAPC) x, 174, 181–5
Worcester, Bob 56
working class *see* class, social (class structure and class politics)

Zagladin, Vadim 119
Zotov, Aleksandr 114

EU authorised representative for GPSR:
Easy Access System Europe, Mustamäe tee 50,
10621 Tallinn, Estonia
gpsr.requests@easproject.com

www.ingramcontent.com/pod-product-compliance
Ingram Content Group UK Ltd.
Pitfield, Milton Keynes, MK11 3LW, UK
UKHW021851210426
5322IPUK00022B/590